The Revolutionary Poet in the United States

EDITED BY FREDERICK C. STERN

The Revolutionary Poet in the United States

The Poetry of Thomas McGrath

UNIVERSITY OF MISSOURI PRESS

COLUMBIA, 1988

Library of Congress Cataloging-in-Publication Data

Stern, Frederick C.

    The revolutionary poet in the United States:
the poetry of Thomas McGrath / Frederick C. Stern.
    p. cm.
    Includes bibliographies and index.
    ISBN 0-8262-0682-4 (alk. paper)
    1. McGrath, Thomas, 1916- —Criticism and interpretation.
I. Title.
PS3525.A24234Z87   1988   88-4846
811'.54—dc19

This book is for Tom, and for (I echo him) "the fighters"

Acknowledgments

THIS BOOK HAS been several years in the making. It is for all those who have helped to bring it into being, a work of scholarship, and, one hopes, a contribution to the understanding of contemporary American poetry. Most of all, it is an appreciation of its subject. I want to acknowledge here the assistance of many people in helping me with this work, in so far as I know, the first full-length book devoted to McGrath's poetry.

My first thanks must go to the contributors to this book. All but one of their essays were originally written for this volume. Without them there would have been no book.

The one piece not originally written for this volume is the essay by E. P. Thompson, which appeared, in considerably different form, before the publication of *Parts Three and Four* of *Letter to An Imaginary Friend,* in Professor Thompson's collection of essays, *The Heavy Dancers* (London: Merlin, 1985). The essay appeared in its present form as "Homage to Thomas McGrath" in *TriQuarterly* 70 (Fall 1987), and is here reprinted with permission. Reginald Gibbons, the editor of *TriQuarterly,* has been most supportive to the publication of the present volume and has my thanks.

Though the other essays were originally written at my request for this book, several of them have appeared in other publications in the interval of time between my request and publication of this book. I wish to express my appreciation to all the writers for their permission to publish their work. I also want to acknowledge here the places where the essays have previously appeared, and to thank the editors and publishers of these publications for permission to reprint.

James Bertolino, "McGrath's Brilliant Brevity" in *Another Chicago Magazine* 17 (November 1987); Joseph Butwin, "The Last Laugh: Thomas McGrath's Comedy" in *North Dakota Quarterly* 55, 1 (Winter 1987); Hayden Carruth, "Tom McGrath is Harvesting the Snow" in Carruth, *Sitting In: Selected Writings on Jazz, Blues and Related Topics* (Iowa City: University of Iowa Press, 1986), p. 69, and *Poetry East* 23–24 (Fall 1987): 98; Gene Frumkin, "Figures and Letters: The Poetry of Thomas McGrath," *American Poetry* 5 (3) (1987); Diane Wakoski, "Thomas McGrath: Orphic Poet of the Midwest," *Poetry East* 23–24 (Fall 1987): 93.

Permission to publish excerpts from McGrath's poetry comes from him, and from his publishers, Swallow Press (Ohio University Press) and Copper Canyon Press. My thanks.

The poem by Pablo Neruda (trans. Ben Belitt) appeared in English in *Pablo Neruda: A New Decade (Poems 1958–1967),* ed. Ben Belitt (New York: Grove Press, 1969) and is published with permission from Grove Press, Inc. The poem by Salvatore Quasimodo (trans. Allen Mandelbaum) appeared originally in English in *The Selected Writings of Salvatore Quasimodo* (New York: Farrar, Straus & Cudahy, 1960), and is here published with permission from the present copyright holders of Quasimodo's poems in English, Anvil Press Poetry, Ltd. of London, England. I thank both publishers.

Many of my colleagues of the faculty of the Department of English of the University of Illinois at Chicago have been patient with me, and have been encouraging as I went about this task. I want to acknowledge special assistance from two of them. The poet and novelist Michael Anania, who was the editor of the Swallow Press when *Letter to an Imaginary Friend, Parts I & II* was published, was instrumental in helping me to decide whom to ask to contribute essays. His vast knowledge of the sociology of and personalities in American poetry was essential for this. He has been helpful in so many other ways that this volume is surely partly his doing, though he is not responsible for any of its limitations. He knows how much I appreciate his support. Ralph J. Mills, Jr., a distinguished critic of poetry who has more recently himself become a poet of increasing power was—as he always is—unfailingly encouraging, thoughtful, willing to make suggestions and read some of my work, and though he too bears no responsibility for its weaknesses, he deserves a great deal of credit for whatever merits this work may have. The Graduate College of the University of Illinois at Chicago has been supportive in helping to pay for some of the word processing costs incurred in developing this book, as has the Department of English. The Head of the Department, John Edward Hardy, has been supportive throughout. Without the department secretaries, the work could not have been finished. I am grateful for their assistance.

A word of special thanks goes to the man whose poetry is the subject of this volume. Tom McGrath has been willing to do whatever I asked of him, despite recent health problems. My thanks go to him for many things—most of all for being the poet he is—but for his cheerful willingness in connection with this book; he deserves my special appreciation.

Members of the editorial staff of the University of Missouri Press have extended themselves to get this work completed. The fact that during part of the production process I was abroad on a Fulbright Lectureship made them especially important. I wish to thank, therefore, Rick Boland, Susan McGregor Denny, Wendy Warnken and the Press' director, Edward King. Professor Jay Rogoff, an early reader of the manuscript for the Press (who permitted himself to be identified) made many helpful suggestions of which I took advantage, and for which I thank him.

My final thanks go to those who never ask that I repay my enormous debt to them. They suffer me through the stages of frustration and chagrin which must accompany the production of any work like this. They are always encouraging, loving—and even willing to read my "stuff" when I need someone to read it. I mean, of course, first of all, my wife Naomi, and also my children and their spouses, Carrie, Kurt, David, Suzanne, Paul, Lisa, Jeremy and Wendy. They ask no thanks, but they have it.

FCS
JULY 1988

Contents

1   The Revolutionary Poet in the U.S.:
The Poetry of Thomas McGrath

WHAT MAKES A POET significant enough to be "worth" a volume of essays concerning him and his work? I suppose each editor of such a volume has his or her own reasons for producing it, and often such reasons are personal as well as aesthetic, intellectual, scholarly. It is my intention here to explore both types of reasons for producing this volume. In the process, I will attempt to "place" the poet, that is, to try to explain where Thomas McGrath fits in the body of contemporary American poetry and to clarify why he plays, at least in the opinion of the essayists in these pages, an important enough role so that he "deserves," as it were, a volume of commentary. If he were as well known as some of his contemporaries, such an explanation would not be needed. Who would doubt that James Wright, Robert Bly, David Ignatow, or Denise Levertov might well be the subject of such a volume of essays? But it is a fact that McGrath's reputation, though widespread among poets and among those who know American poetry of the last four decades well, is very limited among that larger audience of poetry readers who probably know the names of Wright, Bly, Ignatow, or Levertov. This fact itself requires some thought and explanation.

*   *   *

The personal, then. I first learned of McGrath's name in a manner similar to that described in Hayden Carruth's essay—I bought a book of his poems at the Jefferson School's Bookshop in New York. The Jefferson School was a school of Marxist studies, essentially under the direction of the Communist Party and those allied with it. In early 1949 I was taking an evening course there in "The Fundamentals of Marxism." But I was having a problem with my then so newly found affection for radical politics. Though I was, as I am now, thoroughly convinced that Bertolt Brecht's dictum is right, that the world does need changing, and in a socialist direction; though I was then convinced that Marxism presented a world view that could at least engage if not solve, well, "everything," I found myself dissatisfied with the art and literature produced by those who had recently become my political compatriots, and by most of their criticism as well. This disjunction put in question my newfound convictions, and I searched mightily—perhaps even a little desperately—for poetry, fiction, art, and criticism that would somehow satisfy me and yet prove consonant with my political ideology. In criticism I had just found F. O. Matthiessen, whose work was to become a

1

lifelong preoccupation. Then I was delighted to find in the little volume *Longshot O'Leary's Garland of Practical Poesie* some poems I could like, because they seemed to me fine poetry, and yet they were politically acceptable to me.

There were some poems in that book I recognized even then as pretty bad "agit-prop" (agitational propaganda) and many that I am sure McGrath would just as soon forget and has not reprinted since they were published in that fourth volume of his verse. It must be said, moreover, that my own tastes in poetry—I was very young, after all—had yet to be developed by longer and deeper contact than I had then experienced with the works of Eliot and Pound, William Carlos Williams, Hart Crane, Charles Olson, and, perhaps above all, Wallace Stevens, not to mention the contemporary poetry of Europe and Latin America. But there were poems such as "Poor John Luck and the Middle Class Struggle; or The Corpse in the Bookkeeper's Body" (a poem that Gene Frumkin and E. P. Thompson discuss extensively elsewhere in this volume), variations on blues such as "Blues for an Interim," and political lyrics like "Such Lies They Told Us." In the last-mentioned poem McGrath uses his experience of land and nature in ways that were to become, years later, the familiar materials of *Letter to an Imaginary Friend.* Here he also uses the relatively long line, which was to become a hallmark of his poetry as well:

In memory, the wild blue geese, lagging behind the spring,
Seemed all summer long to acclaim our extravagant unselfish notions
Of time—for they seemed eternal, each locked to its changeless image
On the lost lake of the past. And, under that dead sun,
Those kissing hours of illusion blessed our foreheads forever—
Or so we thought. For the years, opening their windows on
That tame image of life, promised us our powers—
Such lies were told us. Signs seen later made us unsure.
In the first fall frost the wild geese flew up, circled,
    were gone.
              (*Longshot O'Leary's Garland of Practical Poesie,* 22)

I had not yet, at the time I first encountered this poem, read enough of Yeats to note its similarity to a poem like the Irish master's "The Wild Swans at Coole." Now such a similarity seems clear and provides evidence of McGrath's consciousness of modern poetry, even when his career as a poet was in its earliest stages. This first stanza of a three-stanza poem appealed to me, and though the poem ends in a third stanza too filled with poetically undigested politics, it seemed to me—whatever I may then have meant by the phrase—"good poetry."

Even more important than these poems was the final poem in the volume, "Blues for Jimmy," McGrath's elegy for his brother, who died in June 1945 while in the Air Corps. As he reveals in an interview elsewhere in this volume, the poet still likes this poem and still finds it emotionally too difficult to read in public. When I first read it, it struck me with such force that I have remembered it ever since. It was this poem, above all else, that convinced me that I had found "my own red poet."

The years went by, and I followed pursuits that took me far away from the study of literature in any formal sense. I lost track of McGrath, especially during the McCarthy period, when "red" was a dirty word and when, I was to discover later, McGrath himself suffered personal difficulties that made his poetry hard to find. When I undertook literary study professionally, more than fifteen years after I had first read "Blues for Jimmy," I began to look for McGrath's work. I wanted to see if the memory I had of this poet would hold true, now that my sense of poetry—as well as of politics—had been honed and modified by age if not by maturity, by years of experience in industrial as well as academic work, by the experience of family, and by a good deal of reading. I mentioned his name to a group of graduate students who were especially interested in contemporary poetry, and on my next birthday they presented me with a copy of *Letter to an Imaginary Friend, Parts I & II,* which had been published by Chicago's Swallow Press some years earlier, when it was under the editorship of my colleague, the poet Michael Anania.[1]

I took the volume home that night and read its 214 pages. I was stunned. Here was a poem in length more or less like Williams's *Paterson* or Hart Crane's *Bridge.* Here was a poem politically left without a doubt, and if not as complex as Pound's *Cantos,* then as politically concerned and at times as forceful in its imagery and craftsmanship. If nothing in the poem struck me with the sense of transcendent beauty and intellectual elegance with which so much of Wallace Stevens strikes me, then its ambition, its force, its American quality, and its wit seemed complementary to Stevens's more involute and Europeanized verse. I was struck by the poem's unregenerate, wisecracking, side-of-the-mouth American humor, its kinship to Mark Twain, even to the best of Finley Peter Dunne, in the midst of its often despairing view of the American experience. Above all, I was struck by the notion that here was a poet to carry forward the Whitman tradition in a fashion no other poet whose work I knew had achieved.

It is this personal history that has made me pursue McGrath's work since my students' gift first put me in touch with it again. I cite this personal history here because, it seems to me, though poetry is the subject of schol-

1. I cannot any longer recall the names of all the students who shared in the giving of this gift, but I am still in touch with two of them—John Jacob, a fine, frequently published poet and novelist, and a teacher of writing at various Chicago-area institutions (including Northwestern University and Columbia College), who is now a doctoral candidate, and thus once again a graduate student, at the University of Illinois at Chicago where I teach; and Kathleen Davidson March, who recently completed a doctorate in American Studies from the University of Iowa and now lives in Madison, Wisconsin, with her husband, Dr. John March, and her two children, Matthew and Maggie. I mention them as token of thanks for the whole group.

arly analysis by the critic, as it ought to be, it must first of all be loved—critically loved, but nonetheless loved—if one is to give it the "passionate attention" fine poetry deserves. I have come to believe, in these years of reading and contemplation since I first encountered *Letter,* that McGrath's poetry deserves such love, deserves such attention. I have met McGrath several times since I read his volume and have come to concern myself with the man who writes the poetry as well as with the poems, though I do not want to claim any intimacy or close friendship. This volume, then, was impelled into being because I like much of Tom McGrath's poetry and find sympathetic some of his ideology—and I think his poetry is important.

Moreover, I believe McGrath's poetry is an unfortunately neglected body of work. His work of recent years—more recent, I mean, than the publication and my later reading of *Letter*—has convinced me of the seriousness of the neglect. *Part III* and *Part IV* of *Letter* have recently been published in a single volume. Thus we now have *Letter to an Imaginary Friend, Parts I-IV,* which I believe is a major work of American poetry, and one that not only will influence those who read it as verse but also will become a significant document about the life of the United States during some five decades. It is a document viewed from the political left, of course, but such a view surely has a place in our poetry. Moreover, I believe the two volumes show that we have among us a poet whose bardic voice should be heard with other such voices of our time—our seers, so to speak—voices such as Hayden Carruth, Muriel Rukeyser, David Ignatow or A. R. Ammons, Denise Levertov or Robert Bly or William Stafford—the list could go on, but the names listed will stand for those others any reader might think worth including.

The primary function of this volume, then, is to "discover" Thomas McGrath's poetry for those who have not yet done so themselves, and in the process to evaluate and attempt to explain and elucidate at least some of it. If while performing this function this volume also pays some tribute to McGrath's poetry, that is only an effort to right the balance a little and, while keeping firmly in mind the proper distance that serious criticism demands, to do what should have been done in years past.

                              *   *   *

What, then, makes this poet "important," not only to my personal life but also to readers of American poetry in general? McGrath cannot claim the "importance" that derives from being as widely known and influential as some of the poets I have mentioned. But is he—as I believe he is—nevertheless "significant"? The question is not simple to answer. Such terms as "centrality," or "renewing the language" or "shaping the national verse" come to mind. In any case, when one makes the judgment of importance about a contemporary poet, one engages in guess work. The instances of the poet (or, for that matter, almost any other kind of artist) who is unknown in his or her own time but becomes important only in later contemplation are many. Conversely, it is not uncommon for the poet who is well known and thought important in his or her own time to fade into insignificance in later opinion. When one is dealing, then, with a poet not very widely known in his or her own moment, the case for importance is especially difficult to make.

In describing "the exacting demands of our poets," M. L. Rosenthal writes:

Even professional critics and poets know the dismay that unfamiliar poetry can arouse at first hearing: another call to the abyss, another reordering of life, of the intelligence. An unexpected widening of sympathies and sensibility threaten to release our dark, subversive, inward self; we fear engulfment by all that we protect ourselves from feeling too intensely. Yet a nagging desire to experience just such a widening persists; we long to face the mysterious depths of self for which the poet speaks with the evasive frankness of our own deepest thoughts. The poet, by bringing the problems of life into his aesthetic orbit, transforms them and reveals far more about our whole contemporary meaning than we ever thought possible.[2]

Though Rosenthal's volume is dated 1960, this is still a useful description of the impact "important" new poetry can have. I am especially taken by the last sentence of the quotation as an appropriate description of precisely that quality of McGrath's verse that, I believe, makes him important.

How does McGrath's poetry achieve importance? First it must be said that, like any poet's, his is a particular view of the "the problems of life" and "their whole contemporary meaning," a view shaped by his experience and his ideology. He sees life in the United States, and indeed in the Western world, as profoundly flawed, as desperately in need of revolutionary change, and locates the possible source for such change in a classically Marxist worker's revolution (though I will modify this somewhat). By saying it this baldly, I run the risk of making McGrath sound like one of those left-wing poets who have contributed very little to the art form except their anger and despair. But that is precisely not the case. One of McGrath's achievements lies in his ability to represent in his verse a world view held by a significant number of people, in language and forms that *are* poetically rich. Moreover, again unlike so many of those who share his political ideas, he makes the connection—carefully, deliberately, and with skill—between his political ideas and their sources in his life's experience, which is rooted first of all in the North Dakota farm experience, in the land, in the landscape.

That such an outcome is McGrath's aim, he himself has made clear. In an "Introduction" to a portion of *Part III* of *Letter,* published before the poem appeared in full, he writes:

How is *Letter* unlike other long poems? In part, perhaps, because it is "pseudo-

2. M. L. Rosenthal, *The Modern Poets: A Critical Introduction,* p. 3.

autobiography." It is *not* simply autobiography. I am very far from believing that all parts of my life are meaningful enough to be usable in the poem. But I believe that all of us live twice: once personally and once as a representative man or woman. I am interested in those moments when my life line crosses through the concentration points of the history of my time. *Then* I live both personally and representatively. I hope to be aware of those moments, because then, I believe, one may be speaking for many people. (*Passages,* 93)

That McGrath is concerned with precisely that expansion of the self of which Rosenthal speaks is clear. Moreover, I am struck with his use of Emerson's pregnant phrase, "Representative Man." The phrase, which gives the title to one of Emerson's most important works, marks McGrath's deep connections with a profound aspect of the American experience and also ties him—whether that is his intention or not—to a strain in Romantic thought, and in particular to its American version. Discussing the issue in his chapter "Representative Men" in *American Renaissance,* in which he compares Emerson's 1850 effort with Carlyle's *Heroes and Hero-Worship,* F. O. Matthiessen writes: "But even before that [Carlyle's book] appeared, Emerson had reached his own position that 'there is properly no history, only biography,' a position that Thoreau, in his confidence, carried to the point of saying, 'Biography, too, is liable to the same objection; it should be autobiography.'"[3]

I would not want to make of McGrath an "Emersonian." His socialism and his general outlook in other ways separate him sharply from Emerson's philosophical idealism. But his sense of the "representative man" in the self does connect him to a notion of history that is similar to Emerson's or Thoreau's, and his insistence on the "pseudo-autobiography" separates him in this regard from some of our confessional poets. The difference is not merely a difference in the use of the "pseudo-autobiography." Rather it is a difference in the forces reflected within the format, which has become one of the major forms of poetry at least since Wordsworth, and more especially so in the twentieth century. If McGrath is not a "confessional poet" like Berryman or Lowell, that is because for him the primary experience of contemporary human beings is not the personally psychological one, which may, in turn, yield insights into history and political life. For McGrath it is the historical and political experience that will help us to understand the personal and private psychological state of the speaker of the poem, and hence of its readers.

The effort to overcome such barriers is most clearly demonstrated in the very next paragraph of the "Introduction" I have quoted above. McGrath writes:

Some other differences from other long poems (perhaps). *Letter* is not a poem that

3. Matthiessen, *American Renaissance Art and Expression in the Age of Emerson and Whitman,* p. 631.

comes out of the sensibility of the city middle-class intellectual. The city is in the poem, of course, but there is a lot, too, of the backlands and of *place*—that "Dakota" which is central to the poem. There is other material in the poem which seems to me more or less new. Work, for example, is not something which most poets write about. Also communality or solidarity—feelings which perhaps are more important to us than romantic love— never appear in our poetry. Perhaps I have begun to identify them. The attitudes toward these materials, also, are not those of the petty bourgeois intellectual no matter how alienated. (*Passages,* 93)

I need not, in this overview, deal with all these aspects of McGrath's claim. Others in this volume do so, and especially Bernard Engel, in his essay "Tom McGrath's Vision and the Hornacle Mine," which is much concerned with work in McGrath's poetry and with the "Dakota" that is everywhere. Suffice it to say that for McGrath not only is the "pseudo-autobiographical" "representative," in Emerson's sense, it is also the voice of a persona who can feel and can explore in language important aspects of "the problem of life." He insists as well on locating these problems in both class and locale in such a way that he separates himself from other poets who have also written long poems in which a single voice, either on its own or by the use of the "pseudo-voices" of others, attempts to explore the situation of the American mind and feeling-state.

McGrath has made the effort, then, out of his sense of "representativeness," to create an American mythos. I will discuss some of the content of this mythos a little further on, but here I want only to suggest that McGrath is very much in the American grain, and very much a descendant of Emerson and, perhaps more crucially, of Whitman. Matthiessen writes, "The circumstances of Thoreau's 'heroic age' called out many independent efforts to create a mythology that would express it, conscious and instinctive, exuberantly playful and highly serious. Between them they give the collective portrait that Whitman wanted, the likeness of 'man in the open air.' Whitman's poetic phrase symbolizes the fact that this age of the rise of the common man was still mainly agrarian."[4]

Diane Wakoski's essay in this volume, "Thomas McGrath: Orphic Poet of the Midwest," explicates some of McGrath's myth-making efforts and demonstrates the deeply pervasive presence in his work of analogies, at the very least, to the central myths of Western Europe. But McGrath is also deeply aware of the *end* of the agrarian mythology Matthiessen discusses, and he seeks to substitute for it another, what we can call a "post-agrarian" mythology. A mythology found in an epic-like poem is, of course, always more than a tale of heroes and heroines. It is also the tale of a people in verse. McGrath sees the voice of his poem not as that of the Homeric bard recording the actions of a Greek demi-god, not as the chanter of an El Cid or an Aeneas, but rather as a late version, perhaps the last serious voice, of the

---

4. Matthiessen, *American Renaissance Art and Expression,* p. 5.

"man in the open air" now forced into Eliot's "brown city." This North
Dakota American knows full well that the farmland that gave birth to the
Whitmanesque myth is no longer what it was:

Had arrived there
            —North Dakota, the farmhouse
                                        the old
Dominion of work and want (but all in a new style now)

and he also writes:

    The road outside the window was "our" road
Once. It is now anybody's road.
                                It is the road
On which everyone went away
                            (*Letter I & II,* 187)

He makes the case for the "pastness" of the past even more manifest in his
description of one of the characters whose voices people *Letter*:

Bill Dee speaking his piece: hard times
In the country.
            Bill Dee: last of the old bronc-stompers
From the gone days of Montana mustangs we used on the farms
For light work and for riding and for the pure hell of having
Outlaws around . . .
                            (*Letter I & II,* 197)

In the following richly described fishing episode, at a time when the speaker of
Letter has returned home to refresh and to replenish a self damaged by the
city—Los Angeles, mostly—and by the ravages of McCarthy-era persecution,
we read how Dee continues to live on the land, a lone survivor. The episode
ends in a description of desolation and emptiness:

And into the Hills lost places: now, following
The river and again buckjumping over the iron, faceless
Ranchroads: opening the gates in the fences, kittycornering and quartering
The waste . . .
            Dead houses here in the bottomlands:
                            an eyeless
Schoolhouse, abandoned, crumbles;
                            undenominational forever,
A church is stumbling into an empty future, lofting
A headless and rotting Christ on the cracked spool of a cross:
Unspinning god at a loss in the psalm of the man-eating wind.

"Ever'body here got blown out in the last of the dusters.
Should never been farmed no-way. The country's sure empty. But me—

I like it this way."

Dee concludes his description of a land now repopulated with wild game with a certainty that "They're comin' back sure—the old days." But the speaker of the poem knows better. "Dreamed it; no doubt," he says, "And dreamed the old days as well: doubtless. / Another fast dreamer . . ." (*Letter I & II*, 199–200).

   Thus, it seems to me, we can see McGrath creating the myth—or charting its end—out of his own "representative man," the "self" of the "pseudo-autobiography" he has constructed. This self, located in passage, takes him from the last remnants of frontier America to the city—and acknowledges the death of the former and horrifying decay of the latter:

"Seems like it was right here somewhere—place we went wrong."
—And the voice of the dead fisherman (still then alive in the future!)
Tears at my ear, at my heart, like a mad bird screaming
Or keening ghost . . .
                    Lost . . .
                         Sunk with all hands . . .
                                        Here.
Somewhere . . .
             My grandfather saw the beginning and I am seeing
The end of the old free life of this place—or what freedom
There was: The round song at least: the solidarity
In the circle of hungry equals.
             Or if there was nothing else—
Resistance . . .
             And of Bill Dee and those others . . .
                                        survivors merely,
Anachronistic.
             Nothing to build on there, though they keep
             (Still!) the living will to endure and resist.
                                        Alone.
             Alive.
                    Outlaws.
                         Riding a cold trail.
                              Holy . . .

In the immediately following section, separated from the above only by six asterisks, McGrath gives us his view of the modern city, the next stage, as it were, from the ending he has just described.

If New York holds history locked in its icy museums
                                        stony
Keeps no wind can shift or shake
                              its falling walls
Spalling
       unspelling the rebel names while the prisoners sleep
In the night rock . . .
                         If Los Angeles' windless calm is only
End of the continental drift

```
                              decaying granite
                                         no house
Will stand
            and change there merely the empty alternatives ranging
The sounding void . . .
                    then what star steers and stands, what mansion
Founded on the fire brightens towards us     what sea will call us
Saying: here is the road to the ancient and future light?
Exhaust these four: what's left?
                              Nothing.
                                         Nothing?
Man is the Fate of his place, and place the fate of the man
And of time
        A beginning then
                         to know one's place.
                                         At least
        That
```

                              (*Letter I & II*, 201–3)

※   ※   ※

I have described McGrath's most frequently used voice as the voice of a self-aware, "representative" speaker. But to leave it at that seems to distort McGrath's work, not only in *Letter to an Imaginary Friend* but also in the totality of his poetry. For if on the one hand he is representative, then on the other hand he is also individual—and it is perhaps in this dialectic opposition that the "unity of opposites" which Hegel and Marx teach us to understand is effected, and McGrath most clearly achieves his place.

That the singularity of voice is a hallmark of the postmodern, and thus of the contemporary in American poetry, my colleague Ralph J. Mills, Jr., makes clear in his important essay "Creation's Very Self: On the Personal Element in Recent American Poetry." Discussing the contrasts between such poets as Roethke, Lowell, Berryman, Shapiro, and others "who began to write in the 1930's" on the one hand, and the masters of the Eliot-Pound era on the other, he writes that the later poets in time achieved

the kind of poetic breakthrough James Dickey calls "The Second Birth"—an intense imaginative liberation, achieved at great personal cost, in which the poet, like a snake shedding his dead skin, frees himself of the weight of imposed styles and current critical criteria to come into the place of his own authentic speech. The secret of this renewal, Dickey observes, "does not, of course, reside in a complete originality, which does not and could not exist. It dwells, rather in the development of the personality, with its unique weight of experience and memory, as a writing instrument, and in the ability to give literary influence a new dimension which has the quality of this personality as informing principle. The Second Birth is largely a matter of self-criticism and endless experiment, presided over by an unwavering effort to ascertain what is most satisfying to the poet's self as it develops, or as it remains more clearly what it has always been."[5]

5. Mills, "Creation's Very Self," pp. 3, 4.

In amplifying this idea, Mills goes on to write:

Contemporary poets, then, with a few forerunners providing guidance, begin to cultivate their own inwardness as material for poetry or to look to the immediacies of their own situation for valid experience. . . . Contemporary poets might take one of their chief mottoes from Wordsworth. In the preface to the *Lyrical Ballads* of 1800, after asking himself "What is a Poet?" and "To whom does he address himself?" he answers unequivocally "he is a man speaking to men." And we can add to this statement—thinking not only of Lowell, Eberhart, or Roethke, but also of more recent poets, of Anne Sexton or John Logan, Gary Snyder or Frank O'Hara, Denise Levertov or William Stafford—that each poet wishes to speak to us, without impediment, from the deep center of personal engagement with existence. For the contemporary poet enters into himself and the particulars of his experience in order to bring into being in his work that true poetic "self which [he] is waiting to be," to borrow a phrase from Ortega y Gasset.[6]

It seems to me that this description of the poet's individual voice is readily applicable to McGrath. The voice is varied of course in time, as must be expected of a poet who writes over a long span—and especially a poet who composes a long poem over many years. But certain aspects of the "self" in McGrath do remain constant and constitute crucial elements both of the individual voice, the "personality with its unique weight of experience and memory," and of the "representative man."

This issue of "voice" is a complicated one in modern and contemporary poetry. Though Mills is quite on target when he describes the poet's effort to speak from "the deep center of personal engagement," it is clear that the voice that *does* speak is a created voice, a "persona" through which the person who is the poet speaks. Indeed, postmodern criticism (and in particular Paul de Man in regard to Shelley and J. Hillis Miller in regard to Wallace Stevens) has dealt with this issue extensively. Though biography—or autobiography—may well be history, as Emerson and Thoreau have it, the speaker of such history is always the maker of a mask made of language, through which the reader must somehow reach—if "reaching" is at all possible—if he or she is to find "meaning," a statement one might make about *all* writing, and not only about poetry. Nevertheless, it is an individual mask, one different, in the significant poet especially, from every other mask, and hence an individual "voice" we attempt to hear and to understand.

The nature of this individual voice and the quality of its "saying" are best apprehended by a reading of the poetry itself. However, we can abstract from it certain attributes, elements that make it what it is.

First comes to mind McGrath's particular agrarian "midwesternism." I do not want to make of McGrath a "midwestern poet," by any means. His

6. Ibid., pp. 6, 7. This essay was originally delivered by Mills as the Cecil Williams Memorial Lecture at Texas Christian University, 7 May 1976. The quote from James Dickey is from *The Suspect in Poetry* (Madison, Wis.: The Sixties Press, 1964). The quote from Ortega y Gasset is from *The Dehumanization of Art and Other Essays* (New York, 1956).

range of locale is very broad, just in *Letter* including Greece, Portugal, Amchitka Island (where he was stationed while in the service during World War II), Maine, Baton Rouge, Oxford, New York, and Los Angeles, as well as the North Dakota of his childhood and youth. Moreover, *midwestern* is a term of peculiar application to the North Dakota farm country west of the Minnesota border where he was raised, since in some designations this portion of the nation can also be seen as the beginning of "the West." Indeed, what Frederick Manfred refers to as "Siouxland," both in his essay in this volume and elsewhere, was described in a collection of essays by its title, *Where The West Begins*. Among localities discussed in this volume are western Minnesota, North Dakota, and some contiguous areas.

In one sense this locale, for McGrath, is the locus of the past. I have already discussed his sense of the past in the agrarian communities of his birth:

Sheldon . . .
            Enderlin . . .
                              bells of the little towns
                                               calling . . .
        Lisbon . . . North Dakota
                                   (*Letter III & IV, 27*)

He identifies them in this way in the Christmas Section of *Part III* of his long poem. But his "North Dakota," as McGrath (as well as Bernard Engel in his essay) points out, "is everywhere." McGrath sees in the towns of his childhood, in the land, in winter travel, in work on the farm, and in nature, in the plants, trees, flowers, in hunting and fishing, the means for metaphor. He also sees in them the background for men and women not completely encoiled in the money ethos he associates with the city. What he often refers to as "the commune" or "the round dance" has its origins in this North Dakota—and it is, or can be, everywhere. It is by no means a romanticized, bucolic landscape he describes. McGrath is far too enmeshed in the hard work of poor farmers, in the need to keep body and soul together while working land that has to be wrestled into yielding cash crops in a commodity-based economy, to grow misty-eyed over it. However, the oneness with the land, the camaraderie of labor, and, most important, the comforts of the united and loving family are, for him, first of all found in North Dakota. Describing Skyros, Greece, on the very first page of *Letter, Part II,* he writes:

Skyros.
      In the false light before sun-up.
I wait while the breeze,
Or a ghost, calls at the shutters.
                        Beyond the window the wild

Salt north 40 of wind and water, the loud, galloping
White maned mustangs of the cold ungovernable sea . . .

Honeysuckle, lavender, oleander, osiers, olive trees, acanthus—
All leafsplit, seedshaken, buckling under the drive
Of the living orient red wind
                                        constant abrasive
North Dakota
                    is everywhere.
                                        This town where Theseus sleeps on his hill—
Dead like Crazy Horse.
                        This poverty.
                                        This dialectic of money—
Dakota is everywhere.
                    A condition.
                                And I am only a device of memory
To call forth into this Present the flowering dead and the living
To enter the labyrinth and blaze the trail for the enduring journey
Toward the roundance and commune of light . . .
                                        (*Letter I & II,* 103)

It is also from North Dakota that McGrath derives his frequent associations with Native Americans, with the Indian lore and history that often form the exemplars of his retelling of the horrors of socio-political life. Often these are metaphoric materials, and sometimes they are the subject of his verse. Indeed, a poetry journal he edited for some years, which is still being published by others, is called *Crazy Horse.* In the history of the Indian peoples native to his home territory he sees examples of the corruption and brutality he associates with much of the United States, and which he frequently discusses. He uses that history as a kind of lode star pointing to future horrors in the American experience, even when the history of his own family is involved:

And my father, a boy at Fort Ransom, saw them each spring and fall—
Teepees strung on the fallow field where he herded cattle.
Made friends and swapped ponies with a boy his own age—
And in the last Indian scare spent a week in the old fort:
All the soddies abandoned, then.
                                        Wounded Knee—
The last fight—must have been at that time.
                                        And now
All: finished.
            South Dakota has stolen the holy
Bones of Sitting Bull to make a tourist attraction!

From Indians we learned a toughness and strength; and we gained
A freedom: by taking theirs: but a real freedom: born
From the wild and open land our grandfathers heroically stole.
But we took a wound at Indian hands: a part of our soul scabbed over:
We learned the pious and patriotic art of extermination
And no uneasy conscience where the man's skin was the wrong

Color; or his vowels shaped wrong; or his haircut; or his country possessed of
Oil; or holding the wrong place on the map—whatever
The master race wants it will find good reason for having.

(Letter I & II, 190)

It is not only the loss of Indian life that the poet mourns. For him, the
destruction of Native American culture, especially as signified by Wounded
Knee—that hideous final death of the Plains Indians—is further metaphor
for the destructiveness of American white culture as a whole. It stands for
the money ethos in its peculiarly American form that is throughout his
poetry "the enemy," that which must be changed if the world is to be properly human again:

Another Hitch Hiker Says

It's been a long time since I was an American
And Wounded Knee was going on long before it was named
In Alabama or elsewhere
Everybody arrives here
On the Road of Tears, The Road of Wounds, on the Cherokee
Road to the Indian Nation
                            prison
                                    good old Highway
66
                                    (Passages, 89)

The city is for McGrath a place of desolation and despair. Though he
can sometimes find in its working people and in his political comrades "the
commune" he has initially located on the North Dakota farm, the constant
and constantly varied figures for New York and Los Angeles—the American
cities most frequently cited in his verse—are sharply negative, deeply involved in money-making, dehumanizing experience:

In New York at five past money, they cut the cord of his sleep.
In New York at ten past money they mortgaged the road of his tongue,
Slipped past the great church of song and planted a century of silence
On the round hearts' hill where the clocktower the cock and the moon
Sang.
        At a quarter past money in New York a star of ashes
Falls in Harlem and on Avenue C strychnine condenses
In the secret cloisters of the artichoke.
                            At half past money in New York
They seed the clouds of his sleep with explosive carbon of psalms,
Mottoes, prayers in fortran, credit cards.
                            At a quarter to money
In New York the universal blood pump is stuffed full of stock quotations:
And at Money all time is money.

(Letter I & II, 127)

Los Angeles fares no better at McGrath's hands. He calls it, variously, "the windless city," the city that is "the end of continental drift," the city "of the Never-Never plan," and other such names.

McGrath is the preeminent poet, in my view, of the end of the agrarian myth and the domination of the urban in American life. As he has lived it in his real biography, his "pseudo-autobiography" puts into poetry a facet of American life composed of the despoliation of the land and the growth of the city that is played against the destruction of the Native American heritage.

McGrath, in that sense as well as in others, is a political poet who would not wish to be known other than as a political poet—and his political stance is an essential aspect of his "voice." Though he is by no means only a political poet—as he is by no means only a midwestern poet—his politics give his work the same kind of ideological underpinning that Christianity gives Eliot's. If Eliot's Christian convictions, especially in the poetry dating from "Ash Wednesday," provide for him a governing ideology that it is *one* function of his verse to explore, then radical politics serve a similar purpose for McGrath's poetry.

McGrath's politics provide not only an ideology for his poetry but also a good deal of material for metaphor and for language-play. It is a politics far more pervasive than the term is usually understood in the American context, having only a little to do with the electoral process or the attendant sense of "party" which goes with that process. It is much more like the politics one finds in European or Latin American writers like O'Casey, Neruda, MacDiarmid, or, in the later part of his career, Salvatore Quasimodo, or even, to deal with a more contemporary figure, Gabriel García Márquez. Politics, in that sense of the term, is an all-pervasive element of McGrath's work, a presence in his thought and in his feeling-states, a source for mood and for emotion, as well as for language. In the extensive discussion of *Parts III* and *IV* of *Letter* that appears in *Passages* he writes:

Finally, the poem is *political*; it hopes to invent and restructure the past and the future by using the narrative line of the speaker of the poem and events from personal and political-social history to create the "legend" of these times. I am aware of how arrogant this must sound. But I think perhaps this is the only *long* poem to make this attempt. (94, original italics)

One might cite *The Cantos* as a similar attempt, from nearly the opposite political vantage point, but in any case the attempt is rare. McGrath's politics are, in a sense, rather old-fashioned. His very language—"labor fakers" and "bindle stiffs," for instance—often turns toward the now all-but-forgotten language of the "Wobblies," the Industrial Workers of the World, a movement with which he associates his father and the agrarian "round dance," and the movement which was in its heyday in the period just before World War I. Often he uses a language that is almost exclusively associated with the Communist Party in the 1930s and 1940s. His references are frequently to labor struggles of one sort or another, to the Spanish Civil War, to the anti-fascist "united front" of the period around World War II, or to other such events and moments in the history of the American Communist Party or of the Soviet Revolution of 1917. Among the characters who people his work are those often associated with the Communist Party and its labor and cultural forces. Sometimes they are clearly named, such as McGrath's friend, the late Charles Humboldt, an editor at various times of *New Masses, Masses and Mainstream,* and the *National Guardian*; and sometimes they are less clearly identified, such as the National Maritime Union leader "Showboat" Quinn and "Mac," who helps the speaker of *Letter* understand both his world and himself.[7] McGrath's politics are not favorably disposed toward the relatively "soft" radicalism of the 1960s, which he sees more as show than as substance, more as a game than as struggle, and he especially notes its lack of attention to class issues.

Beyond the specifics of political commentary, McGrath's poems are steeped in a profound sense of the injustice of the capitalist system, the horror of war, and, Brecht-like, in the need for revolution. He is also aware, however, as he writes in a number of different ways, that the times are not revolutionary in his own America. His dedication to "the victims and fighters" shows in page after page of *Letter* and in most of the rest of his work as well. His hope for revolution is, throughout, undiminished:

Revolutionary Song

Under America's glittering darkness
Assemble the armies of finks and narcs
Who poison the daylight. What's to be done?[8]
Sell all you have and buy a gun!

and, in the last stanza of this four-stanza poem, from a volume published in 1983, he writes:

Only the workers shall remain
When the Black Maria of Time comes round.
Brother, insure that time will come—

7. For identification of some of these voices, especially that of "Mac," see Joe Doyle, "Longshot O'Leary: Tom McGrath's Years on the New York Waterfront," in *North Dakota Quarterly* 32–41. For discussion of terminology used by McGrath particularly associated with the history of the American left, often of the Communist Party, see my "The Delegate for Poetry," in Huseboe and Geyer, *Where the West Begins* (Sioux Falls, S. Dak.: Center for Western Studies Press, 1978), pp. 119–27; rpt. *North Dakota Quarterly* 107–15.

8. The phrase "What's to be done?" is another example of McGrath's use of the language of the Communist left, since the phrase echoes Lenin's famous pamphlet title *What Is To Be Done?*, which appeared originally as a manifesto concerning disputes among Russian Social Democrats abroad in 1902. See, for example, V. I. Lenin, *Selected Works* (New York: International Publishers, 1943), pp. 27–192.

Sell all you have and buy a gun!
                    (*Echoes,* 50)

    Though there is always a modicum of hope for revolution in McGrath, the hope is often very close to despair, for McGrath is always aware that he is writing in his—and in our—late twentieth-century United States. In more lines than one can here recount, the poetry tells of "class struggle" sold out to an economy of abundance or of false revolutionary ideals that cannot lead to the complete revolution McGrath hopes for:

A Note on the Late Elections

Behold, Friends, once more the Revolution has performed its famous
Disappearing act! And never before has one been preceded
By so many prophets! By so many holy books—all in translation!
By so many young men with long hair, so many poets with short
Breath!
        AND the elephant bells!
                Oo la! and incense
                          And
The flowers!
        The flowers, alas, which never found the barrel
Of the gun that power grows out of.

This poem, which comments on the "movement" of the 1960s and the early 1970s ends with the telling lines:

A hard rain is falling; the roads are icing up.
But in every drop of the rain the sailors of the Potemkin wake . . .
                    (*Passages,* 63)

The "rain" reference is, of course, to Bob Dylan's song "A Hard Rain is Gonna Fall," which became a kind of anthem of Viet Nam war–era radicalism, an aspect of which was a break from the more austere and class-related radicalism of the Communist Party and other, similar Marxist groups. The Dylan version of revolution is contrasted here with the 1905 mutiny of the sailors of the Russian battle cruiser *Prince Potemkin,* a mutiny crucial to the "bourgeois" revolution of that year, which was in turn an important precursor of the 1917 Bolshevik revolution. The contrast is instructive and clear. The high point of 1960s and early 1970s political activism seems to the speaker of "A Note on the Late Elections" an inadequate and unlikely scenario for "real" revolution, as the election (one supposes) of Richard Nixon in 1968 showed, while the mutiny of the sailors on the *Potemkin* was the forerunner of a "real," thorough revolution. McGrath's allegiance to a thoroughgoing, communist revolution is an essential component of his ideology and an integral part of his "voice."
    Though McGrath certainly echoes in his verse an American radicalism

that was once central to the American left, it must be said that many Marxists, in the period after World War II, have found themselves deeply disturbed by the actions of the Soviet Union as well as of other ostensibly socialist and communist states. As a result of events as disparate as the Soviet-Chinese clash, the continuing lack of civil and other human rights in most of the Eastern European nations and in the rest of the world's nations governed by avowedly socialist regimes, the clashes in post–Viet Nam war Kampuchea, and too many others to recount here, many Marxists have had to re-think their sense of possible existing models for the societies "the revolution" might achieve. What of McGrath in this regard? I think it fair to say, as I read his poetry, that he has simply not dealt with questions that go much beyond the moment of "the revolution" itself. I do not mean, of course, that the man Thomas McGrath has not thought about these issues; I do not doubt that he has. I do mean, however, that in the verse he has written, in the "voice" of the "pseudo-autobiography," he chooses not to question the outcome of the Soviet revolution or of the desired revolution yet-to-come, but rather to celebrate the revolutionary act itself. In one section of *Letter,* the speaker of the poem is recalled in mind by the name of the North Dakota town of Lisbon to the Lisbon in Portugal, where he was at the time of the revolutionary events that overthrew the successors to the Salazar dictatorship. In square brackets he recalls that revolutionary moment, which ended one of the longest-lasting fascist dictatorships in the Western world:

> [Yes, I hear them now
> In this other time I am walking, this other Lisbon, Portugal—
> Bells of the Revolution, loud as my heart I hear
> Above the continuous bad-rap of the urine colored sea.
> Besides which I am walking through that snow of July leaflets
> In search of the elusive onion to make the home-done sandwich
> Herbaical and vegetable and no doubt even healthy, and certainly
> Hearty-seeming (in mind's tongue) after fifteen K's and quais
> *A la recherche de cebolla perdue:*
>   *Vegicum Apostolicum*
> *Herbibable sancti et ecumenicabable . . .*
>   Meanwhile
> I die on the vine waiting for news from you, Tomasito,
> Waiting for the angel, waiting for news from heaven, a new
> Heaven, of course—and a better world in birth! *Here*:
> Under the changing leaflets under the flailing bells.]
>   (*Letter III & IV,* 27)

The reference to "The International" ("the earth shall rise on new foundations / A better world in birth"), the long-standing anthem of the international communist movements (a song that is discussed in another connection in Joseph Butwin's essay in this volume), together with the wish for news of Tomasito, McGrath's young son, make clear to me that the speaker

of *Letter* is interested in the revolutionary moment itself, finding it the exciting, hopeful event. The speaker perceives the revolutionary action as the
crucial precursor to change for the good because the arrangements of the
capitalist world (and, in the case of Portugal, of a fascist nation) are so devas-
tating that any revolutionary move to the left must at the very least provide
the possibility of improvement. What McGrath is against is clear enough—
it is societies based on the "cash nexus." It is the rebels, the revolutionaries,
the fighters for the needs of poor people, working people, racial minorities,
the colonial oppressed, those who seek a social morality like that of "the
commune," "the round dance" of his North Dakota, whom he celebrates.
He does not feel it the task of the poet, the speaker of the "pseudo-autobiography," to chart the future beyond that. There is some sense in this.
McGrath is, after all, writing poetry and not political philosophy. His
responsibility is to his feelings, his vision, and not necessarily to abstract
political theory. Let others, one supposes him saying, deal with the difficulties the revolution might produce. Let others correct, change, or modify
Marxism. Mine is the seer's task—singing a vision of change; mine is the
task of dealing with

> . . . the false Past . . .
> 	Which we must restructure if we're to create
> The commune
> 	and the round dance . . .
> 			Kachina . . .
> 				the Fifth Season . . .
> The National Past has its houses, but their fires have long gone out!
> 				(*Letter III & IV*, 37)

I have attempted here to deal only with a few aspects of McGrath's
"voice" created, as Mills has it, "from the deep centers of a personal engagement with experience," from "the self which he is waiting to be." If the
aspect of "voice" with which I have dealt is extensively political, that seems
to me an accurate reading of McGrath—and one that he himself prefers. His
is a political voice, then, and a revolutionary political voice; it is a representatively American voice, but also an individual voice of a particular kind; it
is a voice charting the end of agrarian America and despairing of the emptiness and the inhumanity of the urban nation that replaces it; it is a voice
that works to avoid sentimentality about the old agrarian life, but one that
nonetheless sees in it, as well as in the Native American heritage, something
precious that has been forever lost; it is a voice that celebrates the revolutionary moment and does not concern itself with the possible aftermath of revolution—a voice that celebrates all kinds of "victims" and "fighters" in its
search for "the commune." It is, I believe, a unique voice, unique in its
sources from "the tradition" as well as from personal experience, and thus it
is as radical as Whitman's was in the middle of the nineteenth century—and
as "representative."

*   *   *

In the passage I have quoted from Ralph Mills earlier, there is a phrase that I have not yet considered. The contemporary poet, writes Mills, "like a snake shedding his dead skin, frees himself of the weight of imposed styles and current critical criteria to come into the place of his own authentic speech." It is my view that McGrath's "speech" is, indeed, authentic, and if not entirely unique, it is certainly unusual. In its peculiarity, it is rich and gives us one of the grounds for considering him "important."

It is difficult, from such a point of view, to analyze McGrath's style in any brief compass. He has written in an enormous variety of forms, unusual for many contemporary poets. There are very short, epigrammatic lyrics—haiku-like poems—as well as longer poems; there are prosy passages reminiscent of Karl Shapiro's "prose poems"; there are medium-length lyrics; and there is, of course, the book-length *Letter to an Imaginary Friend,* which, though one cannot call it an epic, has attributes as similar to the epic poem as anything written by an American in the twentieth century. There are highly decorated, complexly metaphoric passages that remind one that McGrath comes into his maturity at the time when the metaphysical poets have been rediscovered and are highly cherished by such writers as T. S. Eliot and McGrath's teacher at Louisiana State, Cleanth Brooks. There are also, however, simple, direct statements that take their force less from metaphor than from well chosen, powerful vocabulary and rhetoric. There is in his poetry an effort to capture a variety of speech, of workers and farmers as well as of city trade unionists and middle-class intellectuals. There is the four-letter Anglo-Saxon, French, Latin—and humorously phony French and Latin. The range of tone in his poetry runs from the most serious awareness of horror, death, disaster, to the most witty and humorous, from the romantic love poem to raunchy and sexually suggestive language. There is, in short, a plethora of language so varied in McGrath's large output as to defy any effort to reduce his work in any analysis of "style" or "form" that is more complete than the examination of particular instances.

Several of the essays in this volume deal with various aspects of McGrath's style in some detail. James Bertolino, Robert Schuler, Gene Frumkin, and Joel Oppenheimer—all poets in their own right—consider one or another aspect of McGrath's style in their essays. Hayden Carruth comments in his wide-ranging essay on McGrath's prosody. Joseph Butwin considers humor in McGrath's work in his essay "The Last Laugh," and Diane Wakoski considers his language of romance—his dealing with women—in her essay. In another sense, Carla Kaplan's annotated bibliography demonstrates the variety of formats in which McGrath's poetry has appeared. My intention here, then, is not to provide an overview of McGrath's style, but rather to consider a few issues that, I believe, might be clarified.

The large variety of forms in which McGrath has written require some comment. As one looks over McGrath's poetry, one finds in the early works as well as in the later that from the beginning he has varied the forms in which he has written. So early a work as *Longshot O'Leary's Garland of Practical Poesie* contains rather longer poems, such as the already-mentioned 135-line "Blues for Jimmy" or the 76-line "He's A Real Gone Guy: A Short Requiem for Percival Angelman," as well as the short 8-line "Two for the Show." Not yet to be found in this volume, or in other early works, are the later developments in McGrath's writing, the very short two- or three-line epigram and the very long poem. But the materials for a variety of lengths are present and beginning to develop early in his career. In the 1982 collection *Passages Toward the Dark* and in the 1983 *Echoes Inside the Labyrinth,* both extremes can be found. There are the two- and three-line poems, many of them from a collection of short poems entitled *Open Songs,* and there are longer poems, such as the 96-line "Keynote Speech for a Convention of Arsonists" (*Passages,* 51–54) or the many stanzas of "Trinc" (*Echoes,* 13–18). Thus, from the point of view of length, McGrath has explored every variety imaginable. It seems to me that the epigram, or loosened haiku or senryu forms, are rather later developments in McGrath's work, though the long poem, *Letter* in particular, is something he has had in mind for many years.

If one examines McGrath's work for standard poetic forms, one finds a rather great variety. He writes, for example, poems using folk songs and ballads for structure. "The Ballad of the Blind Staggers" in *Longshot O'Leary* (13), for one instance, consists of four stanzas, each stanza of two couplets, rhyming aabb, aabb, aabb, baba. Each stanza ends in the line "And Christ got back up on the cross again," except the last stanza, which reads "Christ is on his cross and He won't come down." The poem is indeed reminiscent of American folk balladry. A similar item is "A little Song About Charity" (18), which is headed "(Tune of Matty Grove)," a well-known folk song. McGrath uses forms like blues in a number of instances, one of which Studs Terkel quotes in his comments in this volume. There is less of this song-based usage in later than in earlier works, though an interesting exception is the poem "After I'm Gone (Da Da Da Da Da)," in as late a volume as *Passages Toward the Dark* (58), a poem based on the well-known jazz standard "After You've Gone," in which McGrath uses only a play on the title of the standard—and on its rhythm in the "da da da da da" syllables—though the poem itself does not follow the song's rhythmic or rhyming pattern. Thus, McGrath uses a variety of song forms in his verse as "fixed" forms into which he puts his own language.

That is by no means his only formal device of course. I have found only one more-or-less standard sonnet in McGrath's output, but there are poems reminiscent of the sonnet. The fourteen-line poems "The End of the Line" (*Passages,* 66) and "The Histories of Morning" (*Echoes,* 45) do not follow the usual rhyming or rhythmic pattern of the sonnet, though both poems can be seen as having the kind of division between octave and sestet characteristic of the form, albeit at somewhat different points in the poems. There are few other examples of "fixed" forms in McGrath's work. The bulk of his work is in free verse forms, common to contemporary American poets, and, when rhymed, is not set in any particular "preexisting" pattern. Indeed, at times McGrath seems to revel in slant rhyme—or near rhyme or para-rhyme as this peculiar form (almost by definition an irregular verse form) is variously called. He can be quite outrageous in this usage, rhyming, say, "blazing" and "shining" (*Letter I & II*, 192) or playing in one instance with internal rhyme, internal slant rhyme, and alliteration: "Mister/Twister (O Prester John) the master pressman" (*Letter I & II*, 151).

Even in free verse, McGrath's devices are interestingly varied. The lengths of his lines range from quite short, dimeter and trimeter beats, to quite long six-beat lines—the latter the basis of *Letter to an Imaginary Friend*—and sometimes even to lines as long as octometers. It is difficult to scan McGrath's verse in the usual fashion. In his free verse forms, as with most of his contemporaries, he does not necessarily follow a single consistent metric pattern. In "A Note on the Book," introductory to *Letter to an Imaginary Friend, Parts I & II*, McGrath writes:

I think of the metrical base of this poem as being the six beat line. This is not, obviously, true of some of the sections; and even where it *is* true it is not always apparent, since I have sometimes broken the line or cut it in half for what seemed to me the greater value of emphasis. In the last analysis I was more interested in the cadence than the line, but as the poem progresses the autonomy of the line becomes more assured—as I think it should be for the general welfare of American verse.

In discussion with McGrath I have asked him if he still sees the six-beat line as basic to the poem, and he has responded with an unequivocal "yes." In attempting to scan the poem, I have come to the conclusion that although this is generally true, it is difficult to apply usual metric standards to the work, because McGrath is more often concerned with capturing the rhythms of speech rather than with fulfilling any pre-set metric pattern. That is, I can find seven-beat iambic lines, six-beat trochees, and many other metrics often complicated by a kind of caesura in the middle or in several parts of the line indicated by the break McGrath mentions in the quote above, or by punctuation. The variety of line patterns is best seen by an examination of the poem itself, rather than by citing examples. Furthermore, it seems to me that the variety of patterns is greater in *Parts III* and *IV* of *Letter* than in *Parts I* and *II*, though in all parts of the poem the line tends to be rather long.

It is the effort to capture speech patterns that seems to me, from a formal point of view, perhaps the most unusual quality of McGrath's verse. In part, of course, this is a matter of vocabulary and metaphor. Only a few present-day poets, especially perhaps those coming out of the "Black Arts" movement of recent years, have pursued the reproduction of speech in verse as assiduously as has McGrath. What is more, like the "Black Arts" movement poets, and like such writers as Langston Hughes in both poetry and fiction or Nelson Algren in fiction, McGrath is concerned not only with rendering the speech of middle class, highly educated Americans but also with reproducing the speech of North Dakota farmers and city trade unionists, working people with relatively little education not frequently found within the framework of "high" art. If nothing else exemplifies this interest, and the variety of his interests in this regard, the three epigraphs to *Part II* of *Letter* will. The first of these epigraphs is a quote from Brecht, the second is a quote from Lévi-Strauss. But the third epigraph makes my point. It is a quote from "The Joint Is Jumpin'," a "Fats" Waller song: "Don't give your right name! No, no, no!" That is the spoken last line of the recording, and of McGrath's epigraph, from a song that has to do with a riotous party—perhaps one of the famous Harlem "rent" parties—broken up by the police. McGrath is here working in a tradition of major importance in recent American poetry. Especially William Carlos Williams, in his own long poem *Paterson*, makes such an effort continuously. Indeed such an effort is a central part of the poetics of romantic poetry—as Wordsworth's familiar "selection of language really used by men" shows. That McGrath—or Williams, for that matter—is not particularly interested in Wordsworth's effort to render a language "(purified indeed from what appears to be its real defect from all lasting and rational causes of dislike or disgust)"[9] not only indicates how far this aspect of modernism has come since its inception in Romanticism, but also demonstrates conceptions of language that eschew the kind of privileging Wordsworth's phrase indicates. Thus, for McGrath and for others who have taken most seriously the notion of democracy, "language really used by men" *cannot* be "disgusting." For McGrath, as a matter of fact, as well as for the poets of the "Black Arts" movement or for a writer like Nelson Algren and many others, the language of workers and farmers, of the poor and the down-and-out, of slang and jargon, of those *outside* the mainstream, has about it a poetic force and beauty not attenuated by middle-class pretensions, which gives it a very special and important quality. It is part of their *ideology* to reproduce such language.

One can document the varieties of speech in McGrath's work from many of the characters who people his poetry. There is, for instance, Peets, who in the interview later in this volume McGrath tells us "is the landlord I had down in Louisiana, and he first appears in the section [of *Letter*] which deals with the ice storm. He's just one of those voices I keep hearing, a kind of cynical and reactionary voice, I guess, in some ways a counter voice to some of the radical voices in the poetry." McGrath writes:

Then, Asia Street: where I roomed at the family Peets.
A bug mine, a collapsible chamber of horrors

9. Wordsworth, "Preface to the Second Edition of Lyrical Ballad," pp. 300, 301.

Held together by tarpaper and white chauvinism.
There was Peets with his gin, his nine foot wife and his son
Who was big enough to be twins—and stupid enough for a dozen,
And the daughter, big as all three, with a back-side for a face,
With a mouth of pure guttapercha, with a cast, with a fine
High shining of lunacy crossing her horsy eyes—
"Fuck or fight!" I can hear her yelling it now
And out of the room at the back the bed starts roaring,
The house is moaning and shaking, the dust snows down from the ceiling,
The old dog sneezes and pukes and Peets is cursing his wife:
"Teach your daughter some manners, you goddam cow!
Tell her to close the door, and come back to this goddam bed!"

> *(Letter I & II, 60)*

Peets recurs throughout the poem, often with epigrammatic sayings,
when there seems to be reason for a voice like his:

> "Stick out your behind to the North
> Wind and see which cheek gets cold first," Peets says.
> "Know thyself," he confides. "In the dark a wise man
> Can tell his ass from his elbow."
>
> *(Letter I & II, 63)*

And later on, in *Part II* of *Letter* when the speaker of the poem faces a
time of despair in the immediate post–World War II period, he recalls Peets
in another connection:

> "_____ and seems like it was right here someplace—place you git out . . ."
> "Stick beans in your nose and you cain't smell honey." (Peets talking)
> "Ain't no grabirons a man can lay hand to. *I tell you it's* DARK
> DOWN HERE MAN!
>   slippery dark
>   can't see
>   I tell you it's hell—"
>
> *(Letter I & II, 107)*

These quotations seem to me to show McGrath's interest in speech—done
not with the frequently used clumsy changes of orthography but mostly by
means of vocabulary and syntax—not only in the direct quotations but also
in the sections in which the speaker's own voice adapts to the voices around
him, as in the description of the Peets family home.

Another voice heard from time to time in *Letter,* especially in the
Amchitka portions of the poem, is that of Preacher Noone, a fellow soldier:

"Put me down God," Preacher Noone says. "Put me down.
Here am I, 10,000 miles up and I'm flyin' blind;
Got no wings, got no airplane, got no passport—I say to you, God,
Put me down, sir."

In the same passage, we find:

("This train ain't bound for glory," says Preacher Noone.
                         "this train
Ain't bound for glory. Put me down God, please sir")
                         (*Letter I & II*, 73)

and again

                         ("I give you up, God," says Parson
Noone, "I give you up, Sir. You got me cornered
With a Williwaw roaring around my ass and my pants down—
Doctorinal matters blown past at ninety an hour—
I do hereby give you up, sir, truly.")
                         (*Letter I & II*, 75)

Sometimes McGrath uses his quoted passages repeatedly, recalling in one part of this long poem earlier portions. For instance, in the passage following briefly after Peets's "Know thyself" speech, we find the following:

Palaver—
Tradition! Heigh ho! Tradition!
Bobbery! Bobbery. Palaver—
DON'T GO BAREFOOT TO A SNAKE STOMPING!
                         LOOSEN YOUR WIGS!
It's no use hooking them both on the same circuit—
The English and American traditions.
It won't take the play out of the loose eccentrics.
Cattlemen, sheepmen and outlaws, that's American writing,
And few enough outlaws at that.
                         (*Letter I & II*, 63)

The capitalized phrase recurs in the Christmas Section of *Part III* of *Letter,* when the speaker of the poem, recalling through Christmas memories various events in his life and times, recalls the so-called siege of the Pentagon, that crucial event in the history of the anti–Viet Nam war movement:

"Don't go barefoot to a snake stompin'!
                         There's no friends
In Wolf City!"
                         So . . . we go on—passage by night,
By water—but the river is frozen and nothing is charmed or changed
By our little crossing . . .
                         (as, in faery stories: crossing
A stream changes all)
                         as little was changed in that other Crossing
Where we went over the Potomac in the "siege of the Pentagon:"
In '68 I think it was: and got into Second
Bull run by some kind of historical oversight . . .
                         (36)

Thus we can see that McGrath uses individual speech as a prod to memory, as he uses incident and character throughout his long poem, as a means for recalling the past in his "pseudo-autobiography," reminding us of one section of the poem by a speech phrase from another section.

There are many other voices to be heard in McGrath's poems. McGrath's family can be heard. Working people of various kinds speak. Sometimes the enemy, the military, or the rich, or venal politicians are given voice. "Given voice" is the proper phrase here, it seems to me, for McGrath gives us, of course, a created set of voices, the product of his hearing as well as of his imagination, rather than making an effort at some sort of literally linguistic "translation" into writing. He uses these voices as a kind of "found" poetry, analogous to "found" art, reworked by the artist into the design he is weaving. The best-known antecedent in American poetry for this usage is Carl Sandburg, especially in the volume *The People, Yes.* There are other crucial antecedents as well. As with almost everything else in modern American poetry, Pound, Williams, and the Eliot of "The Waste Land" must also be mentioned.

McGrath uses many other language devices as well. He is in control of elevated languages as well as of the speech discussed above, and sometimes he obtains particular effects by the juxtaposition of these two varieties of language:

Meanwhile back among the ranch-type ramblers
The television set loosens the apron strings
Of housewives temporarily widowed
By the same quotidian lion of hard labor.
    ("The Histories of Morning," *Echoes,* 45)

For another example I turn to a very funny, antic poem already mentioned called "Trinc," from a section of it in praise of beer:

    But from beer comes banjos and jazz bands ecstatic
Trumpets midnight Chicago early thirties Bix.
It was Beer that invented Sunday from the long and salty days
of the workday week:
               that from the fast beer on horseback or the warm
Beer of the burning fields of the harvest, when the barley comes in,
Fermented the sabbatarian leisure;
               that, in the eye of the workstorm,
For the assemblyline robotniki and the miner who all week long
Must cool his thirst at the root of the dark flower of the coal
Offered reprieve;
             and for slow men on tractors (overalled
And perpetually horny) turned off their motors for the Sabbath calm.
    ("Trinc *Praises II,*" *Echoes,* 14)

These lines are in many ways exemplary of McGrath's use of language.

Here is his fascination with sound: "banjos-band," "workday week," "cool-root-coal"; his pleasure in playing with word changes: "robotniki," the word "robot" given a mock-Russian ending; his play with "high" language: "Fermented the sabbatarian leisure," in a poem in praise of beer as the working-man's drink; and his use of slang: "perpetually horny." In brief, McGrath is a poet who explores the devices of "the American language" as extensively as, if not more than, any poet who has helped to shape the sense of the varied use of language in contemporary poetry.

Thus, an important aspect of McGrath's "own authentic speech" is his use of the speech of others, characters who people his poetry—language sometimes elevated, sometimes colloquial, but always reworked through the poet's own devices into the substance of his verse.

Such speech, as well as his use of a variety of metaphor and sound devices (which I have not discussed here, since the subject is addressed elsewhere in this volume), the large number of forms in which McGrath casts his poetry, including his use of song, and the complexity of his metric patterns, give McGrath's poetry its individuality. On formal grounds as well as on others, McGrath makes a significant contribution to the body of American poetry—sufficient to make him "important."

* * *

Letter to an Imaginary Friend was first published in 1970 in what was then the totality of the poem, its *Parts I* and *II*. The poem was 214 pages long. *Part I* ends with a place and date designation: "Los Angeles, 1955." *Part II* has a similar concluding line, though more extensive, indicating where the poem was written or thought about or placed, and when it was finished: "North Dakota—Skyros—Ibiza—Agaete—Guadalajara, 1968" (214). McGrath has said that though he thought he was finished with the work, he realized soon after the poem was published that "My God, there's more" (interview). Additional pieces of the poem soon appeared in journals and, in time, in such collections of McGrath's poems as *Waiting for the Angel* (1979), *Passages Toward the Dark* (1982), and *Echoes Inside the Labyrinth* (1983). Finally, in 1985, Copper Canyon Press published *Letter to Imaginary Friend Parts Three and Four*.[10] This volume ends with a place and date designation like that I have quoted from the end of *Part II*: "North Dakota—Portugal—Moorhead, Minnesota / 1984." Thus, we now have the poem in two volumes, one of 214 pages and one of 115 pages, both volumes composed in and having reference to a variety of locales, and obviously composed over many years.

I begin my discussion of the relationship of the two volumes that com-

10. The volume does not use Roman numerals in the poem's title, as did *Parts I* and *II*. They have been used here, however, for consistency's sake, though not when the title of the poem itself is quoted.

prise the poem with this matter of dates because I believe that consideration
of these data gives us an opportunity to examine developments in the
thought, poetic technique, and general poetic stance of the work as a whole.
It is necessary to point out, before proceeding, that the speaker of *Letter,
Parts III* and *IV* is unquestionably the same as the speaker of *Letter, Parts I*
and *II*. That is, though some changes and developments can be observed, the
underlying political ideology, the revolutionary, Marxist ethos central to the
earlier poem is still central to the later one. So is the presentational method
of the poem. *Letter, Parts III* and *IV,* like *Parts I* and *II,* is essentially "pseudo-
autobiography." The persona of both volumes is essentially the same persona, though in the later volume honed—though by no means chastened—
by experience, by time, perhaps simply by aging. The two volumes, then, are
both unified and differentiated, in a variety of ways I want to examine here.

At first glance, one can note a number of significant differences in
form between the two volumes. *Letter I & II* is consistently, throughout,
made up of relatively long lines, lines that look like the lines of a poem and
that inevitably make clear its status, in the era of free verse, as "poem."
McGrath writes, in "A Note On The Book" introductory to this volume,
which I have quoted earlier, that he considers the "six-beat line" as the "metrical base" of the poem.

Essentially the same line as that dominant in *Parts I* and *II* dominates
III and *IV*. There are, however, more variations here. We find, for example, a
kind of Christmas cantata, which begins with a page-long quotation from
Luke 2:8–20, telling the story of the annunciation to the shepherds of
Christ's birth. Assigning parts to various voices—tenor, basso, counter
tenor, and so on—the story is then retold in a variety of styles and "dialects,"
including a kind of pidgin ("'No Scare,' say angelman. 'Got plenty damn big
news, everybody get some. Savior all same Messiah in Bethlehem bime-
by!'"), wordplays of various sorts ("And she brought forth her first born
sonata / and wrapped him in swaddling cloud-berries / and laid him in a
mangonel; / because there was no root for them / in the inoculation"
[65–69]). These are all part of the Christmas scene that is the plot, as it were,
of *Parts III* and *IV*. This portion of the poem does not look like poetry,
though in its split-page section it looks like drama or like the lyrics for choral
music. Nothing quite like this exists in *Parts I* and *II*. Thus, though the six-
beat line is certainly still the "metrical base" of the poem, in *Parts III* and *IV*
variations from this line are greater—with many more examples of such
variation than the extreme one I have cited—than in *Parts I* and *II*.

In *Part III* we also find typographical jokes, which have no counterpart
in *I & II*. For example, there is a kind of Brechtian sign board that sets apart
a funny, even zany story about the coming of the Three Wise Men to a farm
family in a northern, cold climate such as the North Dakota of McGrath's
childhood. The sign, surrounded by a black border and with a sketched
hand pointing to it, says: "The Coming of the 3 Weis Men / A Tale for Good

Little (Red) Indians / And other (Colored) Minorities . . ." (19). A similar sign board appears a little earlier in the poem, following the beginning of a section referring to the disappearing hand of the boy who is the subject or the "protagonist" of the "plot" of this part of the poem. The sign board follows lines that sing the praises of the use of this "hand" for, among other things, sexual exploration. Then with the same hand as in the later board pointing to it comes the sign board that says "Classical Ass / is Hard to Pass" (13). There are other such typographical jokes as well, more difficult to discuss in speech because of their visual nature.

The point I wish to make here is that though basically *Letter, Parts III* and *IV* uses the same long line—the more-or-less six-beat line—dominant in *Letter I & II,* it moves more easily and freely away from the dominant formal line of the poem as a whole than is the case in *Letter I & II.* Combined with the typographical jokes, this less rigorous line form in *Parts III* and *IV* gives these parts of the poem a looseness—though a clearly controlled and purposeful looseness—that *Parts I* and *II* show to a much lesser extent.

This greater looseness of *Parts III* and *IV* is shown in another aspect of the poem. In much of his verse, McGrath likes to joke. Not only does he like the joke for its own sake, but he also ameliorates his ultimate seriousness and prevents it from becoming solemnity by his constant willingness to crack wise, to "kid around," to laugh—though often the laughter is gallows humor. In large part, I believe, this penchant for humor comes from McGrath's sense of self or, if one prefers, from the nature of the persona who is the speaker of most of his poetry. Though McGrath the man is certainly an intellectual of considerable power, a Rhodes scholar, an LSU graduate student who studied with Cleanth Brooks, a university teacher, he is also— as much multiple personality as we all are—the North Dakota farmhand, the shipyard worker, and the New York waterfront organizer. McGrath knows, I believe, and certainly the persona who speaks in his poetry knows, that one of the great saving graces for most people, and one of the great attributes of all Americans, particularly of all working people, is the ability to be funny, to wisecrack, to "kid around." It is no accident, it seems to me, that in this regard as well as in others, McGrath is similar to Bertolt Brecht, a radical and Marxist writer also devoted to humor and to the joke.

In *Letter I & II* humor most often takes the form of the presentation of comic voices other than those of the poem's main speaker. Such figures as "Preacher" Noone or the only sometimes comic Peets can be heard in *Parts I* and *II,* often with extended set speeches. Some elements of these will then recur throughout the poem, becoming, at times, important catch phrases that remind us of previous events in the poem and help to give it unity.

But in *Parts III* and *IV* the humor takes a different, or at least an additional, turn. In the instances I have already quoted—the Christmas "cantata," the sexual joke—and others as well, the humor becomes a major part of the poem, at times pervasive. The entire "plot" of these later parts of the poem lends itself to humor. The story of the Christmas events on the home farm—the sleigh ride to church, the eventual return home and preparation for gift giving, the child's dream—this memory of the childhood of the speaker of the poem, provides what seem like natural opportunities for "kidding around." There is, for example, the already-mentioned telling of the story of the "3 Weis Men," which gives us confusing and amusing mixtures of Irish and Scandinavian Christmas lore, as Sven becomes Ole, as the Scandinavian dialect becomes Irish. Eventually, however, as is so often true in McGrath, the humor takes on seriousness, as the whole scene turns into a reminder of the reality of life on the farm. The characters who speak the story suggest that, instead of three wise men, what they really see coming is "Bill Dee and the Prairie Mule and maybe / . . . Some other lonesome deadbeat staggerin' home from the Hills . . ." (20). Here, concluding this wildly funny passage, the unifying—and serious—function of the poem's humor is shown, as it extends from *Parts III* and *IV* back to *Parts I* and *II*. Bill Dee, whom I have mentioned before, is a figure in the earlier volume, a North Dakota hunter and fisherman who stays on the land after most others "got blown out in the last of the dusters," a man who knows that the land "Should never been farmed no-way" but who believes, contrary to all reason, that "They're comin' back sure—the old days." But the speaker of the poem comments, "Dreamed it; no doubt. And dreamed the old days as well: doubtless. / Another fast dreamer . . ." (199–200). Thus, though this humorous passage in *Parts III* and *IV* is in itself a set piece, one element that helps to undercut any possible sentimentality in the Christmas scene, it is also a unifying passage reminding the reader of important materials in *Parts I* and *II* of the poem. Moreover, it reminds us that though the retelling of this childhood tale has its value, the past is never quite what the past appears to be in memory—as the speaker of the poem in all of its parts and as we as readers as well, sometimes "dream the old days"—like Bill Dee, all of us at times, are "fast dreamers."

McGrath's humor, then, is there not only for its own sake but also for purposes that somehow advance the idea, the structure, or the unity of the poem. Perhaps another example, one so charming that it has caught the attention of many commentators, will make my point clearer. Describing a visit by the boy to the church, the poet focuses on the confessional: "He [Father Mulcahy] takes his fatherly leave of a woman ninety years old, / And gets back to the central business of sinbusting. I'm the next case" (45). The boy then looks for sins to confess because even though " . . . in my child's heart, I do sense sin . . ." he really has no sins to confess. Then he explains—or rather, the speaker of the poem interprets for him—the sins he feels but cannot confess:

> Yes, I do know sin,
> For haven't I felt the whole universe recoil at my touch?

And my mother weep for my damned ways?
                              At my approach
The Sensitive Plant contracts its ten thousand feathery fingers
Into a green fist.
                      I have caused the sudden nova
Where the Jewel Weed's seed-box handgrenade explodes at my touch.
It is fear of my sin that changes the rabbit's color;
                                                      my sin
That petrifies the wave into pelagic trance
Where the deep sea hides its treasures;
                                          It is from fear
Of me that the earthquake trembles in its cage of sleep and ennui;
For me the stars shudder and turn away, closing
Against my image the shining and million eyes of the night . . .
                                                      (46–47)

But those are not the sins Father Mulcahy can consider, nor can the boy confess them. What can he confess for which Father Mulcahy will exact a greater penalty than "three Our Fathers and three Hail Marys. Hop to it."? The boy wants a harder penance because he *feels* his sin and his responsibility for the world's ills, just as he will feel such responsibility as an adult: "As among Spiritual Works of Mercy, Father. To instruct the ignorant. / To admonish sinners. / . . . As among Corporal Works of Mercy, Father: / To bury the dead. To visit those in prison" (48). But Father Mulcahy will not be moved. Then begins the mock confession of sins that grow in intensity, hyperbole, wordplay. The sins are presented in a stichomythic format— contrasting sharply with the poem's usual long line—which gives the confession a rapid-fire quality, enhancing both its comic nature and its intensity:

"I am guilty of chrestomathy, Father."
                              He lets out a grunt in Gaelic.
Shifting out of the Latin to get a fresh purchase on sin.
"And?"
"Barratry, Father.
"And minerology . . . .
"Agatism and summer elements . . .
"Scepticism about tooth fairies . . .
"Catachresis and pseudogogy . . .
"I have poisoned poissons in all the probable statistics . . .
"I have had my pidgin and eaten it too, Father . . .

The list that gives us not only comic sins but also McGrath at his word-loving, word-playing best goes on for several more pages. When Father Mulcahy picks up the game, the sins become an alphabet of animals, beginning with "APED yr elders and bitters with Adders tongue . . ." and ending in "JACKASSed around for Donkey's years . . . ," these later "sins" in a longer than usual line, contrasting cleverly to the earlier stichomythia as the catalog of "sins" develops. But this is all in vain since the only penance Father Mulcahy will give is "Three Our Fathers and three Hail Marys—and get ye gone!" (48–52). What strikes me about this section of the poem, among other things, is how it moves easily from humor to seriousness; how the humor is itself a serious critique of Catholicism and the practice of confession and is, at the same time, a sensitive rendering, though obviously in the adult memory, of the state of mind of a child; how it invokes earlier parts of the poem—the Christmas Cantata, for instance, with its reference to pidgin; and, finally, how, in its totality, in its comic listing of evils, it moves ahead many of the poem's major concerns.

So far I have looked at two aspects of *Parts III* and *IV* of *Letter*—its variations in form and its humor—in examining its differences from *Parts I* and *II* of the poem. I have suggested that in formal ways, as well as in its use of humor, *Parts III* and *IV* has a kind of looseness and easiness in relating to its materials, which sets it off from the more contained earlier part of the poem. I want to suggest that a similar difference can be found in regard to two other matters. One of these is the poem's "spirituality" (although I want to use that term with great care), and the other is its politics, an element without which McGrath's poetry is unthinkable.

The matter of the poem's "spirituality" comes up especially in *Parts III* and *IV* if for no other reason than that in the introductory "A Note on Parts Three and Four of LETTER TO AN IMAGINARY FRIEND," McGrath writes:

> There are some strange names early in Section I of *Part Three*. These are simply the names, according to medieval occultists, for, first the powers of the cardinal directions (Cham is North, Amoyman South, etc.) then of the "infernal kings of the north" then (Azael, etc.) of the four elements, then of the great powers which I associate with the "tetragrammaton" and the Kachina (of which more in a moment). These powers are ambiguous, and, from a Judeo-Christian-Catholic prejudice, demonic. The old Biblical myth gives Adam (and off-spring) "dominion" over Nature. But to have it, the pagan deities had to be demonized or destroyed. Then we had power over the world: it became "dead nature"—so and so many board feet, and so and so much profit and loss. One project of the poem is to "angelize" these (and other) demons. That means: to return us to a view which all primitives, anyone who has spent time in the woods or anyone simply in his/her right mind has always had: that Nature is just as alive as we are. Probably there is an equation there. (unnumbered, ff. dedication page)

The concept of "angelizing the demonic" has been a part of McGrath's thought for some time. The 1979 volume *Waiting for the Angel* contains a version of *Part Three* of *Letter* not very different from the final version. This section of the book is entitled "Half-time at the Funeral" and is dedicated to the British radical historian, leader of the European peace and disarmament movement, and long-time friend of McGrath, E. P. Thompson, who contributes one of the essays in the present volume. The explanation from McGrath I have just quoted and these facts, taken together, seem to me to give a good indication of the nature of the "spiritual matter" in *Letter*.

Such spiritual materials, which seem more pervasive in *Letter, Parts III* and *IV* than in the earlier volume, may appear at first as contradicting the philosophically materialist posture of McGrath the Marxist. I do not think there is any such contradiction. In looking for ways to express *in verse* the desire of the poem's speaker to—I quote Bertolt Brecht—"change the world. It needs it!" McGrath has chosen ancient religious traditions to chart the needed change. After all, if there is a danger of sentimentality in regard to the Christmas story, there is also the danger of cliché in regard to political matter—the very clichés that have made so little poetry from the far left very palatable, or very good poetry. McGrath avoids the trap in part by using mythic, "spiritual" materials to make his point. This is most clearly exemplified by the use of the Kachina. In the "Note on *Parts III* and *IV*," McGrath writes:

> About the Kachina. For the Hopi it is a "God"—a deified spirit of great power. According to the Hopi we now live in *Tuwaqachi,* the Fourth World, but we will soon enter *Saquasohuh,* the Fifth World, which will be much better. This new world will be signaled by the appearance of a blue star. Kachinas are also doll figures which are made to symbolize spirit powers. The Blue Star Kachina will help these spirits to bring the new world into being. I see this as a revolutionary act to create a revolutionary society. All of us should help to make this Kachina. I think of the making of my poem as such a social-revolutionary action. In a small way, the poem *is* the Kachina.

This seems to me quite clear. The Fourth World, *Tuwaqachi,* is, for McGrath, present-day capitalist society, with all the evils—war, poverty, inequality, the destruction of nature, the money ethos—he associates with it. As in the citation given earlier, this is the world in which nature has become " . . . so and so many board feet, and so much profit and loss," language that invokes the Marxist idea of the conversion under capitalism of things—nature included—from use value to commodity value, from useful parts of the natural to means for coining money. The Fifth World, *Saquasohuh,* is for McGrath an eventual socialist world. He invokes the spirit forces from "Medieval occultists" as a means for indicating that powers of various sorts, powers historically conceived of by human beings to explain their world, must now be placed in the service of changing the world. Although in somewhat different ways, one is reminded of Brecht's use of oriental culture, for example the three "gods" who come to visit Setzuan to find a good person in *The Good Woman of Setzuan,* to turn his politics into theater.

McGrath's use of the "nine Heavens" near the end of the poem, has similar purposes. "The 'heavens,'" he writes in the same note, "I have based on the classical-Medieval scheme. I have kept the guardians that the system assigned to the various spheres. This is 'explained' in one of the visions." His reference is to a section near the end of the poem, when the child of the poem—or, in fact, the grown persona of the poem remembering the child—

experiences a dream that takes him from the Christmas of the moment in
"Nineteen Twenty-one or -two of the blithe and fooling times" (4) into the
long visionary dream that concludes—except for a kind of coda—the poem
as a whole. The dream moves the boy from one heaven into another: "And
my first leap is a fall . . . / long fall . . . into / The moonrock of First
Heaven" (89). Each succeeding heaven provides a different vision, a different emotional tone. But those heavens that are salutary and delightful are
ones in which the dreamer cannot remain. He must ascend from the early
Second Heaven where " . . . all's flowering light and the light of flowers!"
(94) to the penultimate heaven, the eighth heaven in which the vision of
apocalypse is patent:

> And a city grows from the smoke: white buildings,
> Spires of light, battlemented turrets and topless towers
> Glow incandescent, aspiring, powered by interior suns . . .
> Then . . .
>   a little puff . . .
>   a small cloud
>   blooms
> Over the city . . .
>   neck like a young girl's . . .
>   but grows—
> Grows: like Fate, an enormous cock, or a woman's head . . .
> And in her coiffeur the nine million swans of Bohr and Einstein
> Are mating in thunder and lightning . . . .
>   the City flashes . . .
>   explodes . . .
> Like a bundle of kitchen matches dropped in an open stove,
> Like a Mexican fiesta
>   Nagasaki
>   fireworks
>   Hiroshima . . .
> Black skeletons of bright buildings . . .
>   ash in the wind
> Like grey snow . . .
>   *a host burning* . . .
>   *nations of smoke.* . . .
>   (105–6)

The Ninth Heaven, the last before *Saquasohuh,* is a heaven the speaker of
the poem is not to be allowed to see:

> Blind.
>   This is the heaven I'm not allowed to see . . .
> Heaven of Transformation . . .
>   SAQUASOHUH . . .
>   the Fifth
> World.
>   Blindfold.

But beside me someone . . .

                              my guide or guard
Steers my progress.
                                    (107)

The description of the Ninth Heaven that follows, at first only olfactory and aural, is soon supplemented by a glance when:

                              The blindfold slips . . .
And I see . . .
            but *what?*
                        Green and gold . . .
                              The fields of a farm!
—Must have been laid out by Grant Wood and Joan Miró—
Dakota abstract . . .
                  and the combines sing as if they were free!
(Or as if they'd at least been paid for) and the fields lie free to the sun.
                                    (107–8)

    In this heaven the land is restored to a kind of pastoral naturalness and beauty, with newborn rivers, with bird and lathe sounds intertwined:

The spirits are alive in the natural world—in wood and water
In the grass underfoot, in the names and colors of winds and directions—
Are they entering again the arts and artifacts of men?
                                    (108)

Thus, the natural world is reconverted in the Ninth Heaven from commodity to artifact and is restored to beauty and to the use of human beings:

No answer from my guide or guard who adjusts the blindfold.
(And the singing is louder—though I still can't make out the words!)
"Your son will see and be where you can not," he says.
"Remember four things: body; and soul; spirit;
And the dirt from handling the world under our fingernails."
                                    (108)

The speaker of the poem then rises out of this Ninth Heaven to *Saquasohuh,* the Fifth World on which shines the Blue Star Kachina. Reverting again to medieval lore, and combining it with the Hopi myth, the speaker sees a flag:

                        . . . —reversed—
Stars for bars!—all ass-over-teakettle!—flag of the Poor!

And now the dance begins in that still unearthly light:
(*AEvum* [L.] or "*AEveternity*"—according to St. Thomas:
"The environment of angels")
                  in the Empyrean.
                              and the Angels dance,

And the Demons—O
                    Samael!
                        Azazel!
                            Azael!
                                Mahazael!
Fire
    Water
        Earth
            Air
                —and the Fifth Element!
Dancing!
        —As they did in the Ninth Heaven!
                                With bird, beast,
Water and flower and the flowering earth of the Republic of Freedom!
And they *shake*hands . . .
                    *take*hands . . .
                            the Angels set free . . .
                                    —the Demons:
                                        angelized!—
                                        (109–10)

Once "the Demons are angelized," the wait for the angel has ended.
This is a spiritual vision indeed, but it is a socio-political vision, though cast
in spiritual terms as it is encapsulated in a dream. It is a vision that main-
tains its awareness of both "body" and "soul," both "spirit" and, in McGrath
always, "the dirt from handling the world under our fingernails." One hesitates to call to mind similarities to Blakean visions, because Blake's visions
were religious, but the similarity is telling. If for Blake the spiritual gave rise
to a vision of a better world in the here and now, McGrath reverses the
field—it is his socio-political vision that gives rise to the metaphoric spiritual
vision. He *uses* his knowledge of Hopi and medieval spiritualism to provide
a poetic, metaphoric dream that will make clear what the larger dream of
the speaker of the poem really is—a dream in which commodity production
is ended and in which human beings are returned to a oneness with nature.
The poem itself and the visionary aspects of the poem *are* "the Kachina" that
is "a revolutionary act to create a revolutionary society." The comparison
with Blake may indicate the degree to which McGrath's view of the world is,
indeed, in the philosophical sense of that term, a Romantic view.

McGrath's use of what I have called "spiritual" material is not only an
issue in *Letter III and IV.* Throughout *Letter,* and in some other McGrath
poetry as well, such materials appear in one or another guise. Already in
Letter I & II we encounter the Kachina—though the concept is not as well
developed as in *Letter III and IV*—as a kind of spiritual icon, and we encounter as well other ideas and figures that can be seen as essentially "spiritual."
To some readers, this may appear to be contradictory to McGrath's clearly
materialist and Marxist impulses. Such a reading, however, seems to me the
result of a misunderstanding of Marxism in general, and American Marx-

ists and communists in particular. Marxists consider religion, in Marx's term, "an opiate" that substitutes "pie in the sky when you die" for the needed improvements of living and working conditions in the here and now. Marxist political activists nevertheless understand the need for ideas and feelings that provide for a millenarian vision of the future, though the envisioned millennium is the socialist one and not a religious one. It is some such vision that inspires radical activists to "keep going," even when the going is tough, as it was for McGrath during the McCarthy period and at other points in his life. If McGrath uses religious symbolism as a metaphor for his sense of a "better world in birth," as the song "The International" has it, that should not be surprising. Religious systems are, after all, the most available set of signs we have in the western world for a "better future." It seems to me that any other reading of McGrath's use of such "spiritual" materials, in *Letter III and IV* or elsewhere in his work, quite misses his purposes. Moreover, the Romantic impulse in most left-wing and Marxist writers, a Romantic impulse I have discussed earlier in regard to language and to the sense of history and autobiography, is present here as well. Blake comes to mind, as do other Romantic reformers and revolutionaries, when we think of visions of a better world. Such visions may well take religion-like form as means for *talking* about a "better world." It is, after all, the *language* of religion that most readily lends itself to such a notion as "inspiration." It is to the *language* of religion, and to its symbol systems, that McGrath turns in finding readily evoked parallels and readily recognized formats for the kind of "inspiration" and hope for a millennium that he seeks to present.

What I have said about the "spiritual" material in *Parts III* and *IV* of the poem will indicate, I think, that the essential politics of the two volumes and four parts of the poem are quite consistent. McGrath is now, as he was when he wrote the 1955 date line for *Part I* of the poem, a committed and convinced radical who yearns for a socialist revolution, an end to capitalism.

Nevertheless, there are some differences in regard to politics between the two volumes worth noting. The first of these is the lack of the frequent references to Communist Party and Soviet history in *Parts III* and *IV* that characterize *Parts I* and *II*. It has always seemed to me that McGrath uses such history in the earlier parts of the poem as a means for explicating his own revolutionary ideas, that his devotion is to the revolutionary moment and that he sees in Communist Party actions and in the history of the onset of the Soviet revolution a kind of icon that he can use to explicate his own hopes for the United States and for the world. In *Parts III* and *IV* it seems to me McGrath has substituted the spiritual material I have just discussed for these devices. If he can use the mutiny on the Russian battleship *Potemkin* as verbal sign in *Parts I* and *II* for actions American workers must undertake to gain power, he uses instead the Hopi myth of the Blue Star Kachina for similar purposes in *Parts III* and *IV*. I do not want to suggest that all reference to Communist history has disappeared from the poem. Early in *Part*

III, for instance, in concluding the section of the poem set during the anti-
Salazar revolution in Portugal, we find:

Time!—to change the angles and angels and to reinstate
Cham, Amoymon, Marx, Engels, Lenin, Azael,
Stalin, Mahazael, Mao, Sitræl—Che-Kachina—
O Yield up the names of the final Tetragrammaton!—
Time! To make sacred what was profane! Time! Time!
Time!
     to angelize the demons and the damned . . .
                                                        (25)

This listing of communist revolutionary leaders, who are identified
here with the demons that are to be "angelized," indicates that the change in
the poem in this regard is by no means total or complete, though I do think
it is real. Reasons for this change may be many, and may be poetic or ideological. I am not prepared to make any definitive statement about what
these reasons might be, but E. P. Thompson's essay is most cogent in this
regard. I do note, however, that lines I have already quoted indicate that the
speaker of the poem is no longer sure that he will really see, really be part of
the socialist world he hopes for, the world of the Blue Star Kachina. The
singing he hears in the Ninth Heaven is louder, he says, "though I still can't
make out the words!" a line followed by his guide's—or guard's—statement
that "Your son will see and be where you can not." It is certainly possible
that the speaker of the poem and perhaps even the poet, having struggled all
their lives for socialism and older now with socialism in this country still far
from likely, feel themselves—Moses-like—privy only to the dream. Perhaps
they believe that they will never be part of the reality, of that "Promised
Land," that Blue Star Kachina.
     It appears to me also that the politics in the later parts of the poem,
more so than in *Parts I* and *II,* are exemplified through the most personal of
experiences. The invocation of McGrath's son Tomasito, the memory of
childhood on the farm, and his family, including brothers, sisters, and parents, play a more important role in invoking the political here than is the case
in *Parts I* and *II.* Memory is the engine that drives *Letter* throughout, of
course, but the more personal quality of the memory in the later parts of the
poem and the willingness to invoke so potentially dangerous—because
potentially so sentimental—a moment as a Christmas scene to make a political statement indicate, I think, a somewhat different methodology for its
unchanging political emphasis. I do not mean that this is exclusively the
case. References to the anti-Salazar revolution in Portugal, already noted,
play a role, and other political events, personalities, and symbols are in-
voked. But in these parts of the poem, political ideology is more frequently
and firmly explicated through the Dakota experiences—a Dakota that, we
already know from the poetry in *I & II* as well as from McGrath's note to

that poem, "is everywhere." These changes give to the later parts of the poem, much more so than is the case in *Parts I* and *II,* an elegiac tone that I have come to think one finds ever more frequently in much of McGrath's recent verse. Again, I do not want to attempt to assign reasons for this change, though it may well be connected with the sense in this part of the poem, already suggested as a possibility, that the speaker of the poem may never see the promised land, the Blue Star Kachina, Socialism—that this new world can only be dream.

It seems to me, then, that in terms of the spiritual material discussed above, and even in terms of politics, *Parts III* and *IV* of *Letter to an Imaginary Friend* are, as they are in regard their humor and form, looser and more at ease with their materials. The older poet, the poet whose craft has now been honed by nearly thirty years of work—if we take the signature dates of *Part I* and *Parts III* and *IV* as our starting point—is prepared to take more chances with the language, the metaphor, even the ideology of his poetry. The younger poet was perhaps more "locked in" to the specifics of Marxist ideology, less experimental, more unwilling to risk criticism from his left-wing friends and supporters for using "spiritual" materials and more unwilling to "kid around" than is the older, more accomplished, more sure-handed poet.

In searching for comparisons, I am reminded of that wonderful set of erotic drawings from late in Picasso's career, when the master painter felt completely free to give rein to his fantasy life and felt so sure of his craft that he could do as he wished, could offer subject matter always in his consciousness, but never as explicitly and as fully presented as in these drawings. I am put in mind also of Beethoven's late quartets—works of such incomparable complexity and such transcendent beauty that they stand by themselves in the history of music—the works of a master so sure of his skills, so certain of his aesthetics, despite the loss of hearing, despite profound political and personal disappointment, that no daring was beyond him. Late in their careers, having mastered craft, having come to certainty about beliefs and sure-handedness in handling such beliefs, some poets—as some other artists as well—have the confidence to create in ways that their younger selves could not quite encompass. The freedom, the ease, the looseness, the delightfully zany humor, the daring explorations of sound and language in *Parts III* and *IV* of *Letter to an Imaginary Friend* seem to me an instance of the additional late flowering of such creativity in the mature artist Thomas McGrath.

*   *   *

If what I have said above, and what other essayists in this volume as well assert about the significance of McGrath's poetry, is true, why isn't he better known? Why isn't he accorded greater recognition? The questions are difficult on the face of it, since "recognition" for any artist is surely in part a

matter of accident—proper placing, being at the right spot to be reviewed in
the right journals. Nevertheless, in the present climate in American poetry,
where there is much critical work and where poets of many persuasions have
obtained recognition, there must be special circumstances that have pre-
vented fuller recognition for McGrath—though I must hasten to add that he
is widely published and widely known among a considerable body of those
who are deeply concerned with poetry.

Three such special circumstances come to mind. The first is connected
to McGrath's politics. McGrath's unregenerate communism and his persecution by the House Committee on Un-American Activities and all that is
associated with that event have certainly harmed his reputation. For some
years after he was fired from Los Angeles State University, McGrath worked
in Los Angeles and elsewhere at a variety of occupations merely to provide
for his wherewithal, which kept him distant from the centers where American poetry is most likely to get recognition. One must understand something of the 1950s atmosphere of repression and fear to understand how this
might have been the case. Even already well-established figures in American
art, literature, and criticism found themselves isolated within their small
coteries, always with good reason, and sometimes with reasons that only
subsequent experience might have made seem less good and might have
made seem self-imposed. In some cases, more drastic results than isolation—suicide, emigration—were the consequences. Thus, McGrath, who in
terms of his age and amount of publication should have been part of the
group of poets whom Cary Nelson has described as those who began the
1960s "with substantial reputations and reasonably well-articulated personal visions"[11]—poets like Roethke, Kinnell, Duncan, Rich, and Merwin,
to cite only those most extensively discussed by Nelson—had not been able
to establish his name as widely as they because in the previous decade he
was, so to speak, "under a cloud," or at least far away from the centers of
American poetry by virtue of work and place of residence.

I do not want to overstate the case here. Before 1970, when *Letter to an
Imaginary Friend, Parts I & II* was published by Swallow Press, McGrath
had already published some seven volumes of verse and had held both an
Amy Lowell Traveling Poetry Scholarship and a Guggenheim Fellowship.
He was by no means totally unknown or unrecognized. But still, it would
have taken unusual daring in the late 1950s or in the early 1960s, prior to the
upheavals in our political life that were to reach their acme in 1968, for anyone to give too much attention to so radical a poet as McGrath, and to one
so radical in such "unacceptable" ways. Indeed, it is to the credit of Swallow
Press and Michael Anania that a poet who dedicated his book to "Eugenia,
[then his wife], Tomasito [his son], Che and the Commune" should have
received book-length publication at all. But the paucity of reviews of the

11. Nelson, *Our Last First Poets Vision and History in Contemporary American Poetry,* p.
1.

book and the relative lack of attention it received upon publication were caused in part, I believe, by lingering political ideas redolent of the recently ended McCarthy era.

McGrath's politics has had a further influence on his reputation, I believe. During the late 1960s and the early 1970s, allegiance to radicalism was fashionable, but allegiance to communism was out of fashion with left and right alike—and McGrath has steadfastly maintained his allegiance to his communism, a communism not always, but sometimes, associated with the American Communist Party and support for the Soviet version of socialism. Thus, while the anti–Viet Nam war poets were holding readings to massive audiences and becoming heroes of the "new left," no one paid much attention to McGrath's form of radicalism, which was unfashionably class-based, old-fashionedly Marxist, and not always very sympathetic to the "long hairs" who gave the police flowers and believed in non-violence. When Eisenhower conservatism held sway in the nation, McGrath was out of fashion in one way; when "new left" and "hippie" ideologies held sway, McGrath was out of fashion in another. He has been, for most of his life, a poet wearing the wrong ideological clothes to meet the moment's modes.

How extensively such political matters harmed McGrath's achievement of a wider reputation than that which he has had I cannot be certain. That some harm resulted from them I am certain. I have found, in part in the correspondence I have conducted with many outstanding poets and critics of poetry in preparation for this volume, that almost all of them know something of McGrath and speak of him in admiring terms, but they claim only limited acquaintance with his work. Only one of the three dozen or so persons with whom I corresponded, some of whom have contributed to this volume, had unpleasant things to say about McGrath, confining him with rather nasty sarcasm to the category "the poet of the proles." As outstanding a figure as E. P. Thompson has written about McGrath extensively and very supportively, as his essay in this volume shows—but then Thompson is himself "of the left" and as an old and admired friend of McGrath's has the distinction of having "Half-Time at the Funeral," the "Christmas section" of *Part III* of *Letter to an Imaginary Friend* (*Passages Toward the Dark*, 91), dedicated to him. But critics whose political outlook is in no way particularly "left" and who are among the best known and most respected academic and non-academic critics now writing about American poetry, as well as a number of outstanding poets, have spoken approvingly of the effort and have expressed a need for carrying out an attempt to establish the significance of McGrath's work in the spectrum of American poetry.[12]

A second problem for McGrath's reputation, and one that further emphasizes the issues just discussed, has been some of the subject matter and

12. I have not mentioned any of the critics and poets with whom I corresponded in this regard by name, because it seemed inappropriate to publish comments sent to me in correspondence not meant for publication.

language of his poetry. This is another aspect of his politics, really. Much of the material of his references—that underlying secondary and allusive text with which every poet deals—comes from his radical politics, his readings in Marx and Lenin, his experiences in the trade union movement and in work associated with labor struggles, and with the American Communist Party; it would take a critic with at least somewhat similar experiences to understand his work without extensive research. Perhaps this is, in part, what has interested me personally in McGrath, since so much of this language and so many of these references are familiar to me from my own early experience. Whether it be a familiarity with the architecture of the National Maritime Union's hall—"(Below Fourteenth) and built them a kind of Moorish whorehouse / For a hall . . ." (*Letter I & II*, 123); familiarity with wobblie or "CP" talk—"branch assignment" or "scissorbills"; a recognition that the phrase "Knowledge of Necessity, All-freeing Power" echoes the Russian philosopher Georgi Plekhanov, much admired by Lenin and his Bolshevik comrades; or that Henry Winston, to whom some McGrath poems are dedicated, was the National Chairman of the Communist Party of the USA; some of his references have been a source of difficulty. Important "taste-makers" who have established the reputations of many of McGrath's contemporaries have much more familiarity with Christian or Jewish thought and referential material, even, recently, with the Black experience as materials for reference, than they do with the often arcane political materials McGrath uses.

This is a matter that has been a disadvantage to him not only with critics and reviewers but even with the younger potential poetry audience of the "new left," which *might* have been a "natural" audience for him in the 1960s and early 1970s had his material of the sort discussed here not been so "foreign" to them. After all, the young women and men of SDS were eschewing not only the establishment, which they saw as source and cause for the war in Vietnam, racism, poverty, and so on, but also the left "establishment," the "old left" from which they attempted to separate themselves and which they held responsible for the failures of past political dissidence. For them, the trade-union movement, "labor"—an important category for McGrath, though he always separates workers carefully from the trade union leadership he considers misleadership—was a failure as much as was American capitalism. It is little wonder, then, that a poet whose language was so often rooted in the language and in the symbol systems of the "old left" failed to appeal to them. It is interesting that the revival of appreciation for McGrath that I see in progress at this writing, in 1987, often comes from these very same "new leftists," now a decade or more older and now prepared to look at the recent past with some re-evaluation in mind, and with some greater breadth than was the case while the political battles that shaped them were under way. But it is not surprising to me that a poet like McGrath was not appreciated or sought after by the "new left" during its heyday. How much of a difficulty this issue might be is hard to assess, of course. The fact that the materials of McGrath's references are frequently so unfamiliar to those who might establish his reputation does seem to present a problem of some magnitude, especially when he already has been somewhat obscured by the externals of political life.

Another issue that seems to be of some moment has to do with where McGrath has been in the last two decades. Since few poets have become wealthy by their poetry and since, indeed, few poets can make a living as poets, McGrath has had to do a variety of things to earn his keep other than writing verse. Writing film scripts or carving wooden animals in a factory are not terribly conducive to the writing of poetry. Thus McGrath, like so many present-day American poets, has held university teaching positions of one or another sort since 1962 (until his retirement in 1983), most of the time at Moorhead State University in Minnesota—pretty close to the countryside of his birth, and the place where he had his first college experiences. Moorhead, Minnesota, cannot qualify as one of the centers for American poetry, despite its many other virtues. Other poets whose reputations exceed McGrath's, of course, have lived in places that are not centers of poetry either—Robert Bly and William Stafford come to mind most readily—but, certainly, absence from the "world" of poetry is a problem for a poet's reputation. Like Bly, McGrath has "done" poetry readings, a form of exposure that has been useful for many poets in our time, but he is not the spectacular performer Bly is, though he reads well, and, as one problem feeds another, he has not had the wide exposure in readings that Bly and others have had. Though McGrath is in person an amusing, charming, and interesting companion, and though he has maintained a wide correspondence—often on ragged slips of paper a more profligate soul might well consign to the wastepaper basket—he is not personally flamboyant, at least in my experience, and does not have so famous a name that readers would come flocking to hear him. Thus, locale has had a negative effect on McGrath's reputation, though, again, the degree to which it has had such an effect is hard to estimate.

Politics, difficulty of reference, and locale, then, are among reasons extraneous to the essential quality of McGrath's poetry that have had a deleterious effect on his reputation. While I am convinced that these issues have had a major impact, I may be quite underestimating one other matter. Perhaps McGrath's work, despite its affinities with the work of his contemporaries, somehow falls outside the canons of taste of the recent past and the present. His determined political position, his "proletarianism," his concern with workers and farmers, his refusal to personalize his despair, all these may also contribute to the lack of extensive recognition I believe is due him.

While the lack of recognition described here is certainly a fact, there has been a sharp change in this regard in the last year or two, as I write this. Early in 1986, the Associated Writing Programs, the association of university teachers of creative writing, recognized McGrath at a dinner in his honor at which poets Michael Anania and Philip Levine, as well as prize-winning writer "Studs" Terkel (whose brief essay appears in this volume), delivered thoughtful and serious tributes to him. An audience including some of our most important contemporary poets and other writers and teachers of writing was present and applauded and cheered heartily, not only the tributes to McGrath but also his reading of his poetry. In the same year, a Minneapolis organization held a "Ceili," a festival in McGrath's honor that was extremely well attended, which proved a joyous and moving tribute to McGrath. At the December 1986 meeting of the Modern Language Association in New York, McGrath was invited to read his poetry and read to a completely packed room. A subsequent panel concerning McGrath's work was also held. The distinguished literary journal *TriQuarterly,* under the editorship of Reginald Gibbons at Northwestern University, published an issue in the fall of 1987 devoted to McGrath and work about him. Thus, it would appear that long-deserved recognition of the sort suggested here is finally coming to McGrath.

*   *   *

I have attempted, along with the other contributors to this volume, to "make the case" for the importance of Thomas McGrath's poetry. I believe him to be a highly significant, perhaps a major, albeit neglected, voice in our poetry.

But I must deal with another matter, one that no scholarship as such can elucidate adequately. Poetry, after all, can do a great many things, but it must above all if it is to be "important" answer to some deeply felt human needs—those needs that have led to the creation of art in all cultures, as long as human beings have had image-making skills in language, plastic media, or sound, as well as sufficient food and shelter to be permitted the luxury of image-making. The most brilliant technical performance examined by the most coldly measuring critical eye must eventually break through to the connection between art and such needs, to those sources in our humanity that command the existence of art and that neither criticism nor science has as yet explained satisfactorily because of their complexity.

I believe that McGrath's poetry is important, finally, because it appeals to those human needs and qualities in special and important ways. His is the revolutionary voice, revolutionary in other than only directly political ways. McGrath, like Brecht, has charted for us, with all the competence of which his language is capable, the profoundest despair of a kind, and yet he has left us with a modicum of hope. He is deeply aware, and he helps us to be aware, that we live in the most brutal of centuries, that the very humanity we all claim to value is threatened as it never before has been threatened in the history of the species. He is deeply aware, and he helps us to be aware, that anomie and alienation are not our only enemies, that for much of the world hunger and hideous dying, war and destruction are far more real than the boredom and ill-ease with which we permit ourselves to be troubled—because we have the luxury of relatively full bellies and tolerable abodes to be so troubled. He is deeply aware, and he helps us to be aware, that the powerful, the owners of the earth, are prepared to destroy us and enslave us if it suits their perceived needs—and that we, who are his readers, have within us also the "beast" that threatens to spring, to turn us into true monsters at any moment, to become Salvatore Quasimodo's "Man of My Time":

You are still one with the stone and the sling,
man of my time. You were in the cockpit,
with the malign wings, the sundials of death,
—I have seen you—in the chariot of fire, at the gallows,
at the wheels of torture. I have seen you: it was you,
with your exact science persuaded to extermination,
without love, without Christ. Again, as always, you
have killed, as did your fathers kill, as did
the animals that saw you for the first time, kill.
And this blood smells as on the day
one brother told the other brother: "Let us
go into the fields." And that echo, chill, tenacious,
has reached down to you, within your day.
Forget, o sons, the clouds of blood
risen from the earth, forget the fathers:
their tombs sink down in ashes,
black birds, the wind, cover their heart.

(161)

And yet McGrath leaves us with hope. The hope is in the mythology of revolution—the same mythology that gives us rebels everywhere, even if the rebels may, in time, find that their newly won victory contains within it the seeds for newly needed struggles, despite the specifics of the revolutionary model the rebel espouses. It is also in the pervasive dark humor of McGrath's poetry, in his ability to laugh—and to help us to laugh—at all that is terrifying, seemingly insurmountable, life-destroying in this world, all of which, McGrath and Brecht agree, need changing. It is also in the warmth of friendship, family, love—the "round dance," "the commune," the "kachina," "the fifth season"—McGrath persists in remembering in the past and dreaming about in the future. His poetry helps us to remember, to dream about, even to act on our awareness that we are, after all, and despite all odds, members of a species that has some glorious history, and helps us to remember that we share a great deal. As Neruda writes:

So wags the world: up hill and down dale
they set up their tables and peddle their masquerades,
the pitchman was there with a different mask for each comer—
a crepuscular mask, or the face of a tiger, the masks

of austerity, piety, family pedigree—
till the full moon moved out of its quarter
and pitch-black in the darkness, we all looked the same.
                    ("Winter Encounter III," 235)

    The strongest argument for McGrath's importance, it seems to me, lies in the underlying spirit of his poetry, in its revolutionary, rebellious, despairing, hopeful reaching for a better world, or at least a livable world. As we move toward the last decade of the twentieth century, such a spirit seems unfashionable, and yet how we need it if we are to survive.

    McGrath's striving toward a fuller humanity is not an easy matter— and he knows it is not:

I'll never get to where I'm going!
No surprise in that . . .
Plugging through this deep snow,
My arms heavy with the weight of the dead . . .
                    ("Everything in Order," *Passages,* 147)

Still, there is such passionate, hopeful, yet patient, desire for change:

How I desire that patience, so faithful and disinterested,
Praying for rain, for the coming of others, for the revolution.
                    ("Chorus for Neruda #1," *Echoes,* 143)

N.B.: "Works Cited" for this essay will be found on p. 190.

2   Tom McGrath Is Harvesting the Snow

AFTER THE WAR, in 1946 or possibly 1947, I first encountered the poems of Tom McGrath in Shag Donohue's bookstore on 57th Street in Chicago. I had been born an easterner, but was from the back hills of New England, not the city, and I had a mixed heritage anyway. My grandfather had founded the first newspaper in the Dakota Territory in 1885, my father had been born in Sioux Falls. My grandfather told me of hearing William Jennings Bryan and of working with Debs in the years before World War I. In other words I had a pretty good dose of prairie populism in my childhood, and actually it fitted quite well with the eighteenth-century libertarianism of the hillside farmers who were my neighbors. Naturally McGrath's poems appealed to me.

But I was puzzled too. Why wasn't McGrath a fixture in *Partisan Review,* for instance, or in the *New Leader?* Why wasn't he right in there with Delmore Schwartz and the rest of the gang? He wasn't, of course. Even though he hewed close to the C[ommunist] P[arty] line in his poems of the late 1930s and during the war, McGrath was still a flyweight corn-hoer to the elite. Do you remember Pound's remark—he who had been born in Idaho—about Harriet Monroe with the "prairie dust swirling in her skirts"? Unless one ascribes rank ingratitude to Pound, which would seem an overreaching, the remark has less to do with Harriet than with some of the poets she had published: Sandburg, Lindsay, Neihardt, who were absent from *The Little Review, Vortex, Transition,* etc., as McGrath was absent from *Partisan.* The New York radical elite, oriented toward Europe, had always ignored "native" radicalism (I mean the continuous tradition of the elite from Johann Most to Alexander Berkman to Philip Rahv). What a pity! I am as strong a proponent for upholding literary standards as anybody, but why should *Partisan* have given us so much warmed-over Sartrean engagement when the conditions of the American working class and intelligentsia were so obviously different? What did Sartre know about the HUAC? And why was *Partisan* so damned eager to publish poems by T. S. Eliot and not Tom McGrath, to say nothing of Dr. Williams?

A significant attempt, perhaps partly unconscious, was made to subvert the tastes and opinions of my generation of American youth, and it largely succeeded.

But not with McGrath. He continued writing, he published his poems wherever he could, he refined his radicalism, moving away from Marxist simplicity toward a functional American anarcho-socialism, and he extended the scope of his poetic vision. For a time he lived on the West Coast and was, at least so I infer, turned on to the pseudo-radical antics of California's senile babies; but his roots were always in the plains. The harsh land had made his sensibility: stone and gravel, wind and snow, rust and poverty. And in the end his sensibility remained faithful to the land. He moved back to Dakota and Minnesota. I don't know exactly when that was, but I think perhaps around 1968.

Let me make it clear that I'm not talking about some social-realist hack. I'm talking about a poet with as great a voice as Whitman's, and with a devotion to the American language (and its English antecedents) the equal of anyone's. A superb talent, a splendid imagination. A *poet.* I give myself the credit of recognizing that from the first; and when I made my anthology (*The Voice That Is Great Within Us*) I tried to indicate it by giving McGrath as much space as most of his contemporaries, Jarrell, Berryman, and the rest. But I've yet to see another anthologist who has picked up the cue, and only very infrequently do I meet young poets who know what McGrath has done.

He has persevered. He has been fantastically consistent, loyal to himself. Here is a poem, a late one, called "Ordonnance":

During a war the poets turn to war
In praise of the merit of the death of the ball-turret gunner.
It is well arranged: each in his best manner
One bleeds, one blots—as they say, it has happened before.

After a war, who has news for the poet?
If sunrise is Easter, noon is his winey tree.
Evening arrives like a postcard from his true country
And the seasons shine and sing. Each has its note

In the song of the man in his room in his house in his head remembering
The ancient airs. It is good. But is it good
That he should rise once to his song on the fumes of blood
As a ghost to his meat? Should rise so, once, in anger

And then no more? Now the footsteps ring on the stone—
The Lost Man of the century is coming home from his work.
"They are fighting, fighting"—Oh, yes. But somewhere else. In the dark.
The poet reads by firelight as the nations burn.

Notice how tenderness for the poet winds into McGrath's desperate anger, almost disillusioned anger. Yet he perseveres. The poem is in hard-sounded prosody, done with perfect verbal tact. This is the poet at work, the poet transmuting his political and social anxieties into *memorable* structures. I emphasize memory. Isn't that what art wants, to make politics a part of culture? Homer could have and would have made as much of Daniel Shays as he did of Odysseus. Here is a poem called "When We Say Goodbye":

It is not because we are going—
Though the sea may begin at the doorstep, though the highway

May already have come to rest in our front rooms . . .

It is because, beyond distance, or enterprise
And beyond the lies and surprises of the wide and various worlds,
Beyond the flower and the bird and the little boy with his large questions
We notice our shadows:
Going . . .
—slowly, but going,
In slightly different directions—
Their speeds increasing—
Growing shorter, shorter
As we enter the intolerable sunlight that never grows old or kind.

Notice here the remarkable rolling control of the long lines. As I have said, Whitmanian. You cannot find more than a few American poets who can do this, though the ephebe says it is easy. Notice also the sentiment, very congenial to a fellow northman, that says the sunlight is intolerable. Is this not the hardihood that old radicals and young poets, who are the same, must assimilate to their deepest impulses? In spite of everything, the whole goddamn mess, McGrath says:

                    I'll have to walk out in the snow
In any case. Where else is there to turn?
So if you see me coming, a man made out of ice,
Splintering light like rainbows at every crazed joint of my body,
Better get out of the way: this black blood won't burn
And their fierce acids of winter are smoking in this cold heart.

No, we have nowhere else to turn, McGrath and I, though we have never met, and when we die our graves will be far apart. But they will be speaking graves, orating graves, sounding forth from beneath the heavy depths of snow. Watch out, all you smushy flatlanders. Fold your dewy palms, and listen to the brilliant voice of midnight.

3   Tom McGrath, His Poetry, A Note

ONE SPENDS A LONG time thinking about what one might say about a man's work, and in the end one can say nothing that the work does not say better, and, besides, it is always too late.

It happens that I found myself, this fall, reading "A Long Way Outside Yellowstone" to a class composed of the under-achieving children of over-achieving parents. It was a class in beginning creative writing, whatever that might mean, and it is my notion that if one can get the kiddies to read some poems while they are trying to write them, they may at least pick up some good habits if only by imitation.

But what was one to do with the children of the rich and the middle class who didn't even know there had been a great depression? And so, blindly, I read the poem to them, and then again. What I have always liked about this poem is its insistence on love, and its insistent—and accurate—arrogance about the fact that love can happen only to people who have some reason to care.

This is the strength in Tom McGrath's poetry that has always moved me, and which I intend to spend a few words paying homage to right now. Whatever his concerns, and they are many and honest ones, McGrath is capable, as perhaps only William Carlos Williams, among Americans, has been, of seeing love as a moving force, and not a sentimental snare.

Jack and Judy "make love against the cold. / He gets the night freight for Denver. She hitches out for Billings. / But now under one blanket they go about their business. / *Suppose you go about yours.* Their business is being human, / And because they travel naked they are fifty jumps ahead of you / And running with all their lights on while half the world is blacked out."

It's remarkable enough, I suppose, that a twenty-four-year-old person could have that solid a perception of the world, rather than ranting in either of the possible directions. It's more remarkable that a poem now close to forty-five years old could use the language solidly enough to hold on to its vernacular and still sing.

Because the poetry is able to fuse such contrary concerns, it has been, for the most part, ignored by those whose duty, not to say function, it is to present it to the American ear. But that's to be expected. We fall so easily for the con jobs and those "with a foreign congeries of literary claptrap, come without courtesy to a strange country. . . ."

Tom McGrath is not strange to this country but is part and parcel of it. *That* is the problem. As it is easy for our historians to excoriate Emma Goldman and praise Andrew Carnegie, it is necessary for them to forget

Debs. The same applies in literature. Let those who come from other places and refuse to see this place be heard, let those who come from this place and refuse to see it be parroted, but God save those who are this place and see it and write it.

This is, as stated, a note. It is also an attempt at an homage, and a repayment as well, for what McGrath stands for in my universe. The body of work is there, it is to be read. It is our loss that we do not read it more, it is our culture's loss that his voice is not heard as "major."

Love, concern, commitment, an eye that sees. These are things to cherish even in the mute. In a poet they are golden.

4 "Clarity Is What McGrath Is About"

TOM MCGRATH IS one of my very favorite American poets. I'll not count the ways. There is no need for that, when a poet offers his personal vision—one that overwhelms a reader. This reader, at least.

Clarity is what McGrath is about. I have no doubt, he could, if he would, be an obfuscatory bard. But he won't. Read him out loud and you find yourself singing a song that surges. Consider one stanza from "Gone Way Blues." It may be out of context, but you'll get the idea.

I have discovered the grammar of the Public Good,
I have invented a language that can be understood,
I have found the map where the body is hid,
And I won't be caught dead in your neighborhood.

Let it go at that. McGrath moves me.

5 McGrath's Brilliant Brevity

THOMAS MCGRATH HAS divided his own work into two general categories, the "tactical" and the "strategic." By "tactical" he means those poems
that have specific political or social occasions, poems intended to comment
on, or affect, particular events or situations. By "strategic" he means poems
that are not "keyed necessarily to immediate events," but in the long run will
hopefully have a positive effect on the general political and social awareness.
These terms are unfortunate in that they are both derived from military
jargon and imply two different levels of confrontation. Many of McGrath's
poems, especially the very short poems, are not in any obvious way confron-
tational and aren't served by these military categories.

McGrath's short poems, especially those of 9 lines or less, are typi-
cally humorous, spiritual, celebratory, puzzling, socio-political, or statements of love. If we consider just his work from the 1970s and 1980s, he
would appear to be one of the main practitioners of the short poem. Though
his 1972 "Collected Poems" volume offered only 17 poems of 9 lines or less,
out of a total of 171, his 1982 collection *Passages Toward the Dark* has 137
short poems out of a total of 180. Consider the poem "Homage" (*Passages,*
147):

To sit just downslope from the brow of a low hill
In the early evening.
To wait for the second song of the cricket—
What a great teacher you were
O my beloved father!

This is a beautiful and slightly mysterious poem. The tone, setting, and the
conceptual space after the word "cricket" are all influenced by the Oriental
poets, yet the voice is casual, very much contemporary American. It is difficult to imagine how either term, *tactical* or *strategic,* would reveal anything
if applied to this poem.

There was a time when very short poems were fashionable, during the
late 1960s and early 1970s, but these days many editors who take themselves
seriously look for poems that average a page-and-a-half in length, ideally
with lines in excess of eight syllables. One might suspect that today's reader
of poetry needs to be given more information in order to be able to grasp
enough of the poem. But more important than the bulk of information is the
quality, and more important than the length of line is the speed of the perceptions. To my reading, altogether too many of the bulky poems published

now in the celebrated journals are slow and burdened with the weight of poor-quality information. They seem like animals that, in their natural state, would be compact and quick but have become ponderously obese through force-feeding. I think of the speed and cunning of the wild boar.

There is a wildness, an unpredictability to many of McGrath's short poems. They shoot out from under cover, do their magical dance, and just as quickly disappear. The level of possibility is very great—under his masterful hand, just about any thing or event, any combination of words or sounds, can be the occasion for an original and memorable poem. McGrath's highly sophisticated intelligence flashes syllable by syllable, and his solid grounding in the "real" serves as platform for great leaps into fancy, invention, even metaphysics. Consider "Revisionist Poem—Octavio Paz," (*Passages,* 74):

The world is an invention of the spirit and the spirit
Is an invention of the body the body
Is an invention of the world

The short poems, more than the longer ones, are poems of discovery. Rather than becoming more predictable and dogmatic as he's matured, McGrath seems more and more open to chance and surprise. In some respects his later work seems "younger" than the earlier work. What *is* consistent, besides the level of lyric mastery, is his disdain for what's fashionable. The totality of his work is almost holographic, in the sense that all the forms, from mid-length poems in free verse to poems in traditional forms and regular patterns of his own invention, from haiku to the vast and ranging *Letter to an Imaginary Friend,* are present in his work, and at almost every stage. In fact, the diversity of forms in the McGrath canon is itself worthy of a major study.

Most important, and always revolutionary, is the quality of McGrath's *being* in his poems. The degree to which he is *there* in all his poems is the measure of his character as a poet, and as a human being. McGrath is arguably the only American poet of the second half of this century whose emotional and formal range, intelligence, longevity, and vitality can reasonably secure him a place in the company of Yeats, Whitman, and Blake.

6 Tom

THE LATE PUBLISHER Alan Swallow of Denver told me about a poet he was going to publish and how high he was on him. When Alan mentioned the title, *Letter to an Imaginary Friend,* I was instantly captivated. Any child with any kind of imagination always has an "imaginary friend" to whom he or she confides all. Flesh friends often turn traitor on one, but never one's imaginary friend.

When Alan finally did publish Thomas McGrath's *Letter,* he sent me a complimentary copy of *Part I.* I had some trouble getting into it at first; it was so very different from what I expected an epic poem to be. It was all very interesting but the long poem didn't fit any form I knew. Gradually, though, on rereading it, the epic took me over. All the wisecracks and the idioms of the day that I'd heard on the farm and in the warehouse in my youth had been lovingly crocheted into swinging lines. I hadn't known that such talk, when woven by a musician of words, could set up a legitimate poetic cadence of its own, as good as the cadences of Whitman and Wordsworth.

Sometime later Robert Bly invited me to visit him on his farm near Madison, Minnesota, some ninety miles north of my Blue Mounds home on the old King's Trail (now Highway 75). Robert had several old shacks on his farmyard in which he housed visitors. I slept in what was once an old chicken coop. And it was at Robert Bly's home that I met Thomas McGrath. Tom had come down from Moorhead with his young wife Eugenia. Also there was the poet James Wright who came out from Minneapolis.

The four of us were about as different as four people could be: Robert the smiling articulate poet politician; James the poet with a fabulous memory and vaulting imagination; Thomas the poet with a quiet smile and measuring eyes. And myself, a novelist.

It didn't take us long to fall into long talks, each taking his turn, while the others listened with glimmer-eyed respect. We talked about our boyhood: Tom telling of how it was in North Dakota, Jim telling of how it was in Ohio, Robert telling of life on the farm in Minnesota, and myself of how it was in Siouxland (Iowa). There were tales of threshing and riding horseback, of fishing and drinking beer, of baseball and horsing around on Sunday.

Sometimes Jim would break out in an orgy of quoting poems that fit what we were talking about: from Yeats, Dante, Whitman, Neruda, Trakl, Rilke. Then Tom would come up with his favorites. And then Robert.

The air would become electrified; full of magnetism. We forgot we were hungry, or had bathroom needs, or that the pebbles in the yard were hot

where we walked barefoot, or that a storm was coming up in the west, drag-
ging its black bottom along the ground and brushing its cumulus head
against the moon and the stars.

Once on a very hot day we decided to go swimming in Lac Qui Parle
Lake. We took a boat out to an island in the middle of the lake and then,
naked, jumped into the lukewarm water. The lake wasn't very deep, only up
to the hips for Tom and Robert and Jim, and just barely above my high
knees. We played like boys again, shooting water at each other with hand
half-cupped and the heel of the palm just catching the surface. When we
looked up from our water battle, we discovered that a boat had drifted into
view around the side of the island. In the boat was a husband and wife fishing. The boys laughed when they saw how I had to skootch down to hide my
shame. I had to kneel around in the water until the boat drifted out of sight.
All the while the husband and wife fished nearby I prayed that a Moby Dick
might show up and that their hooks might catch him and then that he'd drag
them out of sight.

Soon Carol, Robert's wife, came out from the far shore with a picnic
lunch. She discreetly approached our island in such a way that she wouldn't
see us, and hallooed when she hit the island, and left the lunch and tea on a
big boulder, then oared herself back. We climbed out of the water and sat,
each on a huge rock, and indulged ourselves in dried-beef sandwiches.
When the sun sank and cool air descended from the darkening blue sky
above, soothing our white skin, we dressed and climbed into our own boat
and rowed home.

Through it all I became quite aware that sitting in that skull of
McGrath was a watcher, a coiner of well-wrought lines, and a self-made
philosopher.

I saw Tom several times after that: at Bly's home; up in Moorhead
where I went to read; in Minneapolis and St. Paul at parties.

When Tom's *Part II* of *Letter* came out, I was convinced we were seeing
the birth of a remarkable American epic. There wasn't another like it. It
made T. S. Eliot's "Waste Land" look like a pale poorly mixed half-baked
pancake. In that *Part II,* I found all kinds of good grist for Tom's mill, all well
ground and caught up in the matrix of sweet flowing syrup and wild honey.

The story of Jenny the country girl who opened the silky gate for the
hero of the poem and led him through marvelous and terrible thighs to an
ancient and awful world is unforgettable. The Jenny story made all of
Wordworth's little poems about country girls seem like saltless ginger cook-
ies. Jenny carrying ears of corn in her apron against her belly, ears taken
from an enchanted field, still walks in beauty in my imagination, where she
shall never die.

One evening the phone rang in my home on the Blue Mounds. It was
Tom.

"Fred? I just agreed to write the *Conquering Horse* screenplay for Mike Cimino."

Then the phone went dead. Tom didn't wait for me to make comment of any kind, or exclaim, or wonder how come.

When I asked director Michael Cimino about the matter, he explained to me that Tom was known as a very good screenwriter in Hollywood. Mike thought that Tom was more apt to catch what I'd been up to in my novel *Conquering Horse* than anyone else. Like me, Tom was from Siouxland and would know the true feel of the place. Later, when Mike sent me the screenplay I saw right away that Mike had been wise in his choice. It's still the best screenplay I've ever read. Mike has paid us both, but he still hasn't made the movie. (Mike has since made *Lightfoot and Thunderbolt, The Deer Hunter,* and *Heaven's Gate*). Hollywood has a way of ruining good novels, but if Mike finally does make the movie, based on Tom's screenplay, it will be a good movie. A classic even.

Several years ago, the poet Philip Dacey found some money and invited writers from the area, mostly from Minnesota, to the campus of the State University at Marshall, Minnesota. Some sixty poets and novelists showed up for a week. There was good talk, some fine readings, several good panels. One day Robert Bly was holding forth, and after a half hour he got aboard a wild horse and began riding roughshod over us all with his provocative theories and strong opinions. Great stuff, though some of it got to be a bit thick. Tom and I were sitting together, wondering where Robert would fly next and where he would finally land.

Finally Tom had enough. Robert happened to touch on one of Tom's territories with his sharp hooves, and Tom stood up and said in his quiet voice, "Oh, come on now, Robert, that's not true. And you know it." Robert hesitated; smiled; and said, "Well, maybe I'm wrong. But how would you put it?" Tom waved a hand at Robert, smiled, and sat down, as if to say, "It's your show. But be careful what you say around me." Everyone in the audience laughed. They liked Robert's fire, and they liked the way Tom tried to cool him down. Both were loved for what they were.

Robert has several times been heard to remark that he wished Tom would let him edit and cut *Letter.* But Tom has only smiled and has waved him off. Robert likes to cut; Tom likes to sprout many leaves and petals.

On still another evening the phone rang. It was Tom. After I'd said "Hello," Tom said, "Fred, I'm alone again. Eugenia has left me," and hung up. He gave me no chance to commiserate with him or offer him healing words or inquire how it had happened.

The week of October 8, 1977, turned out to be a good one for Thomas McGrath. He was given the Distinguished Achievement Award by the members of the Western Literature Association at their annual meeting in Sioux Falls, South Dakota. It happened that I was asked to make the presentation.

Tom accepted the award in his usual modest manner. At that same gathering Robert Bly gave the banquet address.

The three of us had not seen each other in a while. After the ceremonies, there was a party in Arthur Huseboe's rooms in the downtown Holiday Inn. While everyone was standing around with glass in hand, talking, telling stories, Tom McGrath, Robert Bly, and I rested on a king-size bed. We didn't hear a word said by the celebrants. Heads together, legs sticking out over the edges of the bed, we were commiserating with each other about why all three of us, pretty good fellows really, had trouble keeping our wives happy. We like our wives, loved them, but somehow our marriages were going sour. All three of us wondered if somehow we were at fault; and if we were at fault, what was the fault.

Not one of the scholarly heads above us, sipping from a glass, paid any attention to the quiet scene on that big roomy bed. No one noticed the grave brows, the slowly shaking heads, the slowly articulated doubts, the wrinkled grimaces. I've never forgotten how those three Siouxland fellows, while resting their elbows on the bed and head in their hands, had bared their souls about their sad domestic life.

7 Thomas McGrath:
Orphic Poet of the Midwest

OVER THE PAST few years, I have written a number of essays discussing American poets who fit into the newly identified stream of poetry we can refer to as the Whitman tradition. It is a Dionysian mode of poetry that is involved with ecstatic vision and an intuitive identification with the earth, earthiness, the commonness of nature, accepting death as a natural part of the life cycle, and celebrating, often, madness or drunkenness or conditions outside of society's control. Whitman is the first great American poet who can be identified as embracing this tradition rather than a traditional Apollonian love of order, immortal beauty, or rational control. In particular, Whitman's use of plain or common speech, rather than a language thought to be "poetic"; his interest in proletarian themes like brotherly love, freedom from slavery, giving even the lowliest member of society some human dignity; his long ecstatic lines written in free verse; his interest in sexual freedom and the breaking of sexual taboos; his use of almost exclusively American materials; and his egocentric assertion of himself as the mythic hero of his poems—these are the traits that I see as determining poetry in the Whitman tradition, a poetry that is primarily Dionysian rather than Apollonian. The poems that seem most distinguished in this tradition are long or book-length poems such as "Song of Myself," and the primary examples I will refer to are *Paterson* by William Carlos Williams and *The Maximus Poems* by Charles Olson. In this essay I am treating the myth of Orpheus as Dionysian, even though Orpheus was given his lyre by Apollo. His ending and his descent into Hell are thoroughly Dionysian.

Letter to an Imaginary Friend is a fascinating document in contemporary American poetry. Like Whitman's poem, it is a "song of myself," but, like *The Maximus Poems* and *Paterson,* it is also an attempt to see America, American history, and mythology, as well as economics and politics, through a semi-autobiographical screen, one that allows the power of personal poetry while attempting a much bigger statement. Like Maximus and Dr. Paterson, the speaker of *Letter to an Imaginary Friend* takes on an epic persona. In *Parts I* and *III* and *IV* he is a Christ figure, and in *Part II* he is The Iron Poet, a kind of Orpheus who sees our modern industrial society as a Hell to which he, the poet, will descend in an attempt to lead humanity, which he loves, up and out of this darkness. His vision of light, he claims, is a Marxist one, though in *Part III* he begins to overlay this with the Kachina concept from Hopi mythology; and in *Part IV* he presents a combined vision of the pagan and the Christian.

McGrath, in Book I, through perhaps some of the most vivid and beautiful writing that has ever been done about the American midwest, tells the partial story of his childhood on a farm in North Dakota at just the time in history when farmers were beginning to form their own political movements, uniting against the bankers who held such terrible sway over their lives. One of the heroes from McGrath's childhood is Cal, a farmhand whom he idolized and took as a masculine role model. Cal recurs throughout the long poem, always as an image of the dream, the ideal of both manhood and what a world of brotherhood could be. In that first scene in the book, where the young boy participates in the late summer harvesting and is initiated into manhood, McGrath shows us his first vision of the dark or damned world that he, as a Christ-figure, will set himself up to rescue through politics and particularly through this long poem.

My father took me as far as he could that summer,
Those midnights, mostly, back from his long haul.
But mostly Cal, one of the bundle teamsters,
My sun-blackened Virgil of the spitting circle,
Led me from depth to depth.
                                    Toward the light
I was too young to enter.
                                    (*Letter I & II*, 17)

Cal plays the harmonica and eloquently talks Wobbly politics, which is perhaps an early foreshadowing of the Orphic, the poet whose music can charm even the beasts and force them to listen to reason. But Cal's politics set him apart from the other farm hands, and during the threshing season he is beaten badly by McGrath's uncle and some of the other hands. During the scene of the fight, Cal is portrayed as a figure falling and rising, to fall and rise again, covered with blood. This early image of the resurrection, and the child-McGrath's identification with it, sets up the myth of himself as Christ, and thus it is that throughout the poem McGrath continues to see himself both as the innocent savior and as the charmed bardic rescuer of the human race.

Leslie Fiedler and other critics have commented on the enormous act of both egocentricity and poetic daring that allowed Whitman to claim for himself, in poetic terms, the role of mythic savior of mankind.[1] And it is precisely that sense of the self as hero, of larger than life proportions, which continues to inform and to dominate poetry in the Whitman tradition. Perhaps all epic poems have this task in common, to try to show the patterns of known history so that man can move forward without making the same mistakes; the poet's vision offers a new path or possible way. The *Aeneid,* the *Cantos, Paterson, The Maximus Poems, Howl*: in all these books the

---

1. Fiedler, "Introduction," *Whitman,* ed. Richard Wilbur, The Laurel Poetry Series (New York: Dell, 1959), p. 14.

poets offer a vision of the past, the present, and what a possible future could be. And *Letter to an Imaginary Friend* is no different. The poet feels that the evils of petit bourgeois capitalism, of consumerism, the exploitation of industrial society's workers, are all a kind of Hell that contemporary man, like Euridice, has been snatched down to, and it is the poet who loves us, McGrath, who will go down to that Hell and lead us back up.

However, stronger than the figure of Orpheus in *Letter to an Imaginary Friend* is the figure not of Christ but of the Christ-child. It is the innocent boy, McGrath, who sees the beauty of his midwestern farmland and its exploitation by bankers. Even the sex of young manhood is seen as innocent, pure, without any of the taint that Hell finally puts on it. Cal is a lover of women and thus the model for the young McGrath, who sees this love as freedom and purity, rather than as sin. In Section IV of *Part I,* he presents scenes of sexual initiation that participate in pastoral beauty and wholesomeness, like the preceding earthy threshing scene. First he provides a paean to womanly beauty in general:

> Belly of smokey wheat,
> Alabastrine buttocks, legs like a slow dream—
> Oh as to a citizen of Jupiter's moons,
> Your soft enormous breasts, over the bare horizon,
> Loom, golden and dusky rose, tremendous planets
> Pendulous . . .
> Iris toward the nipple and the nipples pink, veiny
> Shot with faint blue . . .
> *(Letter I & II, 26)*

Then he gives a description of the women of that youth, and finally a tribute to them, as the source for finding the vision of his role in saving the world.

> O small girls with your wide knowledge, you led me
> Into the continent of guilt and forgiving, where love is;
> Through the small gate of your sex I go into my kingdom.
> Teachers of men! O hot, great hearted women
> The world turns still on the axis of your thighs!
> *(Letter I & II, 30)*

Throughout *Part I,* McGrath creates the landscape of North Dakota, even when he goes away from it to college, as the scene of primal innocence and knowledge, as the place of light away from which he must go into the dark of Hell, the real world, the world out of which he must lead his beloved humanity, but a darkness toward which he must go in order to fulfill this promise. When he first goes away to college, it is another dark and Hellish underground he encounters. Coming home at Christmas, he perceives North Dakota as "The rusty ports of the sun" (39) and, even though it is winter and

the light is the "bright enamel / Of the full-filled sentry moon" (39), he understands that the radiance connected with his birthplace (the manger?) will
always be a contrast with the Hell of the real world. He refers to it as
"Cal's lost country" (40) and always thinks of Cal's spirit inspiring the place.
But he knows too that "I am a journey toward a distant wound" (42)
and, partly because there is no possibility of work there, his journey is out to
the darkness of Hell to begin to teach the world how to come back to this
light that he first experiences as a child, the light of sharing, of agrarian
communal existence. It is in going south to LSU to college that he finds
another role for himself, only a slight transition from the Christ-child figure
he holds and returns to in *Part III* and *IV*. It is the figure of Orpheus, the
journeyer into darkness. There he reads poetry and writes it, and he finds a
way to charm both men and women by his speech.

> Toward music, toward speech, drifting
> The night.
> High noon of darkness now and the loud magnolias lifting
> Their ten-thousand candle-power blooms . . .
>
> *(Letters I & II, 61)*

Then war comes, and with it the worst of Hells, the darkness of the Aleutians where he served in the army.

> Then, Night.
> Night, first of the high, great fog: blown down
> From the vast Siberias and freezing unknown lands
> Of the fierce bear and blue shy fox.
> Blown past our sleep
> In the 90 mile wind, a shifting of space itself.
>
> Night of the Army then: its paper snow: proper:
> And its fog of number: cold: and its graceless mossy
> Sleep, like wine in a stone ear.
> Night, too,
> Of khaki:
>
> *(Letter I & II, 82–83)*

In all of *Part I*, McGrath is the Christ figure, always more numinous,
luminous than the dark world he must live in, often with the innocence of
the child-figure, but often too burdened with the weight of knowledge that
he must do something to bring salvation to mankind. And his lot is the same
as the others in darkness. He has the gifts of Orpheus, but he feels himself in
darkness, not in light, and he sees himself and all other workers and poor
people in the world either in the wasteland of the world or its wars, or being
crucified for trying to change things.

> Love and hunger: solidarity and indifference —
> So I ended my journey to the enduring wound,

In the holy and laughing night with the stars drifting
Indifferent;
And myself indifferently drifting
Past the randy Goat and the Water-carrier,
Past Easter, and the high Feast of the Fools,
In the thin rain of the time.

(Letters I & II, 93)

The Iron Poet of Book II is the welder, the worker, the proletarian man, out of World War II, no longer able to see himself as the child-Christ, more haunted with the image of Orpheus underground, who has a mythic vision that,

North Dakota
       is everywhere.
               This town where Theseus sleeps on his hill-
Dead like Crazy Horse.
        This poverty.
              This dialectic of money —
Dakota is everywhere.
      A condition.
          And I am only a device of memory

(Letter I & II, 103)

He refers to himself as "the resurrection man" (105) and is constantly invoking the other voices that invade the poem to keep trying to ascend through the darkness, up into the light. In his own voice he tells the reader, and surely at this point in the poem he is telling himself too, that "North Dakota is everywhere" (103). This is the world of light and purity that he loves, but it is also the world that organized farmers to fight against bankers and started a political party that even ran a presidential candidate in the 1930s. This is the world where his dreams of Cal, himself, as Christ figure began. But now he has a new vision to add to this. It is from Hopi mythology.

The "Kachina," for the Hopi, is a "God," a deified spirit of great power. According to the Hopi, we now live in *Tuwaqachi,* the Fourth World, but we will soon enter *Saquasohuh,* the Fifth World—a much better one. The new world will be signalled by a blue star. Kachinas are also doll figures which are made to symbolize spirit powers. The Blue Star Kachina will help these powers to bring in the new world. All of us should help to make this Kachina. I think of the making of my poem as such an action. In a small way, the poem *is* the Kachina.

(Passages, 95)

While the references in the poem continue to be couched in the European myths of Christ and Orpheus, now the context of the poem is completely replanted in North Dakota, but as Dakota territory, that is, Native

American or Indian territory and mythology. The poet simply slips from
The Iron Poet into his shaman voice.

> Night here.
>   The breathing dark.
> Cave of sleep.
>   I enter.
>   Descending is ascending.

and he concludes this passage with the lines,

> Sing now.
>   We'll make the Kachina.
>   (*Letter I & II*, 134)

The very next line of the poem, which begins Section III of *Part II*, is "Begun
before Easter . . ." (135). Surely the poet, in saying "descending is ascending" (134), has created his transformation from the Orpheus-Euridice myth
to the Christ myth and put them together in a Dionysian frame. To go down
to Hell is the way to eternal life, to salvation, to resurrection. Thus The Iron
Poet who has become the worker, living in Worker's Hells, has also made
himself by descending capable of ascending.

Part III of the poem is in two sections, both called "Christmas Section"
[in versions of *Letter, Parts III* and *IV* which appeared in print before the
book-length volume came out]. McGrath ascends from reality, Iron Poet,
Worker's Hells, to the imaginary landscape of the zodiac and the introduction of Hopi mythology, combining Christianity with cabalism, alchemy,
and Native American lore. He uses his agrarian childhood to focus the rest
of the poem, his journey taking place in a child's sled.

Part III of the poem is a foray into stream of consciousness writing,
using slippages and movements in time and space that are difficult to follow,
though they are often fascinating despite the difficulties. In his note,
McGrath quotes the filmmaker Godard as answering someone who asked
him if he did not think a film should have a beginning, a middle, and an end,
by saying, "Yes. But not necessarily in that order" (*Passages*, 95). Perhaps one
of the problems McGrath began to encounter in writing *Part II* was the narrative burden of working his way sequentially through his life and having no
structural permission to leave anything out or to jump around. Wanting to
talk about ideas much more than wanting to tell his history at that point
overcame him. The poem, I think, suffers from this diversity of the poet's
purpose and method, or perhaps simply from the experimentation with
structure while seemingly still constrained by autobiography.

However, in *Part III* he frees himself from these strictures. He comes
back to the figure of himself as a young boy on his North Dakota farm. The
time is Christmas, and the Christ-child figure is vividly the *enfant terrible*,

already a genius with words, though not knowing what to do with them, not knowing how to lift himself with this gift into a more exalted world. He goes to confession and has nothing to confess in conventional terms. When he says his confession, the priest tells him to say three Our Fathers and three Hail Marys. This seems so inconsequential to the boy that he protests and says that he really has something to confess.

> —and this is insult:
> Our Fathers and Hail Marys—that is the penance
> For children and old ladies! Surely I deserve better,
> I at whom the distant galaxies flare and convulse, shuddering
> At my indeterminate principle and sinister energy potential.
> (*Letters III & IV*, 48)

He wants the dignity of manhood and all it implies. He also is saying that he feels the sense of his destiny's greatness, and he shows us how his sense of being a Chosen One, in this case a Chosen Poet, comes about. What he does is

> call upon all the words
> In the dictionary of damnation and not a damned one will come.
> I pray for the gift of tongues and suddenly I am showered
> With all the unknown words I have ever heard or read.
>
> "I am guilty of chrestomathy, Father."
> He lets out a grunt in Gaelic
> Shifting out of the Latin to get a fresh purchase on sin.
> "And?"
> Barratry, Father.
> "And minerology . . .
> Agatism and summer elements . . .
> (*Letter III & IV*, 49)

This is followed by a virtual bestiary in which the young poet-sinner beginning with the letter "A" starts his way through the alphabet with all the special words he knows, adding poetic constructions and using devices such as alliteration.

This amazing passage of Section 2, Book III is followed by another encounter with the mythic Cal. He is talking about the Christmas story in his poetic slang, "it's the birthday of poor old Jerusalem Slim, / The Galil-lean gandy-dancer and Olympic water-walkin' champ!" (58). This inspires McGrath to continue his own extravagant childhood poetics into a version of the Christmas story filled with puns, crazy jokes, and finally a mock oratorio that begins with the traditional, "And there were in the same coun-try shepherds abiding" (65). The account wanders through such variations as "And she brought forth her firstborn sonata, / and wrapped him in swaddling cloud-berries" (68) and "We're deep into Quantum Country now, Folks, in search / Of the Big Moment—beyond the Eras of Hadron and Lepton—" (69). He concludes the poem with

The dark ladies in their black-as-a-bible robes arise:
In their drizzling dimout and diamond-dazzle of tears . . .
                              Goodnight, sweet ladies.
Goodnight, Mizzez Glorias Mundy and Tuesday.
                    Glad you could come.
                         (*Letters III & IV,* 71)

The last stanza of this section includes an incantation of Latin, French, and Hebrew, implying that the end of the world has finally come, presumably the end of the Fourth World of Hopi mythology, and that we are now moving in the Fifth World. McGrath's desire to show the reader a way, a path to a new world, away from the Hell of this one, now seems grounded in his return to the image of himself, not as The Iron Poet, or Orpheus, or The Blue Kachina, but as the Christ-child, the innocent who believed that words were both his heavenly gift and his ticket to Hell. He has wanted passage to Hell, much as Orpheus did, because it is in Hell that his beloved (humanity) rests, but, unlike Orpheus, McGrath does not find the means of salvation there. If descent is ascent, then he comes back out of Hell in *Part III* into the light of Cal, of the childhood landscape of North Dakota, into the illumination of his amazing vocabulary, his orphic gift of language that charms even the Gaelic priest into playing the game of the words with him. The usual ending to the story of Orpheus, according to Edith Hamilton, is that when he returns distraught to earth, without Euridice, the Gods refuse him an opportunity to go to Hell a second time.[2] He shuns the company of men and wanders the earth alone, singing and playing his musical instrument, until finally he is attacked by a band of Maenads in a Dionysian frenzy, who tear him limb from limb. They fling the severed head into the river Hebrus, which brings it swiftly to the shores of Lesbos where, to this day, the nightingale sings more sweetly than anywhere else.

When McGrath takes the beautiful passage from the *New Testament* beginning "And there were in the same countryside shepherds abiding" (*Letter III & IV,* 65), dismembers it, so to speak, and throws it into the stream of consciousness and the flow of the poem, we finally see, I think, the transformation of the earlier Christ myth structure into the Dionysian/ Orphic myth structure. In this passage, the birth of Christ is announced. But McGrath uses the Orphic or Dionysian frenzy, modeled for us in his childhood confession of (wordplay) sins, to tear apart this text. I see him as tearing apart the old order, the failed one, in order to bring about new beauty in another form. It is this final Dionysian gesture in the poem that

2. Hamilton, *Mythology* (New York: New American Library, 1953), p. 105.

explains to me McGrath's shift from a sequential narrative structure beginning to fail him to one in which a post-Newtonian sense of time is the norm.
For all practical purpose, the Hopi Fifth World comes into being in *Part III*
when McGrath returns to the chaotic but brilliant radiance of this childhood, which is both the beginning and the conclusion of this journey.

In *Part IV* the journey ascends rather than descends as he leaps off the
top of the Christmas tree with the angel, having eaten his grandmother's
magic cookie, "the little Persephone," which allows him to be a disem-
bodied traveler into the Nine Heavens. There he sees visions of all the pos-
sibilities available to the world, including nuclear holocaust. He wakes up
from the dream of the heavens in his child-sled, hearing Cal and his father
talking, as if in song and not in words. He finishes the poem simultaneously
as a child in the dark and as the man, McGrath, hearing a song that is a
blessing, a prayer, a benediction, for the survival of the human race.

Letter to an Imaginary Friend is an epic poem about the Christ child
figure of the poet Thomas McGrath grounded in his midwestern landscape
but using the range of Western myth from Orphic tradition to Hopi proph-
ecy. It glorifies the natural landscape of North Dakota, the agrarian community, and the work ethic, and depicts the fragmentation of modern civilization as well as a vision of wholeness to be restored in a new poetic world
projected by one of the Nine Heavens dreamed at the conclusion of *Part IV*.
McGrath believes that human life is an Orphic journey, "passages toward the
dark," as he calls it, a complete cycle of ascent and descent, fragmentation
and healing.

8   The Last Laugh

JESSICA MITFORD CALLS her memoir of Communism in the 1950s *A Fine Old Conflict* because that is the way she mis-heard the first words of "The International" in English.[1] *La Lutte finale*—the final conflict—becomes for her an invitation to look backward at her own place in what by now has become the venerable history of the left. The anthem itself, of course, goes on to adjure the backward glance at a dismal history whose obliteration it predicts:

Du passé fait une table rase . . .

Mitford's droll error and the contrary assertion of "The International" suggest what I take to be two dominant and possibly conflicting voices in another personal history of the left, Thomas McGrath's *Letter to An Imaginary Friend*. One voice is that of the solemn elegist of the old left, the keeper of what he calls "the winter count" after the record kept in the season of retreat by another diminishing tribe, the Dakota Sioux.[2] The other voice is the mad humorist who has all but taken over the "Christmas Section" of *Letter*. This is the voice that gives us the desperate confession of the blameless boy panting after sin and penitence before a diffident priest:

```
                    "Have you ever
Taken the Lord's name in vain?"
                              "Yes."
                                        "How often?"
"Always."
      "Always?"
            "Always in vain I mean, Father.
It never helped."
—"Ha-r-r-rumph!" (But uncertain.) "Get on"
                              (Letter III & IV, 47–8)
```

And on to a mad catalog of sins from "chrestomathy" to "Anfractuosity" and the "Animal Catechism" that brings *Finnegans Wake* to the prairies. "Parolee and logoklept," the priest calls him, but there is precious little theft in the wonderful abundance of words.

---

1. Jessica Mitford, *A Fine Old Conflict* (New York: Vintage Books, 1978), p. 3. "L'Internationale" was written (in French) by E. Potier at the time of the Paris Commune.
2. See my essay, "'The Winter Count': Politics in the Poetry of Thomas McGrath," *North Dakota Quarterly* 50, 4 (Fall 1982): 59–68.

McGrath's wit plays on failure and turns it into triumph in the way that the clownish pratfall elicits a laugh, which is what the clown was after all along. The boy who fails to impress the priest with the magnitude of his sin enjoys a triumph with his readership that exceeds the minor loss, and this pattern of humor becomes, I believe, a pattern for the whole poem. It is not simply that for the sake of a successful joke the humorist laughs last; the poem uses its humor as another assertion of "McGrath's Law: *All battles are lost but the last!*" (*Letter III & IV,* 14). McGrath's last battle, like the final conflict of "The International," ushers in a new age that may not eradicate past loss but certainly alters its elegiac treatment. The solemnity of the past alternates with humor, political action alternates with religious revelation. Put another way, the elegiac poet whom we might call Thomas trades places with Tom, the fugitive "logoklept" who fuses humor and apocalyptic expectation. Although this essay is largely about Mad Tom, I mean to show his kinship to Thomas and what I take to be the unity of his long poem.

      *   *   *

Parts I and *II* of *Letter to an Imaginary Friend* are, as McGrath says of "our whole history" in conclusion, a "catalogue of catastrophe" and "successions of failures in labor, love and rebellion" (*Letter I & II,* 205-6). The poem was begun in the wake of McCarthyism, 1955, and *Part II* was published in the heat of the Viet Nam War. *Parts I* and *II* take the poet and his generation into time present, those of his generation who survived, that is. And for those who didn't, those in prison, killed in the war, or burned out by endless opposition, the poem is an elegy, from which McGrath emerges as a legendary representative and recorder:

But all time is redeemed by the single man—
Who remembers and resurrects.
                  And I remember.
                           I keep
The winter count.
              (*Letter I & II,* 119)

Part II ends with an uncertain look forward to "the future that never arrived" and promises, at best, attendance and endurance:

We wait: the Eternal Couple: the Fool
           the Woman
           and the Moon . . .
           (*Letter I & II,* 207)

Part III reverts to early childhood and projects a miraculous event on his corner of North Dakota—the birth of Christ that is to be matched by personal resurrection, the infantile triumph over sin. This late access to religion is scarcely a return to the one true church. McGrath translates the miraculous manifestation of a god into the apocalyptic arrival of the Fifth World that he associates with the Hopi *Saquasohuh* but that also resembles the "Fifth Monarchy" and the messianic expectations of revolutionary sects of the seventeenth century. Since in the new age heaven will emerge here on earth (in some unlikely spot), the religious lingo promises its contrary, political revolution. The entire process that McGrath embodies in the four parts of his long poem of the twentieth century brings to mind those rapid alterations of religion and politics that Christopher Hill describes for the seventeenth century and that E. P. Thompson, McGrath's friend—to whom *Book III* is dedicated—describes in his *Making of the English Working Class* as "The Chiliasm of Despair."[3] Thompson offers a pattern for the back and forth passage out of political despair into messianic aspiration that explains the alternation of Methodism and radical politics in the period after the French Revolution. McGrath is no Wesleyan. He emerges from the "catalogue of catastrophe" that concludes *Part II* with a religious image of renewal that is only partly pious.

Early in *Part III* the process of salvation begins in church and ends in a revolutionary festival. He describes himself as "Tom Fool" about to "float into the crocodile's mouth of the Holy Mother Church" high in the rigging

Of the good ship Salvation . . .
                              homeport Jerusalem
                                             outbound
For Beulah Land . . .
                              (*Letter III & IV,* 9)

From this vision we pass to an actual barn where he dances a "fancy fandango, my turkey-in-the-straw" while his father pitches hay and leads him out on a wintry excursion through what has become "a cold kingdom come," where bird tracks in the snow add what looks like Koran and Tao to the holiness of Dakota. A flurry of birds is rising "like sinners snapping at the body of Christ," an "unecumenical" mix of religions that recalls the last harvest, "our sanculotide / Of Fructidore: won from summer, in the Last Days . . ." (*Letter III & IV,* 9–11). The central event is still the revolution linked by the language of religion to the apocalyptic "Last Days." The time past of the poem soon merges with its present—Portugal, 1975, the scene of another revolution, where the snowfall of pamphlets confirms the possibility of winter birth and renewal in political terms:

                    Portuguese winter!
A snow of leaflets falls from the hot and dumbstruck sky.

3. Christopher Hill, *The World Turned Upside Down: Radical Ideas During the English Revolution* (Hammondsworth: Penguin Books, 1974). For "The Chiliasm of Despair" see E. P. Thompson, *The Making of the English Working Class* (Hammondsworth: Penguin Books, 1975), pp. 411–40.

Midnight Mass for the Fourth and Fourteenth of July
(*Letter III & IV*, 23)

What binds politics and religion here is not the solemnity of Thompson's Methodists but the comedy of "Tom Fool" who cannot get over the joke that brings his little corner of the northern plains so close to miraculous transformation. Beulah, that land promised by Isaiah, is, he reminds us between dots and dashes,

> —a little town west
> —toward the Missouri
> (*Letter III & IV*, 9)

and Lisbon is also a little town down the line from the family farm:

Till I hear through the dead-calm new-come night the far bells:
Sheldon . . .
      Enderlin . . .
          bells of the little towns
               calling . . .
Lisbon . . . North Dakota . . .

Along with churchbells in North Dakota he hears in "this other Lisbon, Portugal—/Bells of the Revolution" (*Letter III & IV*, 27).

    This extraordinary linkage of the past and the present and a possible future of secular revolution and religious revival all draws on a geographical and temporal *jeu de mots*. The great change that came to Bethlehem, Paris, and Lisbon could come *here* and *now* out the window, on this page, in "Little East Nowhere North Dakota" (*Letter I & II*, 177).

    If there is a deity that governs where the events that alter world history are likely to happen, such a god would be unlikely to pick North Dakota, a place that American lore has made the subject of both degrading jokes and great expectations. Several years ago midwestern newspapers filled space with a piece on a woman who wrote from Tennessee to the governor of North Dakota that she and her friends questioned the existence of his state. None of them knew anybody who had ever been there. Back in the 1880s when a grand apartment building was constructed west of Central Park in New York, downtown wits dubbed it "The Dakota" by way of suggesting how far it was off the beaten path and how unlikely it was to be inhabited. Before the end of the century North Dakota was to have its day as a result of bonanza wheat farming, but since then its reputation has pretty much returned to what it was. While the population of the United States has almost tripled since 1910, North Dakota has remained the same. Few followed the first waves of optimistic homesteaders and bonanza planters. The recent exploitation of oil in the Williston Basin is not likely to change that, though the population of lonely men has risen somewhat since Hamlin Garland's time.

Garland was one of the first writers to write anything but advertising copy about the Dakotas, but whether what was written in his day was fiction, poetry, or puffery, the early writers were not joking when they applied a national reverie to the northern plains. Whitman, in a revision of *Leaves of Grass,* places his perfect pioneer at home "in Dakota's woods" rather than "Canuck's" of an earlier version. These woods suggest how much "Manhatta" knows of Dakota, but this ignorance does not diminish his expectations. "I strike up for a New World," he writes, where the "vast trackless spaces" change "as in a dream." Here Whitman seems to join the railway promoters for whom Dakota was not simply the "garden" we have come to expect from modern scholarship on the west but also a center of civilization "cover'd with the foremost people, arts, institutions, known."[4]

McGrath is well versed in the literary language that has sentimentalized his west. Thinking of Cooper's Glimmerglass, he reflects on the old romance:

> the deep, heroic and dishonest past
> Of the national myth of the frontier spirit and the free West—
> Oh, nightmare, nightmare, dream and despair and dream!
> <div align="right">(<i>Letter III & IV,</i> 36)</div>

All of this is part of the "Primeinterest Eden" that he describes elsewhere in the section. It is this "false Past," the exploited dream

> Which we must restructure if we're to create
> The commune
>   and the round dance . . .
>   Kachina . . .
>   the Fifth Season . . .
>   (*Letter III & IV,* 37)

How does poetry manage this act of reconstruction? Comedy accomplishes both the reduction of the place and its surprising resurrection as in the several retellings of the birth of Christ, finally in the mock mass that concludes the Christmas Section. The first telling places the three wise men outside any window "in the Anywhere that is Dakota":

> These . . . well . . . *kings,* sort of, mopin' 'n' moseyin' along
> Towards . . .

4. Walt Whitman, "Starting from Paumanok," *Complete Poetry and Selected Prose,* ed. James E. Miller, Jr. (Houghton Mifflin Company: Boston, 1959), p. 15. For a splendid piece of puffery see B. P. Donan, *The Land of Golden Grain: North Dakota: The Lake-gemmed, Breeze Swept Empire of the New Northwest* (Charles Brodix: Chicago, 1883.)

"Ole?"
>(I know it's Sven but *she* has forgotten!)
"Ole?"
>"Yah?"
>>"Some strangers comin' up the coulee . . ."
>>>"Yah"
"Look like three kings . . ."
>>>>(*Letter III & IV, 19*)

The couple shifts from Norse English to Irish; the wise men turn out to include a familiar farm worker from *Part II,* but the fact remains that the biblical Christ was also born on the edge of an empire in a barnyard. There is precedent for the unpretentious legend.

The coming of the wise men is a prologue for the hilarious Christmas Eve confession as well as a preparation for the political epiphany toward which the poem is moving. The catholic international links his parish church with the grand cathedrals of Europe,

>descendant of the tall ships
The cathedrals once were—. . .
. . .
—But here's no cathedral nor all-topsails-set spiritual frigate!
More like a barge or scow tied up for the night,
>>(*Letter III & IV, 44*)

Everything is scaled down for the confessions of our hero except his expectations. His sin "petrifies the waves," makes the earth tremble and the stars shudder:

But the holy father is becoming incensed: against my shame
And my flaming peccadilloes he shakes down his theomometer
And thrusts it into my mouth to see how hot I burn,
What heights I can heat a hell to as spelled on a God-size scale—
"Get on with it boy," he says and I buckle down to my woes.
. . . .
>but all my sins seem so immensely tiny,
Not big enough to swear by: mere saplings of sins,
A pigwidgen patter, no more than jots and tittles
In the black almanac of adult industry: fingerling sins,
Cantlets and scantlings—gangrel and scallywag sins that will never
Come home to roost nor sing for their suppers: a parvitude of sins
>>(*Letter III & IV, 47–48*)

The paltry penance is "Three Our Fathers and three Hail Marys." The avalanche of language throughout this section serves to diminish his sins even further.

It is with similar disproportion that millenarian expectations descend on North Dakota or anywhere the poet happens to be, in one Lisbon or another. The scene that has shifted from the confessional to the revolution in Portugal returns to a circle of men telling folkloric jokes, Ralph Wristfed stories, in the barn. The oracular Wristfed undoes a conundrum by explaining a pious pun in which the resurrected Christ retreats like the groundhog back into his tomb. The joke sobers the men; they pause and wait:

Christcrossed between Christmas and Easter, between this Now and that *Never*
(Between Lisbon and Lisbon, Nothing and Revolution)
Between birth always-and-everywhere and their Never-and-Nowhere—
(Unless Nowhere is *Now here* of the Resurrection)
They wait.
            And are waiting still.
                        As I write this
                                still

In that
        silence
                                (*Letter III & IV*, 56)

One geography is superimposed on another; one means something and the other nothing, just as the word *nowhere,* otherwise divided, becomes its opposite, *now here.* The McGrath that indulges in millennial expectation depends on puns such as this, which are also basic to his humor, even when they do not draw on laughter. There is, in fact, a kind of solemnity about this passage as the men turn in silence from their jokes. In moments like this the two voices that I initially distinguished as Tom and Thomas merge.

The scene of comic storytelling finds him sitting in a circle of friends, and though such a list of names and such a setting recall the elegiac tone of Book I of *Part III,* these are mostly younger friends, poets of his acquaintance at the time of writing. While waiting together they look forward rather than backward, as he puts it in a favorite messianic phrase that gives a name to one of his books:

Waiting for the angel, waiting for news from heaven, a new
Heaven, of course—and a better world in birth! *Here*:
                      (*Letter III & IV,* 27)

In this particular case, *here* is Portugal, but it is in the nature of his messianic expectation that it could be anywhere, in North Dakota, for instance. What is always about to happen here and now for the more buoyant voice has passed and lost its chance there and then for the elegiac.

After the passage in which the circle of men are left waiting in the silent present—"as I write this"—the poetry reverts to recollected narrative. The boy is sent to fetch his father's friend, Cal, whom we know from *Part I* as a hired hand on the family farm, a Wobbly, leading a strike on the harvest crew. His name becomes part of the list and litany of resistance so that when the poet-elegist returns to North Dakota in *Part II,* he is hunting

For the lost sign, blazed tree, for the hidden place
The century went wrong: to find in the Wobbly footprint Cal's

Country . . .
(*Letter I & II*, 133)

Now in *Part III* his errand to Cal becomes "a mission of armed revolutionary memory! / (But I don't know that yet)" (*Letter III & IV*, 57). Cal and his girlfriend resist Christmas in favor of their privacy and moonshine and become for the boy the "Holy Couple" from the end of *Part II*—

The Fool
        the Woman
                and the Moon . . .
                (*Letter I & II*, 207)

Having re-entered the memorial vein with Cal, the poet projects for him an appropriate past:

. . . I'd recall, if I could, a death in the Spanish War,
A valorous, romantic death on the Ebro, or in front of Madrid.
                (*Letter III & IV*, 60)

The projection of death on the Ebro is a bit sentimental—"romantic"—and unlikely.

But he died, will die, I suppose in some nameless struggle;
Or as the poor die: of wear-and-tear of the spirit.
                (*Letter III & IV*, 60)

The poet corrects himself and reflects on his own fate in what amounts to the last purely personal section of the poem. In projecting Cal's death he is fulfilling one of his primary functions as political poet, which happens also to be one of the "Corporal Acts of Mercy" that he has asked the priest to require of him in the mock confessional:

to visit those in prison
                to bury the dead.
                (*Letter III & IV*, 61)

Who will do the same for him? he asks in a line that conjures Tom Fool more than sad Thomas the elegist:

                when all
My mock-hearty hoorahing of hap and hazard will stand in no stead.

His wild side will come to naught, and his sadness will not serve:

But weep just once, Mister Memory, and I'll have your tongue!
                (*Letter III & IV*, 61)

Earlier in *Part III* his inclusion of Bill Dee, another farmhand in *Part II,* among the wise men requires that he catch himself in a similar way:

> If I blink a tear away the world will
> Disappear!
>   But I will not.
>   Nostalgia is decayed dynamite.
>   (*Letter III & IV,* 22)

He cannot afford to weep, but he also cannot afford to forget. As a poet "on a mission of armed revolutionary memory" his job is to keep the "winter count" of what amounts to old loss but not to disarm the enterprise with an excess of sentiment. Mad Tom won't weep, but there is a chance that he also won't remember (or be remembered). McGrath's best jokes and most profound puns cross the boundary of both voices, look forward and backward, reflect and project, record history and introduce fancy, and make of the spiritual world an image of the material.

The sheer length of the poem invites this alteration and defies simple summary. But there are moments when solemnity and comedy merge as I believe they do in a familiar bit of graffiti embedded in Book II of the *Letter*:

> *Kilroy was here.*

Who is Kilroy?—a figure of the war years, seen with a nose, dome, and fingers just over the wall, about to emerge or to disappear and re-emerge almost anywhere. Just when you think you've gone to the end of the earth, so far from home nobody could have been there before, at least nobody you knew, you would find that he had preceded you and left his mark:

> But most of that time I remember
> Kilroy—immortal spelunker! Man I never met
> (Or joke perhaps—ghost-joke: ubiquitous as god His Name
> On every wall later) who in the dark night
> Of the innerbottoms cramped hell crawling worked always ahead
> To scrawl his fame in a rebel joke or slogan, to point
> To the work that had to be done.
>   Where is Kilroy now?
>   (*Letter I & II,* 148)

Here McGrath is a welder delving the labyrinthine bottoms of ships bound for the war, finding his nameless proletarian mate, also a poet and a joker, like the "walking delegates" of the I.W.W. leaving their slogans all over the world.

What does it mean, *Kilroy was here*? It is not a directive of any kind; it is simply an assertion of existence on the part of a fictional character, a rude epigraph for an immortal who, because he never lived, can never die. His immortality (like God's perhaps) is a function of his nonexistence, and yet his very absence prefigures future, miraculous reappearance, anywhere. What we know is that *Kilroy* was not there but that, like the poet, he has momentarily effaced himself into a third person. Kilroy *was,* but the "was" eases itself into the present, as a narrative past intended to convey presence, barely faded like a character in fiction, always potentially *here,* not *there.* Where's Kilroy now? The slogan has petered out, belongs to a period, the past, and a particular culture, pre-War, proletarian, and regional just at the point where narrow localism was giving way to the worldliness of war. McGrath reinvokes his immortal equivalent, the representative, legendary man, gone but always available, here and now.

Kilroy is also the Christ of *Part III,* described by Cal as "poor old Jerusalem slim, the Galilean gandy-dancer," the presiding genius whose signature is both a joke and an elegy, his own "ghost-joke" as well as an assertion of vitality and continuity. You never know where he will show up again or when, asserting last rights to a good last laugh.

9   Thomas McGrath's "green dark"

IN THAT LONG, incredibly imaginative journey toward distant and present wounds, *Letter to an Imaginary Friend,* the lost, questing narrator Thomas McGrath learns that place must become the first element in his new solution of poetics and politics:

Man is the fate of his place, and place the fate of the man
And of time
          A beginning then
                to know one's place
                        At least
That.

Having embraced the sense of place, he soon relearned that the second element must be labor, in all of its true joy:

Here I stop. I begin with identity
And seek the wilderness Trace and the true road of the spirit
I start alone with labor and a place.
                Not much
                    But at least
That.

McGrath is the grand poet of place because of the craftsmanship he brings to his work; McGrath is the poet-worker who makes ideas, events, people, places alive in lines that sing out.

In his poems of place McGrath, burned by the true North, displays a sharpened sense of the real and a consummate understanding of the techniques of traditional poetry, which never sang of "the actual seasons":

Not the threshing floor of Fall nor the tall night of the Winter—
Woodcutting time—nor Spring with the chime and jingle
Of mended harness on real and farting horses,
Nor the snort of the tractor in the Summer fallow.
Not the true run of seasons.

Perhaps the strongest evocation of place in *Letter* occurs in section 6 of chapter 3, *Part I.* Place is presented in sharply cut images that enter with the speed of Eisenstein's montages, the clarity of Pudovkin's, cast in lush, striking patterns of sound, rising and falling rhythms, punctuated by the hushes of silence. Young Tom has been wounded by the first injustice (places howl of wounds: "All this great 'West' is a place of wounds"); his uncle has savagely beaten his friend Cal, a laborer and Wobbly organizer. Unable to understand injustice (who can?), Tom seeks solace in the wild North Dakota woods. Trees, vines, animals, bushes, flowers rise out of the darkness. A poet who knows language like a harpsichordist, let us say Wanda Landowska, understands the keyboards, McGrath charges images with rich sounds. During the first movement of ten lines he plays three major keys, N, S, and K, and two minor ones: O and E. This is a place of "Green Permission . . . ," an Eden, its SS hissing into "Dusk of the brass whistle" and "Gooseberry dark," "dark" echoing "dusk." The OO of "Gooseberry" is soon matched by "Green moonlight of willow." N drones again in "Ironwood," "horny," "June," "thorny," "broken," "king," and is finally and most sharply, as the rhythms rise, accented in "wind-sprung oak," which also completes the pattern of K sounds:

       box-elder; thick in the thorny brake
The black choke-cherry, the high broken ash and the slick
White bark of poplar.
                             I called the king of the woods.
The wind-sprung oak.

Vines and flowers (many of them small, known only to a man who lives with the land, a man who knows that small things are often the real shapers of place) roll out in Rs neatly harmonized with Ks and Ns, the second movement neatly encapsulating the first:

                      I called the queen of ivy,
Maharani to his rut-barked duchies;
Summoned the foxgrape, the lank woodbine,
And the small flowers: the wood violets, the cold
Spears of the iris, the spikes of the ghostflower—

Then McGrath slows us down. The third movement makes us listen. "Runeless" young Tom stands in the "green rain," another chime. More pauses. We must read McGrath's lines slowly, giving silent weight to the spaces between words, waiting; he wants us to hear, to re-enter his scenes, his processes of perception and thought, to be in place. The open O of "Echo" echoes in "horns" and "Then," humming, opens to the whispers, swishes, whooms of animals who move between the sharp Ks and the humming Ns and Ms:

Under the hush and whisper of the wood,
I heard the echoes of the little war.
A fox barked in the hills; and a red hawk boomed
Down on the darkening flats in a feathery splash of hunger.
Silence and waiting.

The rivery rustle

Of a hunting mink.

Shortly after, we hear these lines:

I could not

See in that green dark,

which again ring the main keys of the piece (and foreshadow the predomi-
nant key of the closing movement). "Green dark," a place of growth, of
innocence, of promise. Ks and Ms crackle and sing when he puts his clothes,
"Stinking with sweat," "on a broken stump" and dives "from the hummock
where the cut-bank crumbled." And we are swept into the most haunting,
pausing, heaving, racing lines of the passage: the "Night-Song." The fourth
movement begins by combining a new sound "AH" with the old Ss:

In the arrest and glaucous light

Delicate, snake-like, the water-weed waved and retracted.

The old Ks have come back, preceding a Hopkinsesque flourish of Ws: "the
water-weed waved." Hopkins again: "I roared up out of the river into the
last of the sunlight." Then an eerie incantation of EEs begins and hovers
throughout: "green," "leaves," "mystery," "deep," "teasing," "eves," "seas,"
"weeping," "deeper grieving" (a summary echoing phrase), "heaving,"
"green," "mysterious sea" (emphatically echoing "deeper grieving"). Longer
consonants, Ks and Ts, heave and hold the movement, instants, before it
surges out again:

I heard the green singing of the leaves;

The water-mystery,
The night-deep and teasing terror on the lone river
Sang in my bones,
And under its eves and seas I broke my weeping,
In that deeper grieving,
The long halting—the halt and the long hurry—
Toward the heaving, harsh, the green blurring of the salt mysterious sea.
(Letter I & II, 21)

The boy is washed clean in another place of wounds, "the water-mystery," a place of "deeper grieving" that connects North Dakota to the "salt
mysterious sea," our place of birth, to which we shall return. North Dakota
is indeed everywhere.

Place has been sharply visualized, sharply and hauntingly sounded,
felt, the reader caught in the round dance, the round song. North Dakota is,
will be, everywhere the poem is read, heard, any time, and contemporary

American poetry has its magic passage, an incantation, its ringing music echoing Shakespeare of the sonnets (especially he who made sonnet 129, the magician of echoing Os), Campion, Hopkins, Thomas, sung by a man in love with place, laboring to make song. Work alone is play.

10   Tom McGrath's Vision and the Hornacle Mine

IN THE END, says Mephistopheles, we are all dependent on monsters of our own creation. The avidity with which our ancestors sustained their social and psychological preferences by burning witches and thrilling to tales of "savage" Indians was matched in the 1950s by the zeal of our own Un-American House committees and lives on today in Reagan's fear of that monolithic communism he perceives in all views to the left of those of the Sun King. For English and American poets, a favorite metaphor for whatever condition of men and women and their culture they wish to attack has been that of the wasteland. The abhorred terrain may be the defeated pastoral represented by Goldsmith's deserted village, the Golgotha of James Thomson's City of Dreadful Night, the famously sterile desert of T. S. Eliot's world divorced from divinity, the hysteria-inducing Passaic Falls of W. C. Williams. Wasteland metaphor and imagery depict whatever landscape, geographical or metaphysical, the poet sees as resulting from the beliefs and practices he condemns.

For Tom McGrath, the Dakota poet of the long "pseudo-autobiography" *Letter to an Imaginary Friend*,[1] the wasteland is, quite literally, the waste we heirs of Jefferson have made of the opportunities the new land offered us, our failure to develop a humane community despite our early freedom from "bosses," and our chance to start over in circumstances wherein we could have acted in awareness of our relationship to the universal. The waste is at its nadir in the "granitic" streets of New York and Los Angeles, but it exists everywhere in American life. The undeveloped spaces of North Dakota suggest a faint possibility of starting over, but essentially "North Dakota is everywhere": though its relative emptiness means that its redemptive possibility is not quite entirely stamped out, it shares in the general error. Utopia—Greek for "no place"—is, indeed, as yet nowhere.

To outline McGrath's argument in *Letter* is to reduce to the mechanical a poem that is an assemblage of flashing, darting insights, meditations, distillations, diverse fragments, what the poet terms the "legend of my life and time." The intention is bardic, but this new Whitman believes that we went wrong from the beginning and must start over. We lead our lives not in the joy McGrath envisions in "the round dance and the commune," the existence of shared love and labor that would be his Utopia, but in what he terms "the hornacle mine." Obtaining no explanation of this term from dictionaries, the campus mineralogists, the office of the state mining commis-

1. *Letter to an Imaginary Friend, Parts I & II* and *Letter to an Imaginary Friend Parts Three and Four.*

sioner, or other learned geologers, I telephoned McGrath. He told me that he adopted the word "hornacle" after noting that Army clerks in the Aleutians, misunderstanding military gibberish, typed out supply orders for such objects. (McGrath is not above pulling a leg when dealing with academic literalists. Even though the Army anecdote is probably true, he is engaging in a bit of wordplay. For example, in the opening pages of *Letter I*—in passages purporting to be quotations from an epic, though McGrath says this epic is his own invention—one reads of "hunters of the hornless deer," hopeful emigrants whose goal seems to be contrasted with the hornacles and horn-blowing of Los Angeles.) McGrath uses "hornacle" to mean those goals and goods that people strive for though they lack substance and, by extension, the wasteful, the contemptible, the wrong-headed. The hornacle mine is the experience we live in our variously undeveloped or ruined world. McGrath applies the term to the night streets of New York, alluding, one assumes, to their dangerous frigidity; to the hard life of radicals in Los Angeles in the 1950s, attacked not only by HUAC, the AAUP, and "Establishment Poets," but also by unions they had helped set up; and to higher education, specifically to Moorhead State College, Minnesota, as it was when he was a Depression-era student. For McGrath, the hornacle mine is the inferno we have created on a continent where we could have built a new Eden.

*   *   *

McGrath writes not as propagandist or doctrinaire but as visionary. He tells early in *Letter, Part I* how the first strong impulses from a realm beyond the mundane came to him while, at the age of nine, he was working as "straw-monkey" on a traveling threshing crew. Urged by the boy's adult friend Cal, the crew members decided to go on strike; young Tom watched in dismay as his angered uncle gave Cal a cruel beating. Having, however briefly, traversed the hard route to realization that leads many into the mystical and visionary, Tom went for an evening swim. Once in the water, he found that his grief over Cal faded away under "that deeper grieving," a "singing" of the green leaves on the riverbank, a "terror" that arose in the river, a realization of "the long, halting" hurry toward the sea—the movement, one deduces, of all life toward merger with the rest of what we term the nonliving. The emotion aroused by the mayhem wreaked on Cal had, as critics say, become universalized: Tom had been led to an overpowering emotional conviction of oneness with a realm beyond the individual. The swim had not "reconciled" save to death: he is not writing new stanzas for "When Lilacs Last in the Dooryard Bloom'd." (Sections III and IV of *Letter, Part I*, do repeatedly mention the lilac, a hawk, and Arcturus, however: not exactly the lilac, thrush, and Venus of Whitman's poem, but reminiscent enough of it to suggest that McGrath is perhaps implying comparison and contrast.) The boy had come to understand that life goes on no matter what happens to the individual. Throughout *Letter*, McGrath has one eye cocked at the moon and sun and stars. Their presence seems to remind him that human life is not the whole of existence, that there are other, perhaps greater, participants.

It is this faith in what appears to be a form of revelation—originating in the natural world, not in a supernatural one—that probably accounts for McGrath's interest in the Hopi Kachina as an image of what he desires. To the Hopi, the Kachina is an ancestral spirit who is summoned up to bring rain and therefore functions as a fertility god. For McGrath, one takes it, the Kachina symbolizes renewal.[2] It may seem odd that a white North Dakota poet would find prefigurations of his desires in the metaphysics of a Southwestern Indian tribe, given that such writers as John Niehardt have shown that the tribes of the northern plains had an extensive and available body of lore. Perhaps McGrath, like Willa Cather, Hamlin Garland, and other writers from the cold country, is drawn to the warm southwest. I suspect, however, that whether he read it himself or heard about it secondhand, McGrath was influenced by Benjamin Lee Whorf's well-known discussion of Hopi views of space and time.[3] Whorf wrote that these views constitute a *Weltanschauung* contrasting with both the "naive" views of the English-speaking man in the street and the space-time of relativity theory. (More recently, it has been suggested that Hopi views do not so much contrast with as illustrate relativity principles.)[4] As Whorf writes, the Hopi may appear mystical to the scientist, but the scientist's own views are "*au fond* equally mystical." The Hopi divide experience not as we do, separating past from future and time from space, but into what Whorf terms the "manifested"—inadequately described in English as all past and present events—and the "manifesting" or becoming, which includes not only the future but also what English calls the mental:

everything that appears or exists in the mind, or as the Hopi would prefer to say, in the *heart,* not only the heart of man, but the heart of animals, plants, and things, and behind and within all the forms and appearances of nature . . . in the very heart of the Cosmos. . . . To the Hopi, this is not "subjective" but "intensely real and quivering with life, power, and potency. . . . It is the realm of expectancy, of desire and purpose . . . of thought thinking itself out from an inner realm (the Hopian *heart*) into manifestation."

This existence is not merely advancing toward us out of a future, out of a period separate from ours in time and space, it is already dynamically with us, already eventuating. Such "burgeoning activity," Whorf says, is per-

2. McGrath explains something of his views on Hopi belief in *Passages Toward the Dark,* pp. 93–96, and in *Letter III and IV,* unnumbered, following dedication.

3. "An American Indian Model of the Universe," *International Journal of American Linguistics* 16 (1950): 66–72. The date of composition of the article is uncertain; it was found in Whorf's papers after his death in 1944.

4. Ian Hinckfuss, *The Existence of Space and Time* (Oxford: Clarendon Press, 1974), p. 84.

ceived by the Hopi in "the growing of plants, the forming of clouds . . . the careful planning-out of the communal activities of agriculture and architecture, and in all human hoping, wishing, striving, and taking thought." It is especially concentrated in prayer and in the "communal ceremonies" and "esoteric rituals" of the Indians.

One need not read McGrath as a Hopi theologian. But beliefs like that of the Indians appear to underlie, for example, the telescoping of time in McGrath's hope for "the future that never arrived"—that is, for the heart made manifest. It seems probable that the tribe's belief in a world that, though describable as transcendent, is untainted by Kantian and Emersonian metaphysics, and its emphasis on communal activity and ritual appeal strongly to McGrath. He often mentions details of Hopi doctrine, not only the Kachina but also the several "worlds" of what English divides into past, present, and future existence. The beliefs provide not a Bible or a Koran or a list of commandments he would have us adopt but a convenient set of metaphors for the view of ourselves as a part of the universe and for the sense of human brotherhood he believes we must develop.

      *   *   *

Ideals appropriate to a state that would further human fulfillment come not only from visionary experience but also from the sense of delight that takes its origin in the quite earthly experiences of love and sex and of shared labor. Unsurprisingly enough, the most intense moments of ordinary life come to McGrath's speaker in sexual relations during his teen-age years, and in love and marriage when he is an adult. In a masterful passage opening section IV of *Letter, Part I,* McGrath combines humor—that quality too rare in Anglo-American writing of sexual experience—with graphic but tender description and strength of feeling as he recalls the delights of young women's bodies. His presentation is not a sexist display of himself as triumphant seducer, but a paean to women he has known and to the life that includes such moments. Recollections of Inez and Fay and Rose, of Amy and Sandy and others—there may be a bit of masculine vaunt in this extended roll call—bring up memory of grandfather's hectoring insistence that he ought to be "learning" and lead to the conviction that with the girls he was indeed learning, that not school but women led him to "the continent of guilt and forgiving, where love sits." He values these memories not as an abstract lessening in the characteristics of the passions but as examples of the emotion that a good life should contain: "O hot, great hearted women / The world turns still on the axis of your thighs!" Somehow, the "round dance" that is to be part of human action in his utopia will include warmhearted sex without obligation or responsibility. This is a masculine vision, perhaps, but it is one that many women obviously share.

An almost equally powerful illustration of utopian qualities comes to McGrath in work, particularly in the sharing of hard physical labor. His presentation of the workplace is the most unusual portion of the poem. Few writers have known the feel and sweat of prolonged, everyday work experience. Literary intellectuals who despise all form of manual effort frequently tell us of the horrors of labor on the farm or in mills and factories. But the intellectuals generally turn out to have obtained such knowledge as they have only from summer jobs in their college years, or from a Depression-era year or two on an assembly line. They write not from the point of view of the lifelong working man or woman, but as members of the upper class temporarily slumming. McGrath is no fonder of hard labor than the rest of us, perhaps; and he has not spent an inordinate number of years doing it. But he manages to catch the feel and temper, the oddities and backbreaking effort, the diversity of bosses, the humor that arises not from browbeaten acceptance but from pride in survival—all the accompaniments of labor familiar to the real worker, the "hand" or member of the company "personnel" who may not like his job but rarely wastes time feeling sorry for himself. Aware though he is of faults in the system, he can also be intelligently and ruefully aware of his own failure to "rise" from his condition.

McGrath's assignment at the age of nine to the threshing crew was at first to be only as a temporary replacement, but it turned into a summer-long job. It was not, he says, too hard for him because his father, uncle, Cal, and adults on the crew helped him with the heavier duties. But he was, all the same, "too soon, too early" dragged out of boyhood. Struggling through college in the 1930s he met cheating deans, saw the hardships of the unemployed, sarcastically saluted the economic equality in the poverty into which the Depression forced him and most of his fellow citizens, and decided that "the American Dream," along with Washington, Jefferson, and Madison, is "deader than mackerel."

Yet it was at the hardest of times for him that he experienced a revelation of the ideal condition of labor. Forced early in his college years to winter at home because of lack of money, he went out in the forty-degree-below cold with a wood-chopping crew whose members were as cantankerous as the failing hill farmers and sage rats of H. L. Davis's too little known novel *Honey in the Horn* (1935). With his fellow woodcutters, he complained about the "acetylene" cold, withstood the driving of the always angry boss, and yet somehow knew in the effort "the last years of the Agrarian city," an equality of "swapped labor," a community at the tail end of the frontier, a "Holy City" that was a "commune / Against the cold." The days closed out with an occasional pheasant hunt and perhaps a poker game. Neither the physical circumstances nor the relation with the boss could be described as idyllic; and the work, though primordially useful, was extracting a product that was to be consumed by someone other than the workers. Yet the experience gave McGrath a standard against which to measure other jobs he describes. Brutally hard, at least for anyone not brought up doing manual labor, brutally cold for anyone, the work enforced a deepened sense of brotherhood in shared endeavor that would be a part of the ideal world. The desideratum is not fringe benefits, physical comfort, lessened effort, or schemes for worker-management-owner equality, but the involvement of each person in working toward a goal that is larger than the self. The basis for McGrath's presentation is his own experience. His account supports, however, the hypotheses of Jean-Paul Sartre that "communal work" is a particularly important path toward awareness of participation in an "Us," the human community.[5]

Both *Letters Part I* and *II* review McGrath's wartime experience as an enlisted man, his jobs in Los Angeles, his residence in New York—he says little of his political activities in these cities—and his relationships with his first wife Marian and his second wife, here called Genia (sometimes Genya). McGrath, indeed, comes at his central problem, the presentation of the ways we "went wrong," from as many angles as space permits. His quick cuts from one subtopic to the next and his often brilliant imagery make the poem a version of what has been termed the American surreal—which is to say that it has countless verbal and logical connections that give it a progression more systematic than is typical of the European surreal: like his fellow inheritors of the Puritan ethos, McGrath wants to guide his fellow man and woman as well as to create a work of art.

✻   ✻   ✻

From the beginning of *Letter, Part I,* McGrath's speaker has known that we in America failed in the workplace, developing a class system instead of the "commune" wherein we would share the mutual endeavor that is the action "Nearest to love." By the last sections of *Letter, Part II,* he realizes that we have also gone wrong in love. This is confirmed by his recollection of watching the hired girl Jenny, who when he was thirteen taught him the ways of sex and then half an hour later submitted willingly to a gangbang by a harvest crew. The passage leads not to an editorial on the misuses of sex but to a humorous and proud account of how young Tom carried out the heroic labor of cleaning out the boiler of a steam-threshing rig—an action presented as analogous to a sex act, and one that eased some of the sting of the adult males' refusal to let him share in their exploitation of Jenny's apparently inexhaustible ebullitions. The boy sees that Jenny herself is as lost as he and determines again that our need is to "find among the damned the lost commune," and that his own dedication is "to the lost ones of the world / Forever." These frustrated efforts at unity lead him to remember that the stars, the wind, the night—the permanent expressions of the unity of natural existence—are "all" there is. Again he notes the contrast with the inadequacies of the merely human. Love relationships may, as in his marriage to

5. *Being and Nothingness,* trans. by Hazel E. Barnes (Secaucus, N.J.: Citadel Press, 1974), p. 395 and passim.

Marian, break apart for reasons neither can control—the primacy of money; one's own weakness and corruptibility and potentiality for being lost; and the self-centered nature of present-day love, a nature that, desiring eternal satisfaction, becomes that Eros which desires Thanatos because only death can bring permanency. As men and women part, fail to achieve unity, so most radicals abandon their causes, become suburbanites in Azusa.

The question "What have we, comrades, but love and the class struggle?"—asked again in the Christmas section of *Letter, Part III*—leads not to association of sex and economic analysis but to citation of two other components of transcendental existence, the stars and our hungering bodies. The mention of class struggle is meant as metaphor for that sense of comradeship that could develop if we would end the separations caused by economic inequality. One hesitates, perhaps, to apply the term "moral," but it is accurate for what McGrath seeks: economic reform need not, after all, be inconsistent with moral improvement. The speaker's own "waste" of Marian has been comparable to the waste in the socioeconomic system; with his attachment to Genia, he has a new opportunity, a chance to reenter not innocence itself but "the growth of innocence," to make a new beginning toward development of genuine love. (He never places more blame on Marian than on himself: McGrath is a gentleman in the only sense that word can legitimately have in this context.)

Finding a fulfilling way of love may be one step toward preparing the path for revolutionary change. Another step is to reexamine the beginnings of society by returning to one's own origins. In the closing pages of *Letter, Part II*, McGrath returns to North Dakota to see what the land he knows best can suggest to him. He is no primitivist: North Dakota is not a land offering renewal of pastoral and agrarian values, it is not a refuge (again, "North Dakota is everywhere"). It is simply where his own life and therefore his understanding of American society began: it represents what in another poem he speaks of as the "incubator" wherein he may seek his heritage.[6] He finds in North Dakota two of the causes of our distress. Walking along the coulees on the old family farm on a winter day, he sees that the landscape is as yet little changed, river and earth holding still the emotions of glamour and terror, of the secret and ancient—though his reason notes unsentimentally that a hawk or owl or mink has killed another creature there. He thinks of the Indians whose bones still turn up, of how recently they left and of the desecration whites impose on their remains. Whites learned, he reflects, toughness and strength from the Indians, gained a freedom that they stole—though "heroically"—from the tribesmen. McGrath sees what Roy Harvey Pearce and others insist on, that Americans should recognize that Indian-white relations were not a simple story of good versus evil, that restricting understanding to easy moral judgments will accomplish nothing. Most

6. "Pictures from the Lost Continent of Currier & Ives," *Uzzano* 14: 25.

important for his argument, McGrath sees that white society took its first "wound" from the Indians, that the triumph over the redman "scabbed over" our sensitivity to racial injustice and made it easier to engage in the prejudices and imperialisms of our later conduct.

A second wounding has been imposed by waste, a tragedy demonstrated by the empty farmhouses that result from the blight of our system of "Work and . . . Want." The old settlers have gone west, down the trail that leads not to fulfillment but to nowhere; or into the small towns and bankruptcy; or to the cemetery. Their replacements are fewer in number, work larger farms, and have enough wealth to be "country bourgeois," believers in that "boss culture" McGrath despises. The waste of human possibility is exemplified by Bill Dee, one of a handful of old coots living out their defeated lives in shacks amid the coulees, still counting foolishly on a revival of the past that ground them down. McGrath goes rambling about the coulees with Dee, a garrulous squatter living in defiance of the game laws, a man he describes sarcastically as "the greatest success I know / Out of the old days." Though he is himself an example of the waste that man has produced in Dakota, Dee sees that the settlers "went wrong" at the start, plowing loose the soil that was bound to blow away, taking with it dreams and lives. The one spark left from "the old days" is "the round song," the solidarity of all those in "the circle of hungry equals." The speaker is bemused. North Dakota seems to offer little, New York and Los Angeles nothing, stars and sea are too remote to affect our lives. Control therefore is exercised by the interrelation of people and place: fate is not a remote power, but this relationship. Desperate meditations on place, on our lack of a usable past, lead to the reflection that what the speaker mourns is not the past that was, but the Possible, that what might have been, the manifestation that he again calls the "future that never arrived."

The Christmas section of *Letter, Part III* is a coda, more fragmented in expression, more hysterical in tone. It opens with recollections of a sleigh ride to mass on a Christmas morning in the speaker's childhood, interweaves discussion of missile silos (examples of the domination of society by "law and number"), old Bill Dee, a tentative, somewhat mocking contrast between the world of "Down" (this world) and the world of "Up" (a reordered or ideal sphere), suggestions that in so disordered a territory we might as well set up a "hornacle replicating facility," and a fine passage exploring the move of the human hand as instrument for feeling and work to the "hand" as exploited worker. The ruminations come to the point that no Wise Men have appeared. McGrath now is desperately aware that the ice under us is thin, that survival itself is doubtful. But nostalgia is "dynamite": he will not waste time crying over the past.

As a whole, *Letter* asserts the sense of loss and failure in the American scene. In the ending of *Letter, Part II,* the old radical causes are seen to be defeated: the Wobblies are dead, the Communists imprisoned, the ever more powerful government has "superhighways" to take everyone "to the wall." But though the foxes have stolen the hens, and "it's nearly too dark to say anything clearly," the rooster will go on calling. It is not daybreak that provokes cockcrow, McGrath writes, but cockcrow that drags the daybreak into existence: the revolutionist must rise before the revolution can dawn. Because he will stay "close to the Front," he predicts ultimate "joy"; borrowing Christian belief as metaphor and no doubt having in mind the Irish revolt of 1916, he anticipates an Easter rising, observes jauntily that there is "always springtime in Hell," and closes lovingly urging his "darlings," his fellow radicals—and, by extension, all Americans—to go forward with him. Perhaps all utopias are unreachable because human imagination is circumscribed by its own time and place. As a recent study puts it, "all utopian fiction whirls contemporary actors through a costume dance no place else but here."[7] But though this means that triumph is never attained, it also means that defeat is never total. McGrath will continue to cry out his summons.

*   *   *

McGrath's summons is radical precisely because it demands a cutting back to the *radix,* to the roots of national experience, even a re-ordering of the genes in those roots. As he has summed it up, "We must try to find our real relationship to things."[8] In the invented epic that he pretends to be quoting in the opening of *Letter, Part I,* he speaks of emigrants toiling westward in search of hornless deer, meaning, one supposes, a plenty that would come without the wounding hornacles of our present system, without the class-restricted cornucopia of the consumer economy. McGrath is a radical not in the doctrinaire sense most of us understand as "socialist realism," and not, as the unexamined cant of the 1930s and 1970s put it, because "everything is political" (if everything is political, then the word has no specific meaning). He is political in that he is aware of other people's being, of the community that binds us all. His ideal is a firmer version of the human collectivity that Carl Sandburg, following Whitman, termed "the People," an American presentation of the society that Hugh MacDiarmid sought to develop by urging his fellow Scots to relish the reality of experience.

The idealistic point has been stated by Cesar Vallejo, the Peruvian radical poet who describes the political as including a "passion to love, willingly or by force, / whoever hates me." Quoting Vallejo, M. L. Rosenthal expands the observation: the political, he says, is an "ardor for empathy," an "essential surge of generous, irrational love," a "free energy."[9] Such energy

7. Eric S. Rabkin, Martin H. Greenberg, and Joseph D. Olaner, eds., *No Place Else: Explorations in Utopian and Dystopian Fiction* (Carbondale and Edwardsville: Southern Illinois University Press, 1983), p. vii.

8. "Problems of the Revolutionary Poet in Contemporary Times," a mimeographed paper for a forum of the Midwest Modern Language Association convention in November 1976, 5.

9. *Poetry and the Common Life* (New York: Oxford University Press, 1974), pp. 188–89.

may of course be fascist or militaristic as well as Communist, communist, or communal. Frederick Stern has explored McGrath's move from Communist (that is, Party member) to the "unaffiliated far left."[10] McGrath has taken the path that the genuine artist must take: he has put his art first. If he can also shape it to include and to convey political urging, that is all to the good. But, as he says, in this meteorology the rooster call must come before the dawn.

McGrath's *Letter* meets the definition Rosenthal and Sally M. Gall set up for what they term "the modern sequence": it is "a grouping of mainly lyric poems and passages . . . which tend to interact as an organized whole"; and "its object is neither to resolve a problem nor to conclude an action but to achieve the keenest, most open realization possible."[11] But Rosenthal and Gall study, among others, works by Whitman, Dickinson, Yeats, Williams, Hart Crane, Eliot, Pound, Charles Olson, Robert Lowell, Basil Bunting, and Ted Hughes. Their emphasis is on the subjectivity, the personal sensibility, the desire of the poet to bring the self into a state of tolerable equilibrium in a world it did not make and presumably cannot change. McGrath's self is as harried and nervous as the selves of his peers. But he insists on the possibility of change by an act of will. The urban sophisticate might sneer that this affirmative understanding is possible only for one coming from the rural midwest, that writers living in the up-to-date world of the city have given up on such dreams. McGrath would reply that this argument means that the city is closed to possibility, that though North Dakota has more in common with the city than urban dwellers recognize, its partial separation from the general morass makes it a more likely launching pad for his rocket. Like Czeslaw Milosz in *The Witness of Poetry* (1983), McGrath holds that there is a fusion between the individual and the historical and that this fusion makes it both necessary and possible for the poet today to be committed to causes larger than the self.

*   *   *

McGrath's "essential surge of generous, irrational love" for the "darlings" he addresses causes him in adulthood to envision a transcendental community united in love and labor, a vision prefigured in the glimpse of universal oneness that came to him at the age of nine. In his view, at least, this community can be brought about only by radical action. He has lived long enough to see several specific versions of radicalism dawn, know a high noon, and fade into the night. In his other poems McGrath is often more openly political. In *Letter,* he makes his point effectively because he puts his

10. "'The Delegate for Poetry': McGrath as Communist Poet," in Arthur R. Huseboe and William Geyer, eds., *Where the West Begins* (Sioux Falls, S. Dak.: Center for Western Studies, 1978), pp. 119–27.

11. *The Modern Poetic Sequence: The Genius of Modern Poetry* (New York: Oxford University Press, 1983). The first quotation is from p. 9; the second is from p. 11.

art first: the political understanding arises from the life experience he tells of. His wasteland is the hornacular world that disregards impulses to community in favor of the monstrous selfishness and class snobbery he sees in our socioeconomic arrangements.

11 Figures and Letters: The Poetry of Thomas McGrath

DURING HIS MANY years as a poet Thomas McGrath has given his audience more surprises than most readers of poetry are accustomed to, especially in these doldrum days. For the average poet the plan is to find a style, a groove, and then get the record going, let the needle draw the sound, repeatable and sure (even though the record gets scratchy after a while). Change is not particularly valued because it threatens the writer with dispersal, which might mean some loss of identity, and this in turn could blur his trade mark, the brand name of his work. The emphasis is on holding the line rather than making it new.

Most distinctively in his magnum opus, *Letter to an Imaginary Friend,* McGrath shocks his readers with such a cornucopia of language tones— lyrical, wittily satirical, exhortatory, earthy, and surreal—that the response evoked must surely be, generally and initially, one of amazement. No doubt there are readers who don't want to be caught up in wonder, fearing the sense of bafflement that usually accompanies the wondrous, but the indications are that such readers of *Letter,* the dropouts, are not a significant number. *Letter* is established; it is, along with *Paterson, The Cantos, The Bridge, Kaddish,* and a few other long poems, a monument of twentieth-century American poetry. It is vivid and encompassing, as spiritually efflorescent as *Leaves of Grass.* Anyone who undertakes an enterprise of this magnitude is obviously in the mood to take risks. McGrath has never shirked from breaking molds, not even during his earliest trials as a poet. If his point of view, a Marxist political one, has remained constant, this is a tribute to his courage and maturity. In craft, his work—while coming to finest blossom in *Letter to an Imaginary Friend*—has never lacked authenticity or voice, although it is a voice that we hear through various styles.

This essay will approach the development of McGrath's art via a group of his earlier poems that could be called his Rogues Gallery of Muddled America (his own appellation is Monsters of the Happy Land). These poems, primarily from *Figures of the Double World* (1954)—unfortunately mistitled in the original volume *Figures from a Double World*—are among McGrath's most overt political satires, but they also exemplify several characteristic qualities that appear more subtly in the later poems, including *Letter.* Here is Poor John Luck in his long and short of it:

The clock uncoils the working day
And he wakes up feeling that his youth has gone away.

Over the Eucharist of toast and coffee
He dreams of a Jerusalem where he was happy.
But the cops came and got him while he was still young
And they gave him ambition and a clock to punch.
O poor John! Poor
                    John!
Then he claps him into clothes and he falls downstairs
And the street absorbs him as if he weren't there.
Reassembled in the subway as in the womb
He relaxes on tenterhooks to wait his time,
Reads of Armageddon on the sporting page
And appraises breast and buttock without getting an edge.
O poor John! Poor
                    John!
The street rolls up till his office reaches him
And the door puts out its knob and drags him in.
His desk-trap is baited with the kill of the day.
He sets it off by touching it and can't get away.
So with profit and loss and commerce and knavery
The day is passed in business and thievery.
O poor John! Poor
                    John!
And just when the mind might snap and go sane
The five o'clock whistle brings life back again. (Usury and
simony have buried the day,
The closing stock quotations bear the sun away.)
Into the five o'clock shadow of the bars
Goes good John Luck and his crying nerves.
O poor John! Poor
                    John!
At three past Scotch it is time to go home
To the little woman and the sharp smell of doom
From the over-ripe radio. Free John Luck
Drops a penny from his eye into the magic juke
Box but can't get the number, as he never can now,
Because a witch stole his spell in the long long ago.
O poor John! Poor
                    John!
Then home to his castle and the sacramental beef
And after the dishes to the movies for them both.
Embalmed in the darkness of their deadly wish
The warped years fall at their feet like a dress
While snowed to the bricks, hopped up and heeled,
They throw an endless gun on their Monday selves.
O poor John! Poor
                    John!
But their Tuesday souls will be waiting in the street
When the lights go on and everyone starts
At his naked neighbor. And the lights go on.
The clock starts ticking. And the heart of man
Closes its shutters on its dreaming hurt
As another day falls into the files of the past.

O poor John!
      Poor
           John! Poor
                 John!
("Poor John Luck and the Middle Class Struggle
Or: The Corpse in the Bookkeeper's Body")

This poem confronts us with a day-in-the-life-of situation, a modern soap opera ballad of frustration, ennui, and spiritual stagnation. Not as bloody as "Lord Randall," but quite as damning if one accepts Poor John's generalized lineaments. McGrath's narrative poems of the Rogues Gallery series have this overview perspective, as satire usually does. The ambition of a poem such as "Poor John Luck . . ." therefore differs substantially from the ballad model while echoing the sound of it.

Before giving McGrath's poem full credentials as a narrative, however, it is wise to make special note of the refrain. Refrains are typical of the ballad form, of course, but the Poor John poem falls into an atypical category—not because it contains tongue-in-cheekness (some folk ballads have that too), but because this refrain is both lyrical and satirical, a rare combination. The "O poor John! Poor / John! Poor / John!" at the conclusion plays not only on poor John but also on John poor as well. John deserves our commiseration as well as our disdain: he is a propagator of the system yet also its dupe, its victim. He is a case of moral deprivation whom we are urged to lament as much as condemn. Double entendres like this occur frequently in McGrath's satires, usually handled as here with felicity and subtlety. What often gives them their grace is the songlike counterpoint to the main narrative—satirical theme.

It is also true that character absorbs situation in these Rogues Gallery poems—and in much of McGrath's work before and after. The poems are visualized as human stories generic in their indictment of a society that bends people into the caricatures of their own acts. Poor John Luck is a violated image of God's child, one who wakes up every morning "feeling that his youth has gone away." Paradise is not far in the distance but rather as near as the morning breakfast where "Over the Eucharist of toast and coffee / He dreams of a Jerusalem where he was happy."

The cops in the McGrathian liturgy are the bad guys, the robbers, or the servants of the robbers. They are the various authorities and institutions that compel our obedience and make of us, if they can, the good soldiers of the working day. Theirs is the power of punishment, which may come in the guise of "ambition and a clock to punch."

Poor John, from the start, is a figure staggering through Hell—barely a wage's throw from Heaven. "The subway" and the "womb" are metaphors for the pits, or the Pit. Armageddon, the vicarious bliss of the sports page, provides John with the relief of battle—even if the battle is not the one he himself daily fights—and so does his appraisal of breast and buttock, which represents only another of his impotent pleasures.

The practice of business in this poem is clearly shown as a hostile act against the world; knavery, thievery, usury, and simony have been bred into it, into the genes of private enterprise. It is Poor John's bad luck not to be tough enough to accept and enjoy his work, which results in "crying nerves," the regular Scotch, and the usual little woman, all props in the performance of the diurnal charade. The "sacramental beef" is each night's Last Supper and the "files of the past" soon will run out of days.

On one level the sad facts of Poor John's drudgy persistence are a short compilation of Marxist truisms about capitalist exploitation. If one reads the poem only as message, one will lose most of the sense of its rhythmical life, its song and wit, and importantly its human sympathy. Despite his functional service in which it might fairly be called a functional poem, Poor John is not after all a cipher among the bigger numbers; he achieves a destiny not tragic but fallen; his is the shape of America, host of lost angels. The Marxist truism does, after all, speak a truth.

One of the other figures in the *Figures of the Double World* series is Jason Quint, also based on a general specimen, this time the scientist; but he is a more thoughtful, more resonating type than John Luck. Therefore, Faustlike, his story strikes a deeper vein; McGrath's language here is more textured, witty still but not so dominatingly present. The lyrical gives way, to an extent, to a somber tone disguised by the use of the seemingly light punch lines characteristic of McGrath's writing during this period.

I

Betrayed by his five mechanic agents, falling
Captive to consciousness, he summons light
To all its duties, and assumes the world
Like a common penance. Rust on the green tongue burns
Like history's corrosive on his living tree.
But all the monsters of his sleep's dark sea
Are tame familiars in the morning sun.

II

He sees the nation browse across burnt miles
of toast, toward the time-clock. Deafened, hears
A Gettysburg of breakfast food explode
Against the surd tympanum of air.
The roads outside to No-and-Any Where
Trigger all space-time to a zero Now.
The punctual goddess blossoms on his brow—
Pragmatic emblem of the daylit need.

III

Now with his thought the rank and maundy world
(The lost between quanta and mechanics wave
All pulp and passion sprawls around the globe)

He stiffens, as a hand informs a glove,
And drags each lank potential into form.
This the hieratic arrow of his glance
Creates St. Sebastian Avenue Street Place—
All of sublunary circumstance
Crowds on the casual platform of his gaze.

IV

Like money sealed in a pneumatic tube
He whirls beneath the city's stony floor
To where the cold coordinates of work
Advance their cross-hairs on the target hour.
There surplus value's mathematics flower
(All I squared Y squared like a tesseract
Or ghostly dirigible) grows unseen
Across the lean dimension of in fact.

V

Grows all unseen as Jason Quint pursues
The windy hazard of the Absolute
Through icy tundras, farther than the Horn,
Vaster than Asia in their wuthering snows.
The sweat of progress and humanity
Colors no litmus in those latitudes;
In a rustle of banknotes and casualty lists
The Bomb is shaken from the wrath-bearing tree.

VI

The quitting whistle lofts a flag of truce,
And all hope's flutes and harpsichords compound
The lonely leisure. The Great Nocturnal Drift
Sets to its Deep. He walks the park. Profound
Unease returns to Quint. The sleepy lathes
Of hummingbirds machine the emerald
Of garden silence which his feet confuse.
The statues hoist, on labyrinthine paths,
The mineral grandeur of a public smile.

VII

And the world goes blank, and heavy as stone
Rolls into night. It is the human hour,
Imperfect. Lovers, food, and politics
Command the air, and Jason Quint alone,
Clothed in abstraction, like a bush that burns
In the blind frequencies where none may pass,
Stalks through that only country of the poor—
The lamplit hour the quitting whistle mourns.

VIII

Imperfect. The stability of dextrous stars
Offers him comfort, but their light is cold.
A storm of sentiment, sudden as a cloud
Of migrant birds, sings in his head. Now stirs
The terrible friend, companion of his dreams,
With his emotional algebra of need and loss—

The hateful witness to his mortal part
And confirmation of his loneliness.
("The Little Odyssey of Jason Quint, of Science Doctor")

Quint, the Abstract Man, the Pop Scientist, and the Maker of Bombs, achieves a human and humanistic status because of what he lacks: connection, the Other, the haunting tangibility of which his nightdreams inform him. Basically, the monster poems are about deficiencies in feeling and thought, in the essences of life, induced by a socio-economic code that champions a Darwinian ethic of material and psychic survival. In *Letter* and in other shorter poems, earlier and later than *Figures,* McGrath emphasized the qualities of solidarity, friendship, and love, which must be placed, however foreboding the big picture might be, in balance against our meaner natures. Much of the source of McGrath's hopeful weather emanates from family, lovers, and former lovers, friends of the word and the act and, most particularly in the later work, his young son, Tomasito. His poems find homes not only for such Rogues Gallery figures as John Luck and Jason Quint but also for numerous actual people, often named directly and portrayed in their goodness and health of spirit. Yet Quint deserves our attention because he embodies in a fairly short space McGrath's cosmology of the moral and ethical imperatives.

The first aspect of Quint's dilemma to be noted is the betrayal of his five senses, which have become mere "mechanic agents" of a consciousness that is an entrapment since he refuses to confront "the monsters of his sleep's dark sea." Quint does not deal with his subconscious, or, rather, he deals with it by escaping from it into the daylight where the monsters *appear* to be properly caged. Yet the stifling of nightdreams, no matter how fearful they may be, does not lead to contentment; it leads to distortion, the aforementioned mechanization of the senses and their violent product: civil war within himself ("Deafened, hears / A Gettysburg of breakfast food explode / Against the surd tympanum of the air").

Quint, in his reified abstractedness, is a violent and dangerous man as he "pursues / The windy hazard of the Absolute." Detached as he is—or tries to make himself be—from the uncertainties and, indeed, the perils of the dreamworld, he is forced into another distortion; that is, not only are his perceptions, so to speak, cauterized but even his subconscious "whirls beneath the city's stony floor." Quint's "daylit need" for the "punctual goddess [who] blossoms on his brow," delivers him to a stylization of one-dimensional lifework, described in the arctic language of "cold coordinates," "icy tundras," and "wuthering snows." Possibly McGrath is here confining his portrait too much to the conventional imagery of the stereotypical scientist, one who overstresses mind to the detriment, even to the obliteration, of feeling. The point, however, is not that Jason Quint has lost emotional power but rather that this power is a tiger in chains, straining with mortal animal ferocity to attain its rightful share of the scientist's being. If Quint is dehumanized in his quest for absoluteness and immortality, he is at the same time prey to his own "terrible friend, companion of his dreams," who in witnessing the scientist's ineluctable loneliness confirms that he cannot ever escape "his mortal part." McGrath engages in this poem, as he did in "Poor John Luck..," the schizoidal menace one sees and feels in the American populace. We are a people brought up, generally, to be thrifty with our emotions, to save them, put them in the bank where presumably they will accrue interest while we throw ourselves into the competitive struggle to expand our recognizable daylit egos, no matter how or whatever the expense. Here the Marxist economic analysis that discerns human labor as surplus value for the capitalist is given additional poignancy by the poet, who transforms the equation into a form of psychic dismemberment. McGrath brings into clear perspective the victim-oppressor binds endemic to both white-collar man and scientist, whose values and value as human beings suffer the consequences of their subconscious repressions.

As should be apparent by now, McGrath is a master tactician in developing the political poem into a psychological exploration well beyond any immediate occasion. It is not the surface of political, social, and military events that invites McGrath's pen. He does not cease to be a poet when he undertakes the hermeneutical project of assessing the politico-economic condition of America. He does not usually sacrifice poem to message—a common failing in most politically oriented poems by lesser craftsmen and -women.

But what does it mean not to surrender the poetry to the message? Simply, the writer must subordinate outrage to craft and insight. Although in the two poems examined thus far McGrath utilizes traditional stanzaic patterns, at least roughly, and not quite so traditional rhyme and repetition schemes, he is able to give his work vividness and vitality through his management of a language appropriate to his manner of theorizing. That is to say, his primary subject is people and, additionally, people within a society instead of isolated within the self or with lover, child, or family unit. This being the case, it is probably wise for him to have chosen early on a craft that can take advantage of, and modify as needed, classical prototypes. These models have helped him to carry to his themes a lyrical undertone absent in most satirical poetry, absent even in Pope, who is the model par excellence of such poetry.

This paper has concentrated so far on at least pointing to certain strands of lyricism, wit, and satire in McGrath's oeuvre, in addition to identifying his propensity for dealing with stock figures psychologically as well as politically. Another poem from *Figures* will serve as a transition from the earlier work to the discussion of the later passages from *Letter,* where the cadences move with greater agility and the speech takes on a projective, or open field shape, and where earth tones and surreal undercurrents are more abundantly in evidence. These will perhaps indicate in sharper detail the surprise of the varied styles McGrath can call upon the aegis of his singular voice.

The poem from *Figures* is titled "Monsters of the Happy Land," a poem unfortunately not included in *The Movie at the End of the World: Collected Poems* (1972).

From skies jaundiced with winter, neutral
As the spittle or nuns of children, rain
Falls on the suburbs. Over Skidrow
Night arrives, desperate for wine,
And summons the drifters and the paddy-wagons
and the weedhead whores who all night long
Argue the darkness on the price of love.

Then memory comes back, like the drowned men
Beached on the bar-stools of a savage shore.
Blood has frozen in the veins of neon,
There is ice on Main Street and the echoing ring
Of skates on the pond of my inner ear:
And it is Maine: and the war is coming:
A blond girl's laughter shakes the placid moon.

Or, later, summer, and the war has turned
Sixes to sevens, slain the laughing man
And summoned the sensual to the farthest coast.
Over the headlands the seals lie, waiting
The admiring terror of the summer children.
A dark woman turns a grave face to the sun.
The sea contains an echo of all things.

All things are echoed in the wine's dark sea:
All hope the past conceived, and what was then
Implicit—though we could not image it—
The actual horror of the present hour
And all the monsters that the future holds.
It is not whores nor hopheads nor ourselves
Make the night ugly: but what is still to come—

Some final transformation. Alcohol preserves
The foetus of our hope, sea-changed, and that freak still
To be born between the gin-mill and the morgue.
So, night wears like memory. Skidrow dawn
Withdraws a slack tide to the outer dark
And all sea-monsters hustle from the light
Real as tourists, but diseased with time.
These Presences still haunt the daylit world.

Despite overdependence on that all-purpose word, "dark," the poem succeeds in bringing into an apparently exteriorized context some privacies that, perhaps against the grain of the writer's wishes, contribute an element of mystery absent in the other poems discussed. McGrath has always writ-

ten about the self and about relationship—in fact, as mentioned, some of
these poems exhibit his work's finest qualities—but "Monsters of the Happy
Land" fuses observation with memory to create a different psychic depth:
an overall clarity that is nevertheless furrowed by rivulets of the opaque.
Who is the blond girl whose "laughter shakes the placid moon"? Who is the
"laughing man"? Why has the war (which war?) "summoned the sensual to
the farthest coast"—and where is that? The "admiring terror of the summer
wears like memory" adds a summarizing point to this tour of the mind's
dimly lit basement, from which our monsters come: the private ones and
those we might meet on the boulevard at any time. These references do not
intend to mark weaknesses in the poem's logic, although McGrath might
have felt them to be so in collecting his poems for *Movie*. Albeit the questions above could be answered and meanings assigned, there is enough inde-
terminacy in the passages noted for the reader to perceive them as moving
toward the blending of satire with a broader (almost epical, almost surreal)
lyricism that is one of the salient virtues of *Letter*. The caricatures of Poor
John Luck and Jason Quint give way to the dialectical dynamics of "Monsters of the Happy Land," a poem that serves as their prelude in *Figures*:
which is to say, societal type as against the psyche's individuated hidden-
ness. "Monsters of the Happy Land," in turn, evolves into poetry such as the
following from *Letter*:

Oh night! Night! In the nine hundred countries of the endless war
How cold you come: and sane! John dear, dear
John Thomas what a burning in the snow there! In the blank,
In the year-long dark, in the night when Raisin Jack is your sergeant—
(The squads in the boondack oupposts tip-toeing down to their stills,
And the gone medics—crazy—the needles thick in their skins,
A-dream in each other's arms: the dying already dead
On their clean tables; and out in the storm the mad
Preachers calling curses into the rain)—

Oh holy night: how gone, how long you are!
Then was when I missed her—Marian—in the long missing.
(The long week-end I'd gone on)—missed her most
In that vast waste of the lost, the most abuse of the least,
In the burning and the freezing.
                                        (*Letter I & II*, 83–84)

And:

        And J. J. McJoseph my jingalo johnny gave
Me—as co-conspirators and penance for sins—helpers:
Two (three would have been enough and one too many).
Primero: Coca (a demi-liz para-alcoholic) and Mister
Twister (O Prester John!) the master pressman (consultant
to the three kings of Azusa and Cucamongas royal Raz)

Debile meathead and absquatulant horse's ass!
                                                              Ten times
Around the corner and over the wall: quasiresident
Of the loud funnyfarms. Fat flatulent and phthisic.
                                                              And Coca
The perfect bitch to lead him a dog's life.
                                                         (And *her* ploy
To sink the paper and buy it up cheap with the help of her pressman
Whom she pressed often on the muezzin-screaming leather of the editorial couch.)
                                                         (*Letter I & II,* 151)

Citing these sections must inevitably convey a too-limited impression of the poem as a whole (the first two parts published in book form number 214 pages; *Parts III and IV* another 115 pages). Still, the sampling is enough to show the quintessential level—thematically and musically—on which the satirical thread of McGrath's long work operates. The voice is certainly identifiable from the earlier rhetoric, but here with the avoidance of any more or less recognizable stanzaic repetition McGrath's line opens up to a longer breath and to shorter phrasings within that breath. At times the lines are blank verse or approximations of it; however, there are too many departures from such a scansion for it to hold up. One could say that the blank verse meter hovers as a historical backdrop to *Letter* in a way similar to that of the ballad form which underlay "Poor John Luck" and "The Little Odyssey." While such discriminations do not account for any poem's success or failure, they do assist in differentiating one work's ambience from another's. In this respect, that the passages from *Letter* do not depend on rhyme, slant or straight (generally true of the entire poem despite fun like Mister Twister-Prester-master pressman), also indicates a concern with less traditional shape (although by now Whitman and Williams must be a peculiarly American tradition in themselves).

After other things are said though, McGrath's center of often amusing gravity remains the situation of people formed in a society that does much to deform them (the fact that every society does this does not diminish the culpability of any). But in *Letter* the people for the most part are heroes, fighters against what they know to be the enemy: greed, exploitation, racism, and all those other always-festering wounds of the political body. Mister Twister and Coca are the exceptions, the monsters in what is mainly a memorial to the "saints": Cal, Mac, Charles Humboldt, Don Gordon, students, friends, and mentors. Against the waning revolution they go on living, if not actually then, in the green fields of memory.

Finally, the imagery enlarges on the clear-fuzzy grid of "Monsters of the Happy Land." The satirical thrust is sharpened by a shade of surrealism, as in this section:

Terror of the time clock mechanical salaams low pressure systems
Blowing out of the nightbound heart's high Saharas,

A muezzin of blood blazing in a cage built out of doves . . .
Terror of the noonday bullhorn pulling its string of sound
Out of the lunch box: time where the tides rage off Hatteras
And the drowned locomotives roll like dream monsters slow in the grip
Of the clashing vast deep: and their bells chime: and the whistle rust
Lights submarine tunnels toward dead harbors, sounding far stations
Closed forever . . .
                    retired at sea
                                   their circular shoes
Still
    Terror of the quitting hour, the air full of skinning knives
And the damp buffalo falling through the scaly tenement walls.
Thin-fit lives: tamped matrimonial gunpowder, ancestral pistols.

And the terrors and miseries of the arc of darkness extending past midnight:
Charismatic lightning of alcohol dead in its chapel of glass,
The harping dream-song in the round ditches of revolving roads
Silent. The last ship sinking on the sea of a wounded brow—
All terror and misery present now in the loud and dying
Parish past midnight—a thousand fast mustangs freezing in juke box
Ice, the little shelters built out of temporal wine
Blowing away in the wind the night-bound death wranglers
Stumbling into the day
                            wait.
                                   For the angel.
                                              Wait.
                                   (*Letter I & II*, 126–27)

    McGrath's range is encompassing; it is not only passionate and simul-
taneously witty but also wise in its commitments and fluid in its cadences.
He is not afraid of language, its amplitude, and the amazing ways words can
be alloyed and allied. He has not only written his politics, he has also lived it.
Few of his contemporaries have disdained, as he has, the lure of the literary
establishments over the years as well as today's with its preference for verse
of the single style, the domestic scene, the well-gnawed bones, and sweaty
windows of the shy imagination. Nevertheless, writing counter to the various fashions, McGrath has achieved a measure of eminence—though not
nearly enough. Tom Fool (as he has called himself) has ridden his own crazy
horse through the years and here he is, at the laurel-line, as rich in sound as
anybody around. *Letter to an Imaginary Friend* stands among the poet's
widening circle of admirers as a classic.

12 Homage to Thomas McGrath

IT WOULD BE untrue to suggest that the poetry of Thomas McGrath is without recognition in the United States. On the contrary he has a large and discriminating readership, and the recognition of some fellow poets—even of the odd critic. But the cultural life of the United States is so various, and made up of so many scattered compost heaps, that it is perfectly possible for significant publics to coexist which do not even know of the existence of each other.

In recent years I have come upon distinguished professors of American literature who did not know of McGrath's work and—more remarkable—circles of socialist or radical intellectuals. The East Coast literary establishment, and its opportunistic cousin the *New York Review of Books,* does not know (or does not wish to know) that his work exists.

Yet McGrath's poetry will be remembered in one hundred years when many more fashionable voices have been forgotten. Here is a poet addressing not poets only but speaking in a public voice to a public which has not yet learned to listen to him. Hence not only the poetry but also the reasons for the failure in public recognition demand attention. And this essay must therefore be drawn into a meditation upon obscure alternative traditions within what was once the American Left—contradictions inside a contradiction—a meditation prompted by McGrath's own trajectory.

Let us start by saying that McGrath is a poet of alienation. This puts him at once into a fashionable set. Who, in these latter days, can afford not to be alienated? But, then, McGrath is not, and never has been, a poet in anyone's fashionable party. His trajectory has been that of willful defiance of every fashion. At every point when the applause—anyone's applause, even the applause of the alienated—seemed about to salute him, he has taken a jagged fork to a wilderness of his own willful making.

There is a valuable Selected Bibliography by Fred Whitehead in *North Dakota Quarterly* 50, 4 (Fall 1982) for McGrath. This *festschrift* issue also includes many useful memoirs and essays. *The Movie at the End of the World* is subtitled "Collected Poems," although it is in fact an economical selection from earlier collections. *Parts I* and *II* of *Letter to an Imaginary Friend* have been followed by sections of *Part III* in *Passages Toward the Dark* and *Echoes Inside the Labyrinth.* These are abbreviated in text or notes to *North Dakota Quarterly*; *Movie*; *Letter*; *Passages*; and *Echoes.*

It will be unusually difficult to establish any canon of McGrath's work. From typescripts sent to us in the fifties I have found poems which appear in *Movie* as "new poems," and one or two of them turn up in *Passages* or *Echoes.* This might sometimes be important to the historian, perhaps also to the critic: warning, handle each "new poem" with agnosticism as to its genesis and context. The poet himself appears to have lost some of his own copies, which, however, survive in the hands of friends or in the pages of scores of little journals in which he has published.

This is not (as some critics might plead) because he is just not quite good enough as a poet. McGrath is a master-poet to his last fingernail. He is self-conscious (sometimes too self-conscious) in poetic technique, catholic in his reception of influence: a political poet, very certainly, but a poet whose politics happen in terms of poetry, within the poems, and not as gestures to an ideology happening somewhere outside them. "It is always the texture of a poem" (he wrote to me in 1952) "not what it is 'about' that first catches me . . ."

His vices as well as his virtues are those of a poet. He cannot refuse a pun, least of all a pun which induces a metaphysical vibration, even when the logic of the poem may lead in a different direction. The virtues crowd whole poems, like "Trinc" or "Praises" with sheer fertility of poetic play:

The vegetables please us with their modes and virtues.
                              The demure heart
Of the lettuce inside its circular court, baroque ear
Of quiet under its rustling house of lace, pleases
Us.

  And the bold strength of the celery, its green Hispanic
¡Shout! its exclamatory confetti.

                        And the analogue that is Onion:
Ptolemaic astronomy and tearful allegory, the Platonic circles
Of His inexhaustible soul!

                    O and the straightforwardness
In the labyrinth of Cabbage, the infallible rectitude of Homegrown
                                        Mushroom
Under its cone of silence like a papal hat . . . [1]

At times he fusses and clutters the lines with a surplus of association and imagery: he clowns and asses around with terms and typography (as in some late sections of *Letter to an Imaginary Friend*), arousing and destroying expectations and dancing around the reader in a punning courtship-display. McGrath's is an implacable alienation from all that has had anything fashionable going for it in the past four decades of American culture—and from a good deal of what has been offered as counterculture also. There need be no suspicion that this alienation is worn as a pose, as the distinguished sorrow of a lonely soul; it is *suffered* with bitterness and with anger; it is *opposed*; and the official culture is seen as (without any qualification) menacing and life-destroying, not only in the most direct political meanings but also to historical and literary values:

                        A nation in chains
Called freedom.

  1. "Trinc" is in *Echoes,* pp. 13–18. "Praises" in *Movie,* pp. 157–58.

A nation of murderers—O say, can you see
Yourself among them?
                You?
                        Hypocrite
                            lecteur
                                patriot
                                    (Letter II, 148)

But what is this official culture to be opposed *by*? In some part it is
judged against a past. McGrath's is a profoundly historical poetry. The history is both personal and public, and often both are entwined. His major
long poem, *Letter to an Imaginary Friend* (which after thirty years has
reached only now completion), has an autobiographical structure. But he
describes this as "pseudo-autobiography":

It is *not* simply autobiography. I am very far from believing that all parts of my life
are meaningful enough to be usable in the poem. But I believe that all of us live twice:
once personally and once as a representative man or woman. I am interested in those
moments when my life line crosses through the concentration points of the history
of my time. *Then* I live both personally and representatively. (*Passages,* 93)

In *Letter* (as well as in many shorter poems) the personal meditation
returns again and again to moments of his childhood in North Dakota: the
public meditation returns again and again to moments in the ascendant
labor movement of the late 1930s and early 1940s. Returning (perhaps at the
end of the fifties) to the New York docks—the Chelsea waterfront in Manhattan where he had worked in 1941 (he has called this "the most interesting
time of his life"):[2]

. . . the talking walls had forgotten our names, down at the Front,
Where the seamen fought and the longshoremen struck the great ships
In the War of the Poor.
                        And the NMU[3] has moved to the deep south
(Below Fourteenth) and built them a kind of a Moorish whorehouse
For a union hall. And the lads who built that union are gone.
Dead. Deep sixed. Read out of the books. Expelled. Members
of the Ninety-Nine year Club . . .
*   *   *
                            And many thousands gone
Who were once the conscience and pride of the cold streets of the workers;
Dissolved in numbers is that second Aleph, the Order of Militants,
And the workers defenseless: corralled in the death camps of money
Stoned in a rented dream frozen into a mask
Of false consciousness . . .
                    lip-zipped

2. See Joe Doyle's interesting essay on "Tom McGrath's Years on the New York Waterfront," *North Dakota Quarterly* 50: 32–40.
3. NMU: National Maritime Union.

                                   the eyes padlocked the ears
Fully transistorized
                       —living a life not their own.
Lost . . .

Still, in the still streets, sometimes, I see them moving—
Sleepwalkers in nightmare, drifting the battlefields of a war
They don't even know is happening—
                       O blessed at the end of a nightstick,
Put to bed in the dark in a painting by Jackson Rauschenberg,
Machined to fit the print in a rack 'n' gawk juke box, stomped
By a runaway herd of Genet fagots, shot full of holes
By the bounty hunters of Mad Avenue, brains drawn off
By the oak-borers of Ivy League schools' mistletoe masters.
Everything's been Los Angelized . . .
                       Alone, now, in the street,
What sign, what blazed tree, what burning lightning of the radical Word
Shall write their names on the wall break down that mind-framed dark?

Northern lights in winter; in summer the eccentric stairs
The firefly climbs . . .
                       But where is the steering star
                                         where is
The Plow? the Wheel?
                       Made this song in a bad time . . .
No revolutionary song now, no revolutionary
Party
     sell out
         false consciousness
                       yet I *will*
Sing
     for these poor
             for the victory still to come
RSVP
                                   (*Letter I & II*, 123-25)

     The reminiscence intermixes anger and elegy. The anger falls upon
what C. Wright Mills called "the cultural default":

The Committee comes by with its masked performers
To fire you out of your job, but that's expected.
Money breeds in the dark—expected.
Weeping and loss—expected.
——————What was hard to imagine were the do-it-yourself kits
With 4 nails and a hammer and a patented folding cross,
And all the poets, green in the brown hills, running . . .
                                   (*Letter I & II*, 96)

Or again:

Blacklisted by trade unions we once had suffered to build,

Shot down under a bust of Plato by HUAC and AAUP.4

Outlaws
        system beaters
              we held to the hard road
(While Establishment Poets, like bats, in caves with color T.V.
Slept upside down in clusters: a ripe fruited scrambling of ass holes.)
But it's a hard system to beat: working under the hat
On the half-pay offered to outlaws by the fellow-travellers of money:
                                 (*Letter I & II*, 118)

    Yet anger demands an alternative. If the alternative be only the elegiac recollection of the past, then anger's alternative may only be nostalgia. And nostalgia, even about the Wobblies or labor militancy, offers no threat to the powers which move in the daytime present. This, too, may be coopted, rewarded, assimilated. The characters who recur in the *Letter* as points of reference—his father, farming in North Dakota; his brother Jimmy, killed in the war; Cal, the Wobbly farmhand; Mac, the union organizer on the docks—even these threaten to entrap him in a reputable nostalgia:

                          And always, as I go forward
And older I hear behind me, intolerable, the ghostlike footsteps—
Jimmy perhaps; or Jack; my father; Cal; Mac maybe—
The dead and the living—and to turn back toward them—that loved past—
Would be to offer my body to the loud crows and the crass
Lewd jackals of time and money, the academy of dream-scalpers, the mad
Congressional Committees on Fame, to be put on a criss-cross for not wearing
The alien smell of the death they love [. . .]
                                 (*Letter I & II*, 106)

    His poetry refuses to permit time to cancel experience like a used stamp. It refuses the past tense (the same incidents from the past recur in each part of the *Letter,* as they revolve and are themselves changed by the changing experience of the present). It refuses the placing of a closed moment of experience with its rehearsed response, and seeks to extend the past forward through the present into a round dance of the future. This is why, again and again, themes from his childhood recur: North Dakota farmland, a brief episode in which a local civilization rooted itself, struggled in wind, snow, and debt, and was evicted or emigrated, all within a cycle of three generations: his grandfather, his father, himself, and each generation hard, only half-fulfilled. It is not the finished quality of that experience, but the unfinished quality, the unfulfilled aspirations, which he carried forward:

It is not *my* past that I mourn—*that* I can never lose [. . .]

4. HUAC: House Un-American Activities Committee. AAUP: American Association of University Professors.

—No, but the past of this place and the place itself and what
   Was: the Possible; that is: the future that never arrived . . .
                           (Letter I & II, 206)

But how to carry forward that Possible into the future in the "man chilling" American present? The answer has an effrontery and a chilling courage of its own, in which this poet, who sometimes supposes himself to be some kind of Marxist, puts his boot into the usual Marxist stereotypes:

Well—money talks. It's hard
To say "love" loud enough in all that mechanical clamor
And perhaps the commune must fail in the filth of the American night—
Fail for a time . . .
        But all time is redeemed by the single man—
Who remembers and resurrects.
              And I remember.
                       I keep
The winter count.
                         (Letter I & II, 119)

This is not the posture of an egotist. (No man is less of an egotist of the intellect, less of a poseur—except when he sometimes poses as Tom Fool—than Thomas McGrath). The claim is of a different order, and perhaps it is of two kinds. It is made in *Part II* of *Letter* (written in the sixties) in the aftermath of the defeat and also the (partly self-inflicted) collapse of that part of the Left culture into which the poet had been initiated in the late thirties. The external forces in this defeat ("McCarthyism") are well-remembered, although few who did not endure these years understand the ferocity of its ideological terrorism and the remorseless devices employed to hunt down and harass individual "Communists." What is less well remembered is the internal collapse of that culture of the Left as it disappeared into betrayals, self-accusations and disavowals, "do-it-your-self" Judas kits, meretricious self-justifications, with the alienation of friends and the destruction of associative networks.[5] It was a moment analagous to that of the late 1790s when a combination of Anti-Jacobin ideological terrorism and internal disenchantment with the course of the French Revolution, drove Blake, Wordsworth, and Coleridge (in different ways) into isolation. And it bears analogies with the predicament of any "dissidents" isolated within a conformist society and unable to communicate with any public, upon whom falls the duty of the redemptive memory, the "winter count."

The claim is being made for the unbreakable power of the human mind, which mind, in the end, can never be guaranteed by historicist theories of collectivities, but is an individual mind which, in the winter night of a hostile culture, must stand alone. And, in the second place, the claim is being

5. The evidence is fully presented in Victor S. Navasky, *Naming Names* (New York, 1980).

made for the *poetic* mind, the uncrackable necessity of a poet to defend poetry's own truth and function. In an episode which must have astonished his inquisitors, McGrath, when summoned before the House Un-American Activities Committee, threw down this claim before them:

> As a poet I must refuse to cooperate with the committee on what I can only call esthetic grounds. The view of life which we receive through the great works of art is a privileged one—it is a view of life according to probability or necessity, not subject to the chance and accident of our real world and therefore in a sense truer than the life we see lived all around us.[6]

This unexpectedly Aristotelian view of the function of art may have surprised not only the House Committee but also those of McGrath's own comrades who were dedicated to brutishly utilitarian notions of art and of its instrumental functions in the class struggle. It is in the "privileged" truth of poetry (uncorrupted by the impurities of chance and accident) that its power lies not only to remember but also to "resurrect" and to "redeem." McGrath is not staking a personal claim, but a high (and very generally abandoned) claim for poetry itself, among the most exacting and necessary disciplines of culture.[7] To this discipline he has the humility of a servitor.

The Un-American Activities Committee had hauled him before it in April 1953, during an investigation into "Communist activities in the motion picture and educational field in Los Angeles." The President of Los Angeles State College had promptly decided that he would not have an uncooperative witness on his staff. "There were student demonstrations, etc. but that was it," McGrath recollected. Then he was entered on "the Presidents' List" or blacklist. In a letter late in 1956 he wrote:

> Since the Committee got my teaching job I've been working at several things, mostly very tiring and dull—and also bad paying. A very hard period. I wrote a long poem—about 150 pages—this year . . .

(This was *Part I* of the *Letter*.) Then, back in Manhattan in 1961, he wrote:

> It's been a hard year. I've been working a lot in documentary and other kinds of film, trying to make enough to buy myself a little time for my own stuff. And so far I've lost three jobs this year as a result of committees, blacklists etc. The first two were in colleges and either of them would have been permanent. I like teaching and the

---

6. Reprinted in *North Dakota Quarterly* 50: 8–9.

7. "Probability or necessity"—McGrath here and elsewhere is grounding his view on Aristotle, *On the Art of Poetry,* Chapter 9, "Poetic Truth and Historical Truth": "It is not the poet's function to describe what has actually happened, but the kinds of things that might happen, that is, that could happen because they are, in the circumstances, either probable or necessary. . . . For this reason poetry is something more philosophical and more worthy of serious attention than history; for while poetry is concerned with universal truths, history treats of particular facts." T. S. Dorsch, ed., *Classical Literary Criticism* (Penguin, 1965), pp. 43–44.

security would have allowed me to write. The latest one was doing documentary work for NBC. The pay is very good and I had a dream of doing about three months work a year and having the rest of the time myself. The dream lasted just long enough for them to check their files (I never imagined I'd be there since I've never worked for the likes of NBC) and I suppose it's a duplicate of the FBI file since it's run by retired FBI types. So the dream ended pretty abruptly.

"Thank you," his letter adds, "for the kind words about the value of the poetry, it's hard to believe in it sometimes, the way things are and have been. But of course the Muse doesn't let one quit, the grand old bitch."

> But all time is redeemed by the single man—
Who remembers and resurrects.
> > And I remember.
> > > I keep
The winter count . . .

Against the intolerant orthodoxy of his times McGrath affirmed the "magical" properties of poetry. In the night of a decadent civilization moving toward extermination, the poem might be a charm against evil powers. We have this written out in that fine poem, "Against the False Magicians":

The poem must not charm us like a film:
See, in the war-torn city, that reckless, gallant
Handsome lieutenant turn to the wet-lipped blonde
(Our childhood fixation) for one sweet desperate kiss
In the broken room, in blue cinematic moonlight—
Bombers across that moon, and the bombs falling,
The last train leaving, the regiment departing—
And their lips lock, saluting themselves and death:
And then the screen goes dead and all go home . . .
Ritual of the false imagination.

The poem must not charm us like the fact:
A warship can sink a circus at forty miles,
And art, love's lonely counterfeit, has small dominion
Over those nightmares that move in the actual sunlight.
The blonde will not be faithful, nor her lover ever return
Nor the note be found in the hollow tree of childhood—
This dazzle of the facts would have us weeping
The orphaned fantasies of easier days.

It is the charm which the potential has
That is the proper aura for the poem.
Though ceremony fail, though each of your grey hairs
Help string a harp in the landlord's heaven,
And every battle, every augury
Argue defeat, and if defeat itself
Bring all the darkness level with our eyes—
It is the poem provides the proper charm,
Spelling resistance and the living will,

To bring to dance a stony field of fact
And set against terror exile or despair
The rituals of our humanity.
                    (*Movie*, 121–22)

    This poem is given an uncomplex dialectical structure. The thesis of
the first verse (the wish-fulfillment of romanticism) is easy, fluent, unclut-
tered. The antithesis of the second verse (realism) opens with a memorable
image: "A warship can sink a circus at forty miles." One remembers Mr.
Sleary's circus in *Hard Times* (which, however, was not in the end sunk by
the batteries of utilitarianism); but today I always think also of the tanks
rolling in to extinguish the Prague Spring. If realism surrenders to the con-
tingent ("the chance and accident of our real world") then it betrays the
privileged view of life of art and has not terms for "the potential" ('a view of
life according to probability or necessity'), falling back in the end upon the
lost fantasies of romance. In the final verse McGrath affirms the true magical properties of poetry ("the charm which the potential has"), moving
through a commonplace pathetic image to the sustained and impassioned
synthesis in which the reality of human spiritual forces is affirmed ("in a
sense truer than the life we see lived all round us").
    The poem has an enduring validity. We need not try to fasten it down
into a local context. But it can also be seen within the particular context of
Communist cultural circles to illuminate an internal hullabaloo in which
McGrath was rejecting both of the barren alternatives, "socialist romanticism" or "socialist realism," which were being debated. The argument had
been rumbling and sputtering on since the late thirties. If critics and historians will only lay aside their orthodox or post-Trotskyist almanacs for a
while and look into the evidence, they will find that the real history is many
miles away from the stereotypes. McGrath at this moment was in the belly of
a decaying Popular Front whale, but he was kicking violently at the blubber
around him. This is the way in which most cultural mutations arise—from
the contradiction within the contradiction.

                    ∗   ∗   ∗

    To explain this I must take a detour: first, into a political reflection,
and then into biography.
    The reflection is this: I find, rather often, a curious amnesia within
American radical culture as to certain moments in its own past. There are
matters which, if not forgotten, are rarely talked about or are falsified in
memory. Not only some part of the 1930s but a large amount in the 1940s has
fallen out of polite discourse.
    Orthodox academicism and post-Trotskyist criticism and historiogra-
phy have obliterated this moment under some general theory of the universal
contamination of "Stalinism." Because the American Communist Party and

associated "front" organizations exerted rather extensive influence in the Left press, in cultural journals, films, some trade unions and civil rights movements, a wholesale bill of contamination is issued on all. The errors and illusions of the time are endlessly rehearsed (although, curiously, some of these have a way of returning in more fashionable garb) and the positives pass unremembered. In consequence of this—and also of commonplace pressures upon individuals in their careers—strategies have merged which avoid confronting the historical experience, and which sometimes also (one has to say) avoid confronting or avowing personal histories.

Similar strategies can be observed in Europe, but we do not have the same sense of caesura in our history. It is impossible—although some writers have attempted it—to pronounce the whole history of the Resistance in Italy or France or Spain or Greece or Yugoslavia as contaminated because Communist Parties played a most active role in it. Nor is it possible to hold the hand over the history of Communist Parties themselves, as a distasteful subject fit only for moralistic exercises, when repeatedly these movements have thrown up heresies and heretics. Yet America in that same moment had a very vigorous and influential Left with an international cultural presence. How come that all this, in retrospect, can be analyzed down to an irreducible spoonful of Stalinist tar?

But . . . there is no way that I can get further with this essay except through biography. And a bit of autobiography also. I first met Thomas McGrath when I came across the Atlantic, an aged war veteran of twenty-two in 1946. McGrath had spent some part of his war in the Aleutians. We were both Communists which, please remember, was not only an international "conspiracy," a formal Comintern structure, an auxiliary of Soviet diplomacy, etc., etc., but was also an international fraternity and sorority. Our meetings and occasions and circulations were much like those of other human beings in an affined network. They were not—as a contemporary student might suppose—all structured within 'cells' and disciplined according to rule. We found each other out without the benefit of any Org[anizational]. Sec[retary]. In liberated Italy I would mooch around the town, find the blacksmith's shop—the oxen lifted on a hoist to be shoed—notice the PCI posters, introduce myself as a comrade, and in a trice I would be seated on a bench, incongruous in my British officer's uniform, sampling the blacksmith's wine. It was the same with my comrades in India, Iraq, Egypt. (One good friend of mine, masquerading as a sergeant-major, was able to second himself to work for some weeks with the Communist Party in Calcutta—against British rule!) It was the same also with many of our American comrades, who were moved by the same internationalism and optimism. A million informal transactions and discourses were going on in those years, which historians will never recover and which the hard-nosed Party organizers knew nothing about.

I was passed on to Tom by a mutual friend, an American Communist and poet then soldiering in England. Saul (this friend) had found his way to the offices of *Our Time,* a cultural monthly in London, been introduced to the local beer and company, and thence to myself, and his recommendation took me to the door of Tom and to a week's good lodging in Manhattan. I had just published a short story in *Our Time* and Charles Humboldt, the assistant editor of *New Masses,* liked it well enough to carry it there also. No one in New York knew that it was my only published story; I had that happy misrecognition reserved for travelers and was taken to be a Writer.

Dizzy with success, Manhattan seemed to me to be electric with life. I caballed with poets and pretended to be one. I attended a great rally in Madison Square Garden and heard Robeson, Marcantonio, and Communist Councilman Ben Davis from Harlem. I saw the banners of the Ladies Garment Workers Union waved in defiance of the new Cold War. (For the Cold War was happening already, in 1946, at every street-corner, where the Hearst, McCormack and Scripps-Howard press were howling for an internal terror against Commies and for the atom-bombing of Yugoslavia: yes, I still have my notes.) Above all, Manhattan felt to me then as a great city with an internationalist consciousness; a great anti-Fascist city, its diversity churning into a common torrent of solidarities—whereas now, alas, Manhattan sometimes appears to me as a city of mutually tetchy, self-conscious and self-regarding and sometimes factitious ethnicities. Yet then I have to ask myself—was that cultural moment authentically present, or am I reporting the illusions of my youth?

In 1947–1948 Tom and his wife, Marian, came over to England. He was taking up a Rhodes Scholarship at Oxford, which he had won before the war. Dorothy and I saw them often, and they spent Christmas with us in a croft on the Atlantic coast of the Western Highlands of Scotland. The dark winter days, the treeless landscape, and the windswept sea reminded Tom of the Aleutians. It may be here that he first formed the idea of "Remembering that Island," with its terrible conclusion:

<blockquote>

In a dream as real as war

I see the vast stinking Pacific suddenly awash
Once more with bodies, landings on all beaches,
The bodies of dead and living gone back to appointed places,
A ten year old resurrection,
And myself once more in the scourging wind, waiting, waiting,
While the rich oratory and the lying famous corrupt
Senators mine our lives for another war.

(Movie, 100)

</blockquote>

The friendship between Tom, Dorothy, and myself founded at that time has stuck for more than thirty years. It was a solidarity fiercer than we understood at the time, a commitment to courses which we could not yet

name. The Cold War was closing off all perspectives like a mist at sea. We forget how protracted was the rupture in ordinary communications between members of the European and American left—for some fifteen years, from 1947 until the early 1960s, transatlantic travel was severely curtailed. European Commmunists and ex-Communists insufficiently abject in their penitence could not get visas to the United States. American Communists (or ex-Communists) suffered travel restrictions and the withdrawal of passports.

Defenceless under the night
Our world in stupor lies;
Yet, dotted everywhere,
Ironic points of light
Flash out wherever the Just
Exchange their messages;[8]

During those years, whether just or unjust, we exchanged ironic points of light. At some time around 1960 McGrath at length touched England again, conversed in our New Left coffee bar, and trod the Aldermaston road in support of the campaign for nuclear disarmament. Then the messages came to us not only from North Dakota but from Greece, Yugoslavia, Mexico. We have been poor correspondents. Yet we have felt—certainly Dorothy and I have felt—that all this time we have been walking shoulder to shoulder. And I am proud to find, in a letter from Tom of 1961, "I think of you both there as one of the few solid things in the world."

I do not mean—and it is important to say this—that we have adopted identical political or intellectual positions. But there has been a congruence of ulterior values and commitments, which arose from within the same double-contradiction. McGrath has reprinted in his *Collected Poems,* "Ars Poetica":

Oh, it's down with art and down with life and give us another reefer.
They all said—give us a South Sea isle, where light my love lies dreaming;
And who is that poet come in off the streets with a look unleal and lour?
Your feet are muddy, you son-of-a bitch, get out of our ivory tower.
                                                                    (*Movie,* 59)

But he has not republished "Thomas Paradox's Second Epistle to the Philistines" which probably belongs in the same period (between 1948 and 1953?) with its effective verse:

The poet said to the bureaucrat: man creates
              by the laws of beauty
The artist creates the heart's face: an image
              of all that's human.

8. W. H. Auden. *Selected Poems.* (New York: Vintage, 1979) p. 89.

But he said: I've no time to argue—though it
       sounds like a deviation—
       On a hacienda
       In San Fernando,
I'm making the Revolution.

That is a version of the poem which appears in a raft of typescripts which McGrath sent us from the West Coast in the early fifties. My sole contribution to the full annotated text of McGrath's Complete Works in the Twenty-Second Century (which century neither McGrath nor I expect to arrive) will be this. I cannot prove it, for I cannot find the earlier copy, but this is a West Coast, fifties, variant of a poem which in the late forties (and Manhattan) had ended the verse in this way:

    Desk-deep in class war
      On the eighteenth floor
I'm making the Revolution.

The change was made, as the poet has recently acknowledged to me, for political and not for aesthetic reasons: "by the time the poem got to publication some of the people on the eighteenth floor were in jail or on their way or gone underground; but there were still a good many *one-time* radicals still alive and making money in the shadow of Hollywood."[9]

    This illustrates the difficulties placed not only before an editor but also a critic. McGrath's texts often suggest a subtext which is tactfully diminished or even suppressed because the targets of his intellectual attack—the "bureaucrat," the instrumental Marxist ideologue—were themselves the objects of persecution by media and state. Meanwhile McGrath, himself persecuted by the same forces, was involved in sharp disputes within that cultural apparatus which both presented and contained, both expressed and repressed, an influential part of the American left.

    It is a curious situation, at odds with the stereotypes. On one side McGrath was being hounded by HUAC: "I expect to be fired from my job at the end of this term," he wrote to us from Los Angeles (1951?):

    I'm certain someone will see "Crooked Mile,"[10] read it and decide I'm n.g. Which could mean (this is not for saying aloud) that I might go to jail. Possible.

But he was writing to us the next year:

9. McGrath to author, 27 November 1980. Of his cultural "bureaucrats" V. J. Jerome was imprisoned under the Smith Act and John Howard Lawson was one of the "Hollywood Ten." Navasky has valuable discussion in chapter 9, "The Reasons Considered," of the internal cultural disputes of the CPUSA, especially the "heresy trial" and recantation of Albert Maltz (with Maltz's own recollections). When I first met McGrath in the summer of 1946 the Maltz case had already taken place, and I remember his anger about it.
10. *To Walk a Crooked Mile.*

All in all I think my career as the best or most promising or whatever it was left-wing poet in America[11] is due for some drastic revision. In fact, I feel pretty sure that it is no longer possible for me to publish in the left wing press any more. If that is too pessimistic, then I will emend it to say that it is only a matter of time. I suppose I was always suspect for being "difficult" and for being "bitter" . . . Unless you versify Daily Worker editorials in degenerate Whitmanesque, you're apt to seem like a formalist, and anything that is not a cliché is examined to see whether it might not be a political heresy. This is not just a lament for my own situation. For Christ sake, if you can get anyone to look into the stinking mess here, do so. All the writers I know regard Sillen and the literary commissars (like Fast) as idiots, but the only reaction to them is cynicism, since no one feels that anything can be done. It is absolutely strangling. Unless you are, like Neruda, a senator from Chile in exile, you're in a bad way. If you are Neruda, you get fawned on and editorialized over by bureaucrats who really hate all art but admire anything that succeeds. Help! Help!

But if the left-wing press was "strangling," there was no other: "My novel I think is done for—the pub. house where it was just had a red hunt and the editor was fired etc!"[12]

It was at this time that McGrath, Philip Stevenson, and a few friends founded the *California Quarterly*. It got "a mixed reception" (he wrote to us in 1953):

The agit-prop-and-idiot faction write us letters which say that the stories are negative and that we have no Negro writers—this group is a kind of self-appointed Committee of Public Safety, or better yet the Mrs. Grundys of the Revolution and apparently they never read poetry . . . Another group gives us hell for being so dedicated to uplift and betterment of the human race that we publish a story for its theme . . .

The only salvation of left writing in this country, I think, is to try to break the strangle-hold of the blue stockings who run left editing and criticism. But other editors are afraid to do anything. Unless we hold to orthodox views (views which no left-wing writer in the country accepts, but all are afraid to challenge for fear of a heresy trial) these editors think that Jerome and Sillen and the high panjandrums (Fast et al) will attack and destroy us . . . It's a simply sickening situation. Everyone here assumes nothing can be done about it, refuse to stand together (that would be factionalism!) and adopt an attitude of pure cynicism toward Jerome & Co. regarding *Masses & Mainstream* as the idiot child: lame-witted and a little shameful to be sure, but nevertheless our own.

I am not competent to unravel the inner history of these disputes: I must leave this to others. My sympathies are with McGrath: Yet I do not know that he was always "right," nor that he would always claim this himself.

The protagonists whom he identified most often, among the party of "bureaucrats" or "philistines," were V. J. Jerome, Samuel Sillen, and (on the

11. A jesting reference to the blurb of *Crooked Mile*.

12. A subsequent letter (1952?) notes that "novel now being considered by Liberty Book Club, but editor there wants Sam Sillen to read it to get his opinion—and I figure Sillen will kill it off." It was published in 1985: *This Coffin Has No Handles, North Dakota Quarterly* 52, 4 (1986).

West Coast) John Howard Lawson; and of his own party, Milton Blau and the generous-minded (and neglected) Charles Humboldt:

Now that Charlie Humboldt and Milt Blau no longer have anything to do with *Masses and Mainstream* the present editors choose only the most thinned out kind of material. I pray for a new Duclos letter on American left criticism, but despair of getting it. When Mao wrote it for us (have you seen his pamphlete on Art and Literature?) there was what amounted to a suppression of it—no reviews, no discussion, nothing. Perhaps I am no longer quite sane on the whole subject. The Mao thing especially agitates me, since Mao says the same damn thing about the need for both a tactical and strategic kind of writing which I have argued is the solution to the dilemma of left writing under capitalism . . . I say in dead seriousness that we need help in the worst way.

No doubt the control exerted by the American Communist Party over its own cultural apparatus was unusually disciplinary and its instrumental attitudes toward art may have been unusually bleak. And the self-submission of some intellectuals to the mystique of the historical authority of the Party, as the interpreter of revolutionary and class truth, may have been unusually abject. But McGrath was wrong to suppose that he was facing some local American difficulty, and that help might come from the advice of fraternal Parties ("a new Duclos letter"). Duclos was quite as much part of the problem as were Sillen or Jerome. Little help could anyone in Europe bring as Zhdanovism extended its ideological and disciplinary reign throughout the international Communist apparatus. McGrath was contesting with symptoms which he had not yet diagnosed as those of Communism's mortal crisis; like his own workers he and his fellow protagonists were "drifting the battlefields of a war / They don't even know is happening." And one must add that not only Party discipline (the "fear of a heresy trial") but also a stubborn loyalty to a party—and to comrades—who were the object of incessant public attack inhibited open intellectual confrontations.

Thomas McGrath had rendered his voluntary dues to the Party's Caesar. He had offered to compromise with Caesar's demands, by developing a theory of "tactical" and "strategic" poetry. "Tactical" poetry might be about immediate political events: "the poet should give it as much clarity and strength as he can give it without falling into political slogans." "Strategic" poetry ("a poetry in which the writer trusts himself enough to write about whatever comes along") should be open and exploratory, "consciousness raising or enriching."[13] In 1949 he had unleashed a splendid charge of his own tactical cavalry in *Longshot O'Leary's Garland of Practical Poesie*. The title of this book has probably lost meaning to today's

13. When McGrath first tried out this not-very-threatening revision in *New Masses* he "got a terrific shower of shit as a result"; see interviews in *Another Chicago Magazine* 5 (1980), and in *Cultural Correspondence* 9 (Spring 1979), *North Dakota Quarterly* 50: 28. I have not tracked down the original exchanges in *New Masses*.

readers, although the fiercely political surrealism of the poems has enduring vitality. What has been forgotten is the precedent charge of the heavy brigade of T. S. Eliot, stationing their chargers on every campus and in every literary review. After the *Family Reunion* (1947) and the *Notes Towards a Definition of Culture* (1948) had come the reissue of *Old Possum's Book of Practical Cats*. McGrath's contestation with Eliot can be detected throughout his poetry of this decade, as allusion, irony, echo. And against Old Possum he sent out Longshot O'Leary onto the field.

These "tactical" poems McGrath wrote as immediate polemic. He did not expect them to last. His savage poem on the Marshall Plan, "First Book of Genesis According to Marshall," is—he wrote to us in 1948—"going to be completely useless in a few months possibly." But it has, in fact, long outlasted the Marshall Plan, perhaps because of its hilariously inventive surrealist polemic; and the poet has acknowledged this by including it in his (highly selective) "Collected Poems" (*Movie*, 55–56).

But even poems such as these could not get into *Masses and Mainstream* by 1952–1953. They were too "bitter." And where else could they find an outlet? I cannot, even today, turn away without a wry smile from the recollection of those know-all High Marxists and political Heavies who suppressed verses because they were *too bitter!* "Comrades, you must be more positive! You must have confidence in the international working-class movement!" And what if that movement was collapsing in ruins and bad faith all around us, did not poets then have the duty to warn?[14]

McGrath was right. But that did him no kind of good. Come 1956 and all that, and surely McGrath was at last liberated, freed from the Stalinist shackles, in touch once again with the new and ebullient radicalism of the 1960s, in accord with an audience once more? Well, no. That wasn't how it was. How exactly it was I do not exactly know. But a little I remember, something is in his letters, more is in his poems.

McGrath's break with the Communist Party was never as sharp or as polemical as was ours. This was partly plain pig-Irish stubborness. When some of those very commissars of culture with whom he had been wrestling for years (in private) suddenly flaked out in public confessional mood, accusing "the Party" of their own sins, he sat in the same place and was privately sick.[15] He had never, unless in one or two poems in *Longshot*

14. McGrath recalls the years after 1946: "There was nothing to do to prepare, except as an isolated individual. All one could do was to warn, and those were warnings that no one wanted to hear, often seen as a kind of pessimism or defeatism" (*Cultural Correspondence* 9, 43).

15. Tom does not recall exactly when he left the CPUSA. Around 1955–1957 he was quarreling with West Coast organizers about cultural matters and trying to transfer from an "intellectual" to an industrial branch. When this failed, his membership lapsed but he continued to write for *Masses and Mainstream* and *People's World*. He became a sort of "charmed quark" on the unaffiliated far left, and was interested for a while in the Progressive Labor Party until it turned out that his main contact was an FBI spy (conversation with author, 1980).

O'Leary, romanticized the Soviet world.

His stance, in the matter of the Soviet Union, had, and maybe still has, a source in pure curmudgeonly opposition. If the official culture of the United States of America, which he found to be foul and mendacious, wanted to name Communism as its Satanic antagonist, then he was willing to vow himself a Satanist and place himself directly in front of Orthodoxy's polished self-satisfied nose.[16]

There was, in any case, a brief moment of honor in the American Communist Party in 1956, a revolt within the *Daily Worker,* a stirring of authentic self-reflection in the Party. Tom was, with Charles Humboldt, one of the boarding-party who tried to set *Mainstream* onto a socialist humanist course. When the attempt failed he simply removed himself quietly and without public statement from the snarling comrades. In a letter which I cannot exactly date (probably 1961) he gave a rundown on the previous five years:

I'm afraid that long letter will never arrive—somebody not paid by the post office dept here must have found it interesting reading. But anyway you must have gathered the main strands—and it's dreary to go over them (some jobs lost thru automation and some thru the high spirits of various quasi-governmental bodies: schools, films, etc. etc. . . .) In the last three years I've moved around a lot— hardly six months in any one place—following jobs like a bindle stiff . . . To bring you up to date. For some years I was looked on by the *Mainstream* people as a very bad cat— largely because I had been fighting with John Howard Lawson, the grand panjandrum on the West Coast, a great culture faker. Then it was officially discovered that a lot of mistakes had been made etc. etc. Humboldt went as editor of *Mainstream* and asked me to join up with him, which I did. Then, over a period of time things went back to what they had been; it became more and more difficult for Humboldt to do anything with the magazine; there was a show down and he lost. So I dropped off also—I was only a "contributor" whatever that means. I've had no organizational connection with the party for years, and the last years when I did have such a connection—god knows how long ago now—were ones where I spent most of the time fighting expulsion. Since then I've free-lanced in a few tactical things with other dissidents—there are a lot of us but there seems no way of getting everybody in any kind of concerted motion, although a few of us did dream for a while of organizing the Ramshackle Socialist Victory Party (RSVP). Somehow it seems that this might still be done, but I don't see how. Still, with all the trouble there was with the organization, the fact that it has had such a terrible fight in the last years and has lost so much in members and power (more from bad politics than terror) has left a terrible terrible emptiness in the whole life of the country, an emptiness which I think everyone feels without knowing why. And an emptiness which has left a lot of writers and intellectuals in a bad way. I

16. See *Letter I & II,* p. 150: ". . . having come by blacklist degrees / To the bottom: dropped out of the labor market as unsafe / To a government at wars ie the cold, the Korean, the Pretend / (Against Russia) the Holy (against Satanic citizens the likes of / Myself)."

This suggests that the Pretend War against Russia was only a cover for the holy war of internal social and intellectual control. Cf. *The Gates of Ivory, The Gates of Horn* (New York, 1957), p. 100 (Rpt. Chicago: Another Chicago Press, 1987), where the generals come and ask the Sybil "How long will the Pretend War last?" and the Sybil replies: "How long do you want it to last?"

don't mean the ones who were in the organization (although they've been hard hit too); what I am thinking of is the kind of intellectual who never was with the organization and was always critical of it and even opposed to it. *But* who felt some kind of sense of comfort that on many of the big issues where he himself might do nothing, there was a group that was fighting for good causes . . .

Northern lights in winter; in summer the eccentric stairs
The firefly climbs . . .
                                                      But where is the steering star
                                                                              where is
The Plow? the Wheel?
                                      Made this song in a bad time . . .
No revolutionary song now, no revolutionary
Party
        sell out
                false consciousness
                                      yet I *will*
Sing
      for these poor
                              for the victory still to come
RSVP
                                                      (*Letter I & II*, 124–25)

So McGrath returns in the *Letter* back to Manhattan, the "stone city":

                              An age of darkness has entered that stone
In a few years between wars. The past holds
Like a sad dream trapped in granite: what foot can slip free what trail
Blaze in that night-rock where the starry travellers search?
                                                      (*Letter I & II*, 125)

But before he returned to Manhattan (1960–1961) something had happened in his last years on the West Coast: no less than a Renaissance! In 1958 he wrote to us about "a whirl of work"—a speaking-reading tour up the Coast, poetry with jazz in a nightclub, a record with Langston Hughes: "mean-while I'm broke." Yet as this "Renaissance" bloomed, McGrath once again turned abruptly away on his own jagged fork. If anything he had found the civilization of the West Coast more threatening than the East. Los Angeles gets a singularly savage handling in the *Letter*:

Windless city built on decaying granite, loose ends
Without end or beginning and nothing to tie to, city down hill
From the high mania of our nineteenth century destiny—what's loose
Rolls there, what's square slides, anything not tied down
Flies in . . .
        kind of petrified shitstorm.
                                                      (*Letter I & II*, 112)

He recalled his time on the West Coast as:

Ten years—doing time in detention camps of the spirit,
Grounded in Twin Plague Harbor with comrades Flotsom & Jetsom:
Wreckage of sunken boats becalmed in the Horse Latitudes
Windless soul's doldrums LosAngeles AsiaMinor of the intellect
Exile.

(Letter I & II, 111)

The "exile" was made the more anguished by the loss of his two most valued and sustaining relationships: with Marian, and then with his second wife, Alice. It was made endurable by the small "commune" of resistance, the "Marsh Street Irregulars," the circle of friends, fellow-outlaws and poets, which he was later to recall in elegaic mood.[17] But the pervading memory is one of nightmare, the nightmare of *The Gates of Ivory, The Gates of Horn* (1957). This terrible futuristic extrapolation of a capitalist consumerized subtopia, governed by the invigilations of a surrealist HUAC, ought never to have passed out of print. Much superior to *Animal Farm* (that exemplary case of ideology masquerading as art), its fertile symbolic code disallows any simplistic ideological printout—when published in Czech it was no doubt read as a savage satire upon Stalinism. It carries no local political "message" but a warning that human creativity was under threat from external repression and internal self-betrayal, and that civilization might pass "into some kind of surrogate existence."

McGrath's hostility to West Coast civilization extended not only to its dominant consumer culture but also to a good part of the self-styled oppositional culture also—an "opposition" which he often gestures at as one of "culture-fakers," exhibitionists, egotists, and "the dreamers, crazed, in their thousands, nailed to a tree of wine" (*Letter I & II*, 116)—an "opposition" only too easily to be bought or co-opted by money and power. What happened to destroy McGrath's accord with the West Coast "Renaissance" I do not know. But he explained some part of it to us after his return to New York in 1960. For a while he had "had some hope" for "the Beat mob":

There was in fact a lot of social critical thinking in the group (never a group, just a bunch of people who were on the scene). Then *Life-Time* discovered the thing and invented their own version of it. The censors helped by making *Howl* and Ginsberg into an icon. Barney Ross of Grove Press and Lawrence Lipton (he wrote a book called *The Holy Barbarians*) cut the balls off the "movement," substituting "disaffiliation" and (as if there weren't enough to go around) "alienation," dada, obscenity etc. etc. The Beat Movement became a little club of crazies, very exclusive; and the younger ones accepted "disaffiliation" etc. etc. as the official program, grew beards, went back to the big war against their parents and all social content was lost. All positive social content anyway. What a son-of-a-bitch Rimbaud was! He gave a program to a century of petit bourgeois psycho-anarchists.

17. See "Return to Marsh Street," *Movie*, pp. 142–44; *Letter, Part II*, pp. 120–22; Gene Frumkin, "A Note on Tom McGrath—The Early 50s," *North Dakota Quarterly* 50: 46–55.

*   *   *

What! All those years after the Annunciation at Venice
And no revolution in sight?

                              And how long since the lads
From West Stud Horse Texas and Poontang-on-the-Hudson
Slogged through the city of Lost Angels in the beardless years
Led by a cloud no bigger than an orgone box, whence issued—
Promising, promising, promising (and no revolution and no
Revolution in sight) issued the cash-tongued summons
Toward the guru of Big Sur and San Fran's stammering Apocalypse?

I do not know how long this thing can go on!
—Waiting for Lefty, waiting for Godot, waiting for the heavenly fix.
In my way of counting, time comes in through my skin—
Blind Cosmos Alley, charismatic light
Of electric mustaches in the Deep Night of the Gashouse gunfire
From enormous imaginary loud cap pistols of infinitely small caliber
Anarcholunacy—how long, in that light, to read what signposts?
When all that glows with a gem-like flame is the end of Lipton's cigar?[18]
                                                      (*Movie*, 162)

For a year or two (1960–1961) he was back in New York now with Genya, an unaffiliated and agnostic revolutionary:

I remain unconvinced of everything except that (under what auspices now I cannot imagine) the revolution has got to come. And it had better come pretty soon here or we will have passed into some kind of surrogate existence—unless we have already—in which regeneration is impossible . . . We live in Manhattan—lower East side—lower than it's ever been, very poor, luminous poverty and a phosphorescence of non-literary alienation in the streets. We have a terrible sort of place. Would be unbearable to think of living here for a long time—but I feel that way about the whole city.

And, in the same letter;

No movements about. The pacifists keep fairly busy and I've given them a hand on a few things now and again. The biggest thing I think that has happened in quite a while is the action which the women took a couple of weeks ago. Demonstrations took place all across the country, some of them pretty sizeable (a couple of thousand Americans involved in a *good* cause is pretty sizeable to us nowadays).

Several letters exchanged at this time related to his attempt to visit—perhaps to stay a while and work—in Cuba. We furnished credentials from *New Left Review* for Tom and Genya to serve in Cuba as, respectively, jour-

18. "After the Beat Generation," *Crazy Horse* 1, no date (but published from Tom and Genia's address at 220 East 14th Street, New York, which they left in 1961 or early 1962); also *Movie*, p. 162.

nalist and photographer, but to no avail: the State Department evidently consulted up-to-date files and permits were refused.

It is at around this time that McGrath's pessimism about urban American civilization appears to deepen: "I don't belong in this century—who does?"

Now, down below, in the fire and stench, the city
Is building its shell: elaborate levels of emptiness
Like some sea-animal building towards its extinction.
And the citizens, unserious and full of virtue,
Are hunting for bread, or money, or a prayer,
And I behold them, and this season of man, without love.

If it were not a joke, it would be proper to laugh.
—Curious how that rat's nest holds together—
Distracting . . .
                    Without it there might be, still,
The gold wheel and the silver, the sun and the moon,
The season's ancient assurance under the unstable stars
Our fiery companions . . .
                              And trees, perhaps, and the sound
Of the wild and living water hurrying out of the hills.[19]
                        ("Poem," *Movie*, 130–31)

Later, back in North Dakota, in one of his rare essays on his poetic intentions, he discussed the matter:

What is there, out here on the edge, that makes our experience different from that of the city poet? First there is the land itself. It has been disciplined by machines, but it is still not dominated. The plow that broke the plains is long gone and the giant tractor and the combine are here, but the process of making a living is still a struggle and a gamble—it is not a matter of putting raw materials in one end of a factory and taking finished products out of the other. Weather, which is only a nuisance in the city, takes on the power of the gods here, and vast cycles of climate, which will one day make all the area a dust bowl again and finally return it to grass, make all man's successes momentary and ambiguous. Here man can never think of himself, as he can in the city, as the master of nature. Like it or not he is subject to the ancient power of seasonal change: he cannot avoid being *in* nature; he has an heroic adversary that is no abstraction. At a level below immediate consciousness we respond to this, are less alien to our bodies, to human and natural time.

The East is much older than these farther states, has more history. But I believe that that history no longer functions, has been forgotten, has been "paved over." In the East man begins every day for himself. Here, the past is still alive and close at hand—the arrowheads we turn up may have been shot at our grandfathers. I am not thinking of any romantic frontier. The past out here was bloody, and full of injustice, though hopeful and heroic. It is very close here—my father took shelter with his family at Fort Ransom during an Indian scare when he was a boy. Later he heard of the massacre at Wounded Knee. Most of us are haunted by the closeness of that past,

19. But I think this poem also dates back to the fifties.

and by the fact that we are only a step from the Indian, whose sense of life so many of the younger people are trying to learn.[20]

* * *

> Why my grandmother saw them—
> And saw that last one perhaps: ascending the little river
> On the spring high water in a battered canoe.
> > Stole one of her chickens
> (Herself in the ark of the soddy with the rifle cocked but not arguing)
> Took the stolen bird and disappeared into history.
> > > (*Letter I & II*, 190)

But it was not only that in the cities the sense of history was "paved over." McGrath also argued—and perhaps still argues?—that urban civilization in the United States had entered into a "surrogate existence."

Supposing he already knows the facts of life and the class struggle, the poet has nothing to learn from the city. Where once it was a liberating place it is now a stultifying one. Only in the ghettos is something "happening," as the great proliferation of Black, Chicano and Indian poetry shows. For such poets the ghettos are a source of strength. But the white poet can enter the ghetto only with great difficulty and in any case the ghettos are only beginning to work through to revolutionary politics. At the moment they are still involved (with important exceptions) in cultural and political nationalism, dead ends which it seems must be explored before a serious politics becomes possible. When that time comes the cities will again be the place of the central experience of the time and the poets will have to go back . . .
    The point is to find, during these years of "wandering in the desert," the link with the revolutionary past in order to create, invent, rescue, restructure, resurrect the past. This may be our gift to the city.[21]

Yet McGrath did not retire from New York to North Dakota gracefully and in elegiac mood. He stormed out with the first number of an irregular journal, *Crazy Horse*, "edited by a dead Sioux chief"—the chief who helped to defeat General Custer. *Crazy Horse* announced that it wasn't interested "in either the shrunken trophies of the academic head-hunters nor in those mammoth cod-pieces stuffed with falsies, the primitive inventions of the Nouveau Beat. We believe that poverty is real, that work is real, that joy and anguish and revolution are real."

We, the Irregulars of Crazy Horse, Ghost Dancers of the essential existential Soli-

20. "McGrath on McGrath," *Epoch* 22 (1973): 217; also in *North Dakota Quarterly* 50: 23–24.
    21. *Epoch* 22: 218–19. See also "Poetry and Place," interview McGrath and Mark Vinz, *Voyages to the Inland Sea* 3, ed. John Judson (La Crosse, 1973), pp. 33–48.

darity, now summon into being the hosts of the new resistance. Give up those bird-cages built for lions! Alienation is not enough![22]

McGrath's own poems and those of Alvaro Cardona-Hine came closest to meeting the extravagant prescriptions of the manifesto. There is a violence of desperation, a mood of willful self-isolation, invective and blasphemy about this moment: a total rejection.

Crazy Horse was published sporadically over the next years, from North Dakota, and then passed from Tom and Genya's editorship into other hands. McGrath half turned back to his own state and he was half-driven there. First the University of North Dakota and then Moorhead State University (Minnesota) to their honor (and their own good fortune) found places for this most distinguished poet. In the past twenty-odd years there have been dark patches and patches of sun, and in all times McGrath has continued to be prolific, innovative, poetically "Live-O." These years are still too close to both of us to discuss with objectivity.

*   *   *

As I have followed the tracks of this remarkable poet through a dozen tiny and short-lived journals on the margins of official (or "official" opposi-tional) culture it has been impossible not to reach for a comparison. The experience of isolation, of the loss of relations with a public, of blacklisting, and of survival through a succession of casual jobs,[23] is one which calls into mind the experience of many Czech intellectuals who were evicted from their professions in the "normalization" which succeeded upon 1968. McGrath has been the outlaw of American normalization.

Of course, the proper and important qualification must be made. McGrath was hounded around the place but he was not imprisoned, his work was not actually suppressed (except by the self-regulating censorship of editors and publishing-houses), and if he was hounded at length back into North Dakota, Dakota—he would be the first to insist—is no Siberian gulag. He has even, of late years, received a little recognition: an Amy Low-ell and a Guggenheim Fellowship came his way.

Yet, for all that, the trajectory of his life and work offers the sharpest

22. Most of the Crazy Horse manifesto is in North Dakota Quarterly 50: 10. I am indebted to the archivists at the poetry collection in Brown University Library, where I consulted some numbers of Crazy Horse, the California Quarterly, and Witness to the Times!

23. McGrath's work ranged from some pulp-writing and movie moonlighting (see Mike Hazard, North Dakota Quarterly 50: 101–6) to casual labor and semi-skilled work in fur-niture and ceramics workshops. He found the physical work ("if it is not too bloody phys-ical") pleasant and compatible with writing poetry. He commenced Letter, Part I, while working "in a little factory for making decorative sculpture—the things we were working on were beautiful things . . . it was a very good situation:—and completed it in a few weeks": interview in Dacotah Territory, pp. 8–9, cited in North Dakota Quarterly 50: 122 and McGrath to author (1980).

kind of critique of the dominant culture. His work has been barely permitted to continue, sometimes circulating to a readership of a few hundreds on an outlaw margin. Students in the next century may savor the "metaphysical" wit of the poet who, hounded from one job to another in California in the 1950s, wrote "Figures in an Allegorical Landscape" from his temporary refuge as a board marker on the Stock Exchange:

Where number farmers plant their hope
In the dark of the moon of ignorance,
He guards their fractionated sleep:
A sad vaquero, riding fence

Like a good shepherd. Sacred cows
Graze on the ranges of his lack.
In his high patrol he binds the strays
From Anaconda to Zellerback,

While all Dow's children clap their hands
For the Eucharist of their golden feast.
But he is bound in stocks and bonds,
Who writes the Number of the Beast.[24]

And I will predict with greater confidence that students will read with pride McGrath's multi-faceted refusal to cooperate with the House Un-American Activities Committee in 1953, as a teacher, poet, and citizen; a statement which commences:

As a teacher, my first responsibility is to my students. To cooperate with this committee would be to set for them an example of accommodation to forces which can only have, as their end effect, the destruction of education itself . . . I am proud to say that a great majority of my students . . . do not want me to accommodate myself to this committee. In a certain sense, I have no choice in the matter—the students would not want me back in the classroom if I were to take any course of action other than the one I am pursuing.[25]

And they will note with pleasure that McGrath's students fulfilled his confidence in them, publishing a tribute to him in the form of a collection of his own poems, *Witness to the Times!* In a "Comment" prefaced to the collection, McGrath wrote:

I hope that the poems will be a witness to a continuing liaison with the world, an

24. "Figures in an Allegorical Landscape: Stock Brokerage Board Marker," typescript in our own collection. Ironically his job as board marker was one of the only ones he was not blacklisted out of. He was simply "automated out."
25. *North Dakota Quarterly* 50: 8–9. McGrath refused to cooperate with HUAC as a teacher and as a poet. "When I was notified to appear here, my first instinct was simply to refuse to answer committee questions out of personal principle and on the grounds of the rights of man and let it go at that." However, on "further consideration," and to support the stance of other witnesses, he also cited the first, fourth, and fifth amendments.

affair that is not without its ups and downs but which is as secure as a sacred marriage. I believe that this figure of the world's lover is the best image for the poet—that he may succeed where the Neutral Man (whom it shall not profit to gain his soul if he lose the world) is certain to fail. The poet always has this task, it seems to me: to bear witness to the times; but now especially when the State is trying by corruption, coercion, and its own paltry terror to silence writers, or dope them or convert them into the bird sanctuaries of public monuments—now especially the artist should be responsible to the world.[26]

McGrath's good friend and mentor, Charles Humboldt, had a more savage comment on "the witnesses" who made their terms with "the confessors of the sacred state."

Now they are kind to children and at the least
Rebuff burst into tears, reproach and follow
The hunted as though they were being holloed
Through halls and borders like a tired beast.[27]

"Why does the persecution in mass of Communist and progressive intellectuals arouse no protest among the partisans of the liberty and integrity of the individual?" he asked. And he indicated the "latent conservatism" of even the "pseudo-revolutionary" movements of modern art, "self-absorbed and devoid of all realistic material perspective":

Their goal was freedom *from* society, not freedom *within* society to be won in alliance with its progressive forces. After all, one could still crawl in the cracks of the police state. So the fire eaters now drink at their masters' tables while the prophets compose cautious prayers for their own salvation.[28]

McGrath perhaps will have said "amen" to that, yet it will not have satisfied him. He was not euphoric about "the progressive forces" of society, and his "realistic material perspectives" lay more in the past than in the present or future:

I sit at the beach, in the light of a gone day,
And I wait for the hunters. [. . .]

Dark, now, all the States
And night on the west coast.
Darkness and exile [. . .]

For they will hunt you, O revolutionaries!
Hunt you in darkness—the slogan chalked on the wall
Is your magical sign, icon of terrible love,

26. *Witness to the Times!*, a mimeographed typescript "conceived and edited by students of Thomas McGrath," Los Angeles, 1953 or 1954.
27. *California Quarterly* 2, 1 (Autumn 1952): 50.
28. *California Quarterly* 2, 2 (Winter 1953): 8–9.

The dark of the calendar. They hunt you, listening
For a sound of gunfire.

But, now, the silence, and the neutral stars on the sea.
Sirens. Waiting. The waves' long lamentation.
Endured by millions—this darkness and the hunting:
Capture Death Victory. Like the struggle, the changeless sea,
Like the constant stars: Endure Resist Endure.[29]

Here, waiting for the hunters, he turned inward upon himself and commenced the *Letter to an Imaginary Friend*. In such a moment of isolation and defeat, Wordsworth at Goslar in 1799 commenced *The Prelude*, a poem to which *Letter* can be justly compared. There is the same autobiographic structure (and the same indefiniteness as to biographic detail); the same recovery of childhood experience, seen both through the child's eye and the adult poet's; the same central concern with political experience, the same strenuous attempt to settle mythological accounts with the poet's own time.

Yet to mention *The Prelude* in the same breath as *Letter* is not only to provoke academic hilarity. It is also to snag one's foot on the widespread misunderstanding that *Letter* (in its "valid" parts) is some kind of "pastoral" offering from "the West." It is this (I suspect) which has closed the urban and academic readership against a due recognition of the poem: it is difficult to perceive that a poem with "agrarian" themes, by a poet who has chosen to "withdraw" to North Dakota might possibly be addressed to their immediate history and their own malaise. When McGrath published *The Movie at the End of the World*, a selection from a lifetime's verse, the *New Republic* noted that this revealed the poet as "an old-time dustbowl radical out of the Dakotas of the '30's" who had passed through "characteristic romantic progression from illusion to disillusion" (21 April 1973). Seven years later the *New York Times Book Review* got around to awarding the same book the high fame of a seven-line notice (13 April 1980) which said that "the spirit that animates [the poems] is of the West, whether it is in the form of tough modern verse or that of the simple, oldtime ballad."

The misrecognition here is spectacular. McGrath's first published poems belong to the last years of the thirties. His first volume, *First Manifesto*, was published by Alan Swallow at Baton Rouge in 1940, and a brief scrutiny will show that dominant influences upon the poems were those of Hart Crane and of the English left-wing poets of the thirties: Auden, Day Lewis, Spender, MacNeice. It is not so much the "oldtime ballad" as Auden's reinvention of it in *Look, Stranger* and *Another Time* which gave to McGrath an

29. From sections 1 and 4 of "The Hunted Revolutionaries," first published in *California Quarterly* 4, 1 (1955). Sections 2 and 3 are republished in *Movie*, pp. 172–73, dedicated to Henry Winston, the black national chairman of the CPUSA who lost his eyesight while in prison under the Smith Act: see Frederick C. Stern in *North Dakota Quarterly*, 50: 108. I do not think that sections 1 and 4 have been republished.

inspiration for his own reinventions in *Longshot O'Leary*. In McGrath's subsequent poetry he draws upon Western agrarian themes and a Wobbly vocabulary, but the poetic and intellectual influences are in no way "regional." A very long way back there may be Whitman, or the voracious appetite and universal self-license of Whitman, but

Whitman, he thinks, deserves to be sung.
His imitators should all be hung.[30]

Influences which I have myself noted include Lorca, Elouard, Neruda, Brecht, Pasternak. The strongest intellectual influence of "Marxism" came to him, not through Marx, but through Christopher Caudwell:

Longshot O'Leary Says a Square Is a Person
Who Cannot Read Caudwell.[31]

Among his contemporaries he was clearly in touch with the group of British poets of the left around *Our Time* and *Arena* (some of whom he had met in 1947–1948): Edgell Rickword, Randall Swingler, Jack Lindsay, Hamish Henderson, Arnold Rattenbury, Jack Beeching, Roy Fuller. And close poetic colleagues and friends in America are often summoned into the round dance of his verse: among them Charles Humboldt, Edwin Rolfe, Naomi Replansky, Don Gordon, Alvaro Cardona-Hine, Robert Bly.

But I have written myself into a ridiculous corner: in noting influences which might be overlooked, I have suggested far too narrow a grid of reference for this deeply cultured mind. He has received, no doubt, two hundred influences per week, and some he has received and rejected (as Eliot, Pound, and Beckett) while others, like the *haiku*, he has submitted himself to as a discipline.[32] His poetry is enriched by sufficient mythic and literary (as well as political) allusion to keep, alas, whole Eng. Lit. Faculties at work through the twenty-first century. I wish only to emphasize that *Part II* of *Letter*, which some people suppose to be "about" North Dakota, is signed off "North Dakota-Skyros-Ibiza-Agaete-Guadalajara, 1968." It is true that McGrath's *politics* are given a very distinct American location; they are not the extrapolation of some theorized cosmopolitan prescription. But these are interpreted through a poetic grid of reference which, if not universal, is as universal as his selection of poetic values allows it to be.

As he insists, "North Dakota is everywhere." And what is "everywhere" is not that complacent and self-important entity, "the human condi-

30. Alice McGrath, "Longshot O'Leary Says It's Your Duty to Be Full of Fury" (November 1952) in *North Dakota Quarterly* 50: 45.
31. Ibid., p. 44.
32. See *A Sound of One Hand* (St. Peter, Minnesota, 1975) and *Open Songs* (Mount Carroll, Illinois, 1977).

tion," but the condition of men and women in their labor, in their love and their loss, in their "somatic" relation to nature, in their exploitation and oppression, in their thwarted aspirations for "communitas" (their faculty for dreaming and myth-making), and at times very specifically in their common imbrication in the capitalist nexus.[33]

Nevertheless, it is *Dakota* which is "everywhere," and if we are to understand the *Letter,* that is where we must start. The history of the Dakotas and the biography of the McGrath family is an extraordinarily compressed episode, almost a parable of capitalism. His grandparents on both sides were Irish and on his mother's side (the Sheas) were Gaelic-speaking. His maternal grandfather came, by way of Ellis Island, up to North Dakota, working on the railway, carting and freighting. His paternal grandfather came through Canada, carrying with him savage anti-English recollections of the Great Famine; he also came following the railway, doing freighting work with a contractor of oxen. Both pairs of grandparents became homesteaders, the Sheas in the neighborhood of Sheldon, where McGrath grew up. The family passed on to the growing poet a vigorous inheritance from the Irish oral tradition. His paternal grandfather was a notable "curser"[34] and his father a great teller of "tall stories"—such stories as recur in *Letter,* as when the winds from the dust bowls of the West darken the Dakota skies:

And the dust blowing down your throat like a fistful of glass—
And *that* not so bad, but pushing down on your hat
Were the vagrant farms of the north: Montana, Saskatchewan,
With the farmers still on them, merrily plowing away,
Six inches over your head . . .
                                                    (*Letter I & II,* 47)

In the evenings at the farm, when the battery-set ran out, his father would entertain the children with songs and stories, some traditional, some (about local personalities and events) of his own making. To this McGrath could add the scanty resource of the local school—Pope's *Iliad,* Halkett and Laing versions of the classics, *The Burnt Njal:* and the ambiguous inheritance of the Catholic church, which is resurrected and roasted in *Letter:*

And now comes the Holy Father a-flap in his crowdark drag!
                                                    (*Letter III & IV,* 62)

The Dakota farms are laid out like geometric patterns on a drawing board, allocation upon identical allocation. They seem to have been planted on top of the natural environment, not to have grown up in relation with it. Here and there are densely packed clumps of woodland ("woodlots"), for

33. See interview in *Voyages,* note 17 above.
34. Extravagant play on his grandfather's alliterative cursing is in *Letter, Parts III* and *IV,* pp. 50–52.

homesteaders who agreed to raise timber received a small additional grant
of land. The trees do not follow the lanes and hedges, they are simply
dumped into isolated corrals: utility plants for fuel. Here a civilization was
planted, with immense hardship, in one generation; struggled to maintain
itself in the face of dust bowls and mortgages in the next; and gave way to
collapse and emigration in McGrath's own generation. Moreover, the first
generation entered into that hard world of labor only after expelling their
forerunners:

It was here the Sioux had a camp on the long trail
Cutting the loops of the rivers from beyond the Missouri and Mandan
East: toward Big Stone Lake and beyond to the Pipestone Quarry,
The place of peace.
                    A backwoods road of a trail, no tribal
Superhighway; for small bands only. Coming and going
They pitched camp here a blink of an eye ago.
＊   ＊   ＊
From Indians we learned a toughness and a strength; and we gained
A freedom: by taking theirs: but a real freedom: born
From the wild and open land our grandfathers heroically stole.
But we took a wound at Indian hands: a part of our soul scabbed over:
We learned the pious and patriotic art of extermination
And no uneasy conscience where the man's skin was the wrong
Color: or his vowels shaped wrong; or his haircut; or his country possessed of
Oil; or holding the wrong place on the map—whatever
The master race wants it will find good reasons for having.
                                        (*Letter I & II*, 189–90)

And, even more savagely, in *Part III*:

            . . . the deep, heroic and dishonest past
Of the national myth of the frontier spirit and the free West—
Oh, nightmare, nightmare, dream and despair and dream!

A confusion of waters, surely, and pollution at the head of the river!
Our history begins with the first wound: with Indian blood
Coloring the water of the original springs—earlier, even:
Europe: the indentured . . .
                                        (*Letter III & IV*, 36)

It was in his father's generation that this episode came to its climax. Yet
the climax was not one of promised prosperity after hardship and toil, not
that of prairie middle peasantry or New England individualists. What took
place instead was a climax of exploitation, by banks, millers, dealers, and
railways, leading these Irish, Scandinavians, Germans, and assorted Americans into a huge social movement of wrath and solidarity. The Dakotas and
Minnesota, so easily to be seen from the East or West coasts as being way out
there beyond the uttermost sticks, were in fact the heartland of a great and

effective popular movement, inadequately described in the misty all-inclusive term as "populist." It was an active and democratic movement; the North Dakota Non-Partisan League was socialist in its origins, and demanded the state ownership of banks, grain elevators, etc. In 1919 the NPL caucus dominated the state legislature, created a state bank and grain elevators, imposed income and inheritance taxes, introduced assistance to home buyers, legalized strikes, and brought in mines safety regulations. In the judgment of a contemporary historian, "no more dramatic demonstration of democracy has occurred in American history."[35]

This movement was one of the few great impulses on the North American continent in the twentieth century which afforded premonitions of an American socialism or "communitas." And it contained within it even sharper forms of political consciousness. McGrath's father read the *Industrial Worker* and the migrant farmhand, Cal, so important in the structure of *Letter,* is a Wobbly and McGrath's childhood mentor. It is from Cal also that young Tom first encounters the savage scepticism of the freethinker in the face of the Catholic formation of his boyhood.

"All peace on earth for about five seconds."
(*Letter III & IV,* 58)

These are some of the materials for the "pastoral" (or sometimes "anti-pastoral") themes of McGrath's poetry. And there are in fact many themes, which the urban reader—encountering coulees and horses and Indians and the stars—allows his eye to pass across too inattentively. Not one of them should be treated with that kind of disrespect, and least of all McGrath's horses, which are sometimes horses, sometimes nightmares or outlaws, and very often Pegasus, the Crazy Horse. (In one of his first published poems he noted: "I have known personally horses / Who were more alive than many college professors.")[36]

Within this "pastoral" mode we find, certainly, the keenest eye for natural beauty and for the rightness, but also mercilessness, of natural things: a "somatic" sense of human transience, a cutting-down of humankind to size against the cyclonic weather and the stars; a sense of contest, the small farmsteads pitted against the vast Dakota winters. And we find other things also. We find the central theme of labor, a male world of agrarian labor with its glimpsed solidarities; and the theme of exploitation, for the winds which blow incessantly over Dakota are two, the wind of nature and the wind of *money,* of mortgages and interest-rates and bankruptcies, "continual wind of money, that blows the birds through the clocks" (*Letter I & II,* 92). There are other themes also, among them the glimpsed "communitas" of the

35. David Montgomery, in *In These Times,* 8–14 October 1980.
36. "Letter to Wendell" in *First Manifesto* (Baton Rouge: Swallow Pamphlets No. 1, 1940).

Farmer-Labor alliance and the Wobblies—a communitas which found, in
the thirties, a further and sadder extension in the moments of solidarity of
the unemployed.

So this is not altogether what one has come to expect from the term
"pastoral." "*Letter* is not a poem that comes out of the sensibility of the city
middle-class intellectual" (*Passage,* 93). Yet this is not pastoral's negation,
anti-pastoral, or urban face-making either. The moments of agrarian experience—of joy, terror, hardship in labor—are unqualified values. In *Letter I,*
there is a moment of sudden transition when McGrath moves (1939) from
Dakota to his first contact with High Culture in Louisiana:

                     And they got hold of Agrarianism—
Salvation—40 acres and a mule—the Protestant Heaven,
Free Enterprise! Kind of intellectual ribbon-development [. . .]
*   *   *
                                   And all of them
On Donne. Etc.
   And all of them sailing on the Good Ship Tradition . . .
For the thither ports of the moon.
                                   High flying days
I'll tell you right now!
                     And me with my three ideas
With my anarchist, peasant poverty, being told at last how bright
The bitter land was.
How the simple poor might lift a laud to the Lord.
*   *   *
O architectonic colloquy! O gothick Pile
Of talk! How, out of religion and poetry
And reverence for the land the good life comes.
Some with myth, some with Visions out of
That book by Yeats would dance the seasons round
In a sweet concord.
                     But never the actual seasons—
Not the threshing floor of Fall nor the tall night of the Winter—
Woodcutting time—nor Spring with the chime and jingle
Of mended harness on real and farting horses,
Nor the snort of the tractor in the Summer fallow.
Not the true run of the seasons.
                                   (*Letter I & II,* 60–62)

Labor, then, the "real and farting horse" (which might still be Pegasus),
exploitation (the "wind of money"), glimpsed communitas:

But I was a peasant from Sauvequipeuville-
I wanted the City of Man.
                     (*Letter I & II,* 60)

All these are at odds with customary urban expectations. For McGrath's

pastoral verse lacks one almost-obligatory element, that of ultimate reconciliation (of man with nature, or of men and women in a shared consensus). I
can point to this by means of a contrast with Robert Frost's "The Code," a
poem which I highly regard. Frost often acknowledged in his poetry dimen-
sions of labor and of hardship. In this poem we have a moment of sudden
conflict between a small working farmer and his hired hand. Storm clouds
threaten the taking-in of harvest: the farmer urges on and chides his skilled
laborer who, sharing equal commitment to the task and equally aware of the
weather's threat, knows better than to change his steady, measured pace,
since there is no way in which that long-learned pace can be mended. At
length the laborer is goaded to throw down the whole load upon the farmer's head. But, then, notice how the poem ends:

"Weren't you relieved to find he wasn't dead?"

"No! and yet I don't know—it's hard to say.
I went about to kill him fair enough."

"You took an awkward way. Did he discharge you?"

"Discharge me? No! He knew I did just right."37

The poem has established conflict to the edge of murder, but has then reconciled that moment within a shared consensus of values, of shared agrarian
skills, which are acknowledged by both master and man.
     Contrast this with the episode of Cal at the opening of *Part I* of *Letter*:

>   Then, one day—windy—
> We were threshing flax I remember, toward the end of the run—
> After quarter-time I think—the slant light falling
> Into the blackened stubble that shut like a fan toward the headland—
> The strike started then. Why *then* I don't know.
> Cal spoke for the men and my uncle cursed him.
> I remember that ugly sound, like some animal cry touching me
> Deep and cold, and I ran toward them
> And the fighting started.
> My uncle punched him. I heard the breaking crunch
> Of his teeth going and the blood leaped out of his mouth . . .
>   (*Letter I & II*, 18)

The episode violates any notional consensus of agrarian values, not only as
between employers and hands, but also carrying the conflict right into the
poet's own family, for McGrath's father quarrels with his brother:

Outside the barn my father knelt in the dust
In the lantern light, fixing a harness. Wanting

37. Robert Frost, *Selected Poems* (1936), p. 190.

Just to be around, I suppose, to try to show Cal
He couldn't desert him.
                                     He held the tubular punch
With its spur-like rowle, punching a worn hame strap
And shook the bright copper rivets out of a box.
"Hard lines, Tom," he said. "Hard lines, Old Timer."
I sat in the lantern's circle, the world of men,
And heard Cal breathe in his stall.
                                     An army of crickets
Rasped in my ear.
                                     "Don't hate anybody."
My father said.
I went toward the house through the dark.

That night the men all left.

There is a reconciliation here between son and father, for both carry the conflict unresolved inside them. But for that conflict itself there is no resolution:

There were strikes on other rigs that day, most of them lost,
And, on the second night, a few barns burned.
After that a scattering of flat alky bottles,
Gasoline filled, were found, buried in bundles.
                                     (*Letter I & II*, 23–24)

And never, in any poem, is it resolved. The past is never "paved over" and finished. It remains, tormented by conflict, but also pregnant with "the possible that never was." It is this which confronts the expectations of pastoral verse and which prevents McGrath's *Letter* from being nostalgic, a retrospective meditation upon or a celebration of a finished way of life. Both conflict and potential coexist in the poem's present tense.

The theme of the potential indicates the point at which McGrath departs from prevalent notations—and also anxieties—as to what is called "populism." He has always been more watchful, more accusatory of the "cultural default" of the intellectuals than the default of "the people." The Western intelligentsia has increasingly found refuge in theories (some of these even in the form of Marxisms) which predicate the inexorable determinist force of structures to expropriate the people of self-activity. The people are thus regarded as stamped with an ideologically confected false consciousness, leading to the view that "populism" is always threatening and only the islands of intellect, the reviews and academies, are able to liberate themselves from determinist process. McGrath has, in contrast, held the intelligentsia as themselves co-partners of the expropriators and co-authors of false consciousness. Even the revolt of the *New York Review of Books* intelligentsia during the Vietnam War did not convince him:

Out of so much of this temporary "war politics" rises a terrible spiritual smell which signals to the enemy: "I'm not really like this. Just stop bombing Hanoi and I will go back to my primary interests: flowers, early cockcrow, the Holy Ghost, wheelbarrows, the letter G, inhabitable animals, the sacred mysteries of the typewriter keyboard, and High Thought including the Greater, the Lesser, and High, Low, Jack-in-the-goddam-game mysticism." Worthy enough subjects in themselves . . .[38]

I am not wholly clear what is being argued here. Perhaps it is that the "revolt" engaged with certain symptoms—symptoms too embarrassing to ignore—but did not identify nor engage with the cause? Perhaps that the cause, if identified, would have indicted the artificers of false consciousness themselves? Maybe the criticism is even more bluntly political?

I suppose I ought at once to name the villain who has stolen our past—or tried to steal it: we don't admit anything but temporary defeat—in order as soon as possible to activate the rage of those critics and those readers who feel that politics is vulgar and revolutionary marxism anathema. The villain is capitalism in all its material and magical forms. How sad for me that I cannot name something nicely and safely metaphysical![39]

Yet McGrath's political stance derives less from revolutionary Marxist theory than he may himself suppose, simply because it does not ultimately derive from theory at all: "in the beginning was the *world!*"[40] And the "world," the experience in which his politics are rooted (and which his poetry strives to recover) is "a very *American* kind of radicalism":[41] not that of "populism" but of the most radical—sometimes socialist, sometimes anarcho-syndicalist—and the most militant anti-capitalist affirmations within Labor-Farmer, Wobbly and early American Communist traditions. In retrospect he has become critical of the Popular Front of the thirties and early forties: "the more sectarian politics before the Popular Front were more 'American' than the politics which followed."

In the '20s the Left had many of its origins further west than New York, and out there some of us had been living with the dark side of the American experience for a long time. In the late '30s and even more the '40s the Left got corralled in the Eastern cities. And I think some of the writers were unprepared for the late '40s and '50s because they had taken in too much of the Popular Front and watered down their radicalism . . . It led people into an optimistic notion of what *was* going to happen, although after 1946, it should have been perfectly plain what was going to happen. Perhaps it was some sense of this that made me, if not prepared for the long night, at least unsurprised.[42]

38. *Epoch* 22: 214.
39. *Measure* 2 (Bowling Green State University, 1972), unpaginated.
40. *Epoch* 22: 213.
41. *Voyages,* p. 38.
42. *Cultural Correspondence* 9, 43.

The radical intelligentsia inhabited an exciting metropolitan culture, taking some of their bearings from a cosmopolitan Communist mythology, and found themselves quite unprepared for the "man-chilling dark" of subsequent decades. They were unprepared for the mercilessness of American capitalism "in all its material and magical forms." Nor were they sustained by the experience of the solidarity of anti-capitalist struggle (although the poet himself had found this in dockside Manhattan in 1940) and its glimpsed "communitas." For radicalism had begun to drift, from the Popular Front onward, into complicity with the same divisive ego-psychology that is the legitimating operating drive of capitalist ideology itself: the multiple "I wants" of the claims to equality of ego-fulfillment. And working-class militancy itself was engulfed as the full employment and easy money of the war years dissolved the bonds of solidarity:

Out of the iron thirties and into the Garden of War profiteers.
Once it was: *All of us or no one*! Now it's *I'll get mine*!
(*Letter I & II*, 146)

"Here's the first / Sellout from which the country is a quarter century sick," and one made the more possible because Popular Front radicals turned away from the class war to "that other war / Where fascism seemed deadlier and easier to fight—but wasn't" (*Letter I & II*, 147–48).

Against this loss of militancy and solidarity, McGrath's poems perform their incantatory charms, searching backward for the "we" of shared labor and hardship, the "we" of active democratic process, the "we" of historical potential, the "we" of casual labor sawing wood in the bitter cold of a Dakota winter, when "the unemployed fished, the fish badly out-numbered"—among the coffee-guzzling Swedes, the moon-faced Irish, the lonesome deadbeats:

Those were the last years of the Agrarian City
City of swapped labor
Communitas
Circle of warmth and work
Frontier's end and last wood-chopping bee
The last collectively stamping its feet in the cold. [. . .]

The solidarity of forlorn men [. . .]

The chime of comradeship that comes once maybe
In the Winter of the Blue Snow.
(*Letter I & II*, 45–46)

This sense of solidarity . . . in the community is one of the richest experiences that people can have. It's the only true shield against alienation and deracination and it was much more developed in the past than it is now.[43]

43. *Voyages*, p. 41.

Communality or solidarity—feelings which perhaps are more to us than
romantic love . . .

(Passages, 93)

So he recalls—writing in Los Angeles in 1955—the rising mood of militancy, solidarity and hope of the late thirties, in poetic mood half angry,
half-elegiac:

Wild talk, and easy enough now to laugh.
That's not the point and never was the point.
What was real was the generosity, expectant hope,
The open and true desire to create the good.

Now, in another autumn, in our new dispensation
Of an ancient, man-chilling dark, the frost drops over
My garden's starry wreckage.
                              Over my hope.
                                                Over
The generous dead of my years.
                              Now, in the chill streets
I hear the hunting and the long thunder of money. [...]
                              To talk to the People
Is to be a fool. But they were the *sign* of the People,
Those talkers.
                              Went underground about 1941
Nor hide nor hair of 'em since; . . .

(Letter I & II, 52–53)

As I have gone over this lifetime of work and have touched upon some moments when the poet's life intersected with the crises of his own society, I
have been more and more possessed by a sense of the stature of McGrath's
achievement. I will say without qualification that we are dealing, with
McGrath, with a major talent. To sustain over forty years a principled alienation from the dominant culture; to turn away from every seduction which
could have co-opted him to the modes of an official opposition, a "two-
party system"[44] of Academy and anti-Academy which the dominant culture
could accommodate; to face directly the terror and defeat of those years in
which that culture seemed to move inexorably toward an exterminist con-
summation; to refuse romanticism or easy answers, and yet at the same time
to refuse the options of pessimism or empty face-making—all this is an
achievement to which I do not know an equal.

A major talent, who has marked his trail through the forest of forty
dark years with the blazes of his poems. But can we say that the achievement
of his art has matched the achievement of his integrity? It is my own view
that we can; that McGrath must be measured as a major poet. But I am
perhaps too close both to the poet and to the times to be the necessary

44. McGrath, "Some Notes on Walter Lowenfels," *Praxis* 4 (1978), p. 90.

"Good Critic who, even now, may be slouching towards" his poems.[45] His
shorter poems employ the whole keyboard of techniques and tone: lyrical,
polemical, satirical, meditative, elegiac, metaphysical. They convey, cumu-
latively, a unique and consistent view-of-life and, with this, an inversion of
official descriptions of reality, a demystification of American normalization:

The street rolls up til his office reaches him
And the door puts out its knob and drags him in.
His desk-trap is baited with the kill of the day.
He sets it off by touching it and can't get away.
("Poor John Luck and the Middle Class Struggle," *Movie,* 89)

From this "Poor John Luck" of the forties to his most recent poetry, there is a
characteristic McGrathian imagery of determinism, in which persons are
acted upon by impersonal forces:

The streets bulge with ambition and duty—
Inhaling the populace out of exhausted houses.
The drowsy lion of money devours their calendars [. . .]
                    ("The Histories of Morning," *Echoes,* 45)

—until the metropolitan civilization itself carries its inert human freight to
disaster:

          Below me the city turns on its left
Side and the neon blinks in a code I can all too clearly
Read. It will go down with all hands.
          ("The News Around Midnight," *Movie,* 138)

And yet, with swift inversions, these massive determinist structures themselves are seen as resting upon the frail spiritual and emotional powers of
those who inhabit them:

The city lifts toward heaven from the continent of sleep
This skin of bricks,
                    these wounds,
                              this soul of smoke and anguish,
These walls held up by hope and want [. . .]
                                        insubstantial
Structures, framework of dream and nightmare, a honeyed static
Incorporeal which the light condenses.
                    ("Dawn Song," *Passages,* 9)

I do not know any contemporary poet with comparable range of tone

45. *Epoch* 22: 208.

and theme, and sureness of touch with all. Nothing is predictable. On one page we have a hilarious celebration of beer ("*Guinness Stout* with its arms of turf and gunfire"; "Trinc: Praises II," *Echoes,* 17), on another a meditation upon the Heisenberg Principle ("Living on Faith," *Passages,* 48). The characteristic imagery invites by turn the description "metaphysical" (by bringing into conjunction opposing mythologies or belief-systems) and "surrealist" (by implanting will and intention to inanimate objects): one is tempted to coin, for McGrath, the term "metasurrealist."

From start to finish of his oeuvre there is one recurrent theme: war, the losses of war, the threat of nuclear war, the celebration of war, and the means of war in the official culture of the "heavy dancers." And here also "Dakota is everywhere," for, if Dakota were to secede from the United States, it would be, with its battery of Minutemen, the third most powerful nuclear state in the world:

As in the silos waiting near Grand Forks North Dakota—
O paradise of law and number where all money is armed!
                    (*Letter III & IV,* 5)

But even this terrible theme—and a distinct essay would be needed to follow its development—is handled with extraordinary versatility, like a crystal tossed into the air so that the sun glints now from one facet, now from another. He can move from lament to jest to invective to the quiet and beautiful "Ode for the American Dead in Korea" to the low-keyed meditation of "The Fence Around the H-Bomb Plant." "The fence proclaims / A divorce between yourself and a differing idea of order."

[. . .] it creates out of your awareness a tension
Wire-drawn, arousing a doubt as to whether
It is the bomb that is fenced in, you free,
Or whether you mope here in a monster prison

As big as the world may be; or a world, maybe,
Which has everything but a future [. . .]46
                    (*Passages,* 56)

"A world which has everything but a future." Is it possible for a poet who is ever sensitive to that threat to write great poetry? It is a question which McGrath has asked himself; he has spoken with respect of poets (his contemporaries) who, overcome with the sense of political emergency, set

46. For lament see among other examples his poems for his brother Jimmy, "Blues for Jimmy," *Movie,* pp. 73–78, and "The Last War Poem of the War," p. 180; for jest, see "Mottoes for a Sampler," p. 159; for invective, see "Song for an Armistice Day," p. 161, and *Letter, Part II,* pp. 147–48. "Ode for the American Dead in Korea (subsequently changed to "Asia") is in *Movie,* pp. 102–3, and also "Reading the Names of the Vietnam War Dead" ("thousands of dense black stones fall forever through the darkness under the earth"), 180–81.

aside their talents for more direct forms of engagement.[47] And the injury of living in such times can be sensed within his own poetry. The times offered to him few affirmative evidences capable of carrying authentic symbolic power. There are such evidences to be found, for example, moments in *Letter, Part II,* when the movement of the sixties can be felt:

> I tell you millions
> Are moving.
> Pentagon marchers!
> Prague May Day locomotives
> With flowers in their teeth!
> (*Letter I & II,* 107)

But the weight of evidence falls always the other way, and he has been too honest to romanticize the record.

He has turned in his verse to three kinds of affirmatives. First, to the elementary alphabet of love, of work, of the rightness of natural things, and, more recently, of his growing son, Tomasito. This is always effective. Second, to a more metaphysical assertion of the exploited as the absolute negation of capitalist process: "Labor His Sublime Negation," "the accursed poor who can never be bought" (*Movie,* 57), who must ultimately confront their exploiters. This (it seems to me) comes through with increasing strain, as a proposition whose confirmation by history is continually postponed, and hence can only be affirmed by recourse to the past, and sometimes to an antique Wobbly vocabulary of the "bindle-stiffs" and "jungling tramps." McGrath has perhaps less emotional insight into newer and more complex forms of social contradiction: his world of labor and of exploitation is predominantly male, and (as we have seen) he has considered "cultural and political nationalism" to be "dead ends" which must be worked through before "serious politics" is reached:

> At the congress of the color blind
> I put up the communist banner my father signed and sang:
> LABOR IN A BLACK SKIN CAN'T BE FREE WHILE WHITE SKIN LABOR IS
> IN CHAINS!
> (*Letter I & II,* 130)

Yes: but something of the positives of "black skin" civil rights has been left unsung. And there is at times a dated stereotyping of gender roles—perhaps authentically recollected from his Dakota youth—which suggests a pose of tough masculinity which undoubtedly presents a resistance to younger readers. (They should overcome their resistance, since a refusal of McGrath's

---

47. *Cultural Correspondence* 9: 42, and *Praxis* 4, 1978, where he writes "there are some particularly interesting examples in England," perhaps thinking (among others) of Edgell Rickword's long poetic silence?

verse on these grounds—even if the grounds have some validity—is bigoted and to their own loss.)

The third affirmative is central to the organization of the *Letter to an Imaginary Friend*. It consists in the magical or "charm" properties of poetry itself:

It is the charm which the potential has
Which is the proper aura for the poem . . .
("Against the False Magicians," *Movie*, 21)

The poet, in revealing the human potential, is the vector of (we remember) "a view of life . . . in a sense truer than the life we see lived all round us." He prefaced to *Letter, Part II,* a passage from Claude Lévi-Strauss as a figure of the poet:

[T]he man who wishes to wrest something from Destiny must venture into that perilous margin-country where the norms of Society count for nothing and the demands and guarantees of the group are no longer valid. He must travel to where the police have no sway, to the limits of physical resistance and the far point of physical and moral suffering. Once in this unpredictable borderland a man may vanish, never to return; or he may acquire for himself, from among the immense repertory of unexploited forces which surrounds any well-regulated society, some personal provision of power; and when this happens an otherwise inflexible social order may be cancelled in favour of the man who has risked everything. (*Letter I & II,* 102)

This rather grand prescription is perhaps cited, not as an exemplar for the poet so much as an indication of poetry's function. But it is important that McGrath sees the "immense repertory of unexploited forces" as lying in the unrealized *past*. It is the past which is the reservoir for potential for the present and the future.

[. . .] I am only a device of memory
To call forth into this Present the flowering dead and the living
To enter the labyrinth and blaze the trail for the enduring journey
Toward the rounddance and commune of light . . .
(*Letter I & II,* 103)

From the past also the poet draws the resources for the mythic or magical properties of poetry. In the *Letter* these come in three forms: autobiographical; in terms of Hopi myth and the *kachina* ritual; and in terms of the Christmas ritual. The balance of these three varies in the long period of the poem's composition—about thirty years. And the tone of the poem varies markedly. In a sense, *Letter, Parts I and II* is a different poem from *Letter, Parts III and IV,* although there are autobiographical and thematic bridges which carry us from one to the other. In my own view some of the very finest work belongs to *Part II,* and *I* and *II* are intellectually the most taut, as well as the most engaged. They are poems of resistance. *Letter, Parts III* and *IV* have surrendered nothing to no one, yet there is a sense in which they have passed beyond polemic and resistance to a "philosophical" acceptance of the tragi-comedy of things. In the first volume the injustice and repression of the rulers of this world made McGrath angry and embattled; in the second volume it can as often make him laugh.

In conception the poem was to be structured by reference to Hopi myth: "it is concerned with the offering of evidences for a revolutionary miracle and with elaborating a ceremony out of these materials to bring such a miracle to pass" (*Letter I & II,* "Note," unnumbered). Yet while this myth is remembered in *Part IV,* it has come to share its place with the Christmas myth (which was scarcely evident in *I* and *II*).

In origin McGrath's use of myth may have been influenced by Christopher Caudwells's *Illusion and Reality,* and perhaps by the discussions around the book in England and New York in the late forties. Caudwell's was a heavy book to throw at the heads of the philistines and bureaucrats of the Communist Party. It provided a full charter against utilitarian views of art, and the most complex claims for the function of the artist then available in the Marxist tradition.[48] To simplify, *Illusion and Reality* offered a materialist vindication of the primacy of spiritual forces in human development. The function of poetry and art was seen as partly "adaptive," socializing and adapting the "instincts" to changes in material being; and partly that of summoning up the spiritual energies of the group prior to any collective action. *Part IV* of *Letter* is preceded by a passage from Caudwell describing how, through verse or dance, the "simplest tribe" creates emotionally a collective "phantastic object"—such as the anticipated harvest—in order to summon up the energies to grow the real harvest. In this sense the phantastic world is more real than the material world of social being, which depends upon "magic" to give it form and energy.

Caudwell's speculations on the origin and functions of art were enforced at the end of World War II by advances in scholarship, by the discovery of the treasury of cave paintings at Lascaux, and by the publication (1948) of G. R. Levy's *The Gate of Horn,* with its examination of totemism and cave art. The totem is "a focus of the life-energy of a group embodied in the immortal ancestor":

> That is why art is necessary to such a religion, and why approach to the forms or symbols is so strictly guarded, since they are nearer to reality than the separated lives.[49]

Perhaps it was in the postwar excitement of the debates around Caud-

48. I have discussed this moment in "Caudwell," *Socialist Register* (London, 1977). McGrath has not revised his high opinion of Caudwell.
49. G. R. Levy, *The Gate of Horn* (1948), p. 39.

well, Levy, and Lascaux that McGrath grounded his materialist vindication of poetry's spiritual power and function. In his encounters with utilitarian "politicos" he was able to argue "that I was the *real* political type and that they were vulgar marxist." He refused to accept the loftier authority of the political theorist: "It would be a good thing if both sides recognized that while they're both politcal animals, one is dog and one is cat."[50] And this Caudwellian respect for the powers of magic will have predisposed him to borrow from Hopi myth those symbols of ressurection and renewal which recur in *Letter, Parts II, III,* and *IV*. Yet these symbols are embodied in the spirits of the past, "that power of the dead out of which all life proceeds" (*Letter I & II,* 104), a power which can be liberated by the ceremonies of poet or artist. This task is

> . . . not so much [one] of rescuing the past (and not just my own) but of *creating* it, since it was stolen from us, malformed, a changeling substituted. I do this, of course, as do all my comrade Kachinas and resurrectionists, to rescue the future.[51]

And the "ghost dances" or *kachinas* of the Hopi provide a vocabulary of symbolism for this, since "*kachinas* are properly not deities . . . They are respected spirits: spirits of the dead . . . spirits of all the invisible forces of life."[52] Tom's father and Mac and Cal and all the *dramatis personae* of *Letter* may therefore be called up into the dance. A blue star will signify the transition from the Hopi's Fourth World (McGrath's capitalism) to *Saquasohuh,* the Fifth World:

> The Blue Star Kachina will help these spirits to bring the new world. . . . All of us should help to make this Kachina. I think of the making of my poem as such a social-revolutionary action. In a small way, the poem *is* the Kachina. (*Letter III & IV,* "Note," unnumbered)

It is a happy conceit to warm the poet at his work, although I am less certain that so contrived a conceit can operate as warmly on the feelings of the reader. It is perhaps for this reason that the poem seems to change direction midway. Between *Parts II* and *III,* Hopi mythology is supplemented by important-sounding personages from medieval occultism, and the *kachina* plays (in *Letter III & IV*) a less significant part in the structure of the poem than may at first have been intended. It is replaced by the more familiar vocabulary of Christmas ritual, which affords the narrative structure for both *Parts III* and *IV.*

At the most lucid (and beautifully recovered) level this Christmas narrative spans both books in the sled ride of the poet as a young boy from the

50. *Another Chicago Magazine* 5 (1980): 73.
51. *Measure 2* (see note 39 above).
52. Frank Waters, *Book of the Hopi* (New York, 1963), p. 167.

family farm to his grandparents' home in Sheldon, the nearby town; confession and midnight mass; the boy's recollections and vision (and the grown poet's reflections on the boy); episodes, anecdotes, and a Homeric Christmas dinner at Sheldon; and the return to the home farm. At another, polemical level the poem explores the child's notions of Christian mythology and satirizes Catholic faith and ritual. Christmas brings two opposed worlds into tension: the "World of Down," a world of natural things, of the child's excitement, of commensality, of the (somewhat pagan) Christmas tree; and the "World of Up," a world of false consciousness, draining the spirit:

Upward.
          Outward.
                    Away.
                              Toward the black hole of Holy Zero,
To that Abstract absolute of Inhuman and Supernatural Power:
Not Father nor Mother nor Son nor Daughter but old Nobodaddy . . .
                                        (*Letter III & IV*, 63)

And in a complex dance, occult personages, revolutionary heroes, and Hopi incantations join with Christian symbolism to reconcile the opposing worlds. This is to be done by acknowledging or "angelizing" the demons of the natural world, and demystifying or "demonizing" the abstractions or the "Heaven-Standard-Time":

And so, act unto act, we pass through the ancient play
And the little godlet tries to be born to our fallen world,
To the poor in this ramshackle church, to insert himself, crisscross,
Between this world of the poor and that Heaven & Earthly World
Of Power and Privilege owned by the eternal Abstract One
Who is not even the Father.
                                        (*Letter III & IV*, 63)

Is *Letter* a major poem, a "great" poem? Does the spirit-dance of incompatible mythic personages convince? How can anyone tell yet? Such matters take time to settle. *Parts III* and *IV*, in particular, have a complexity of reference which must be tested by a discourse among readers.[53] There are places where I must confess to my own difficulties: places where the poet appears to lose direction, passages of "mock-hearty hoorahing" (his own self-criticism). There is a tendency to fall back on revolutionary incantations ("to free the Bound Man / Of the Revolution," *Letter I & II*, 209) which arouses suspicions. It suggests a philosophical or political irresolution—an inhibition against working through in public his accounts with the illusions and self-betrayals of his own tradition of the Left. The "Bound Man of the

53. The most helpful guides as yet known to me are Dale Jacobson, review of *Letter, Parts III* and *IV*, and Joseph Butwin, "The Last Laugh: Thomas McGrath's Comedy," both in *North Dakota Quarterly* 55 (Winter 1987).

Revolution" is proposed as self-evident proletarian Natural Man who is everywhere in chains; but the evidence of the past half-century must call in question any such Natural Man.[54] One wonders at times whether those occult personages or the blue haze of the Hopi's *Saquasohuh* might not be put in there to obscure the fact that the poet has found certain matters too painful to examine.

But if there are evasions these are not of such an order as to diminish the poem's stature. *Letter to an Imaginary Friend* is a remarkable achievement. It tears down all the curtains which lie between "poetry" and "life"; it opens directly upon the pandemonium of reality, the stubborn issues of history, work, morality, politics. It discovers a long, broken, accented rhythm of extraordinary versatility, which can pass from invective or humor into lyrical or contemplative mode. The childhood recollections (especially in *Letter, Parts I* and *III*) bear comparison with the early books of *The Prelude*. (But Wordsworth would never have been capable of the hilarious passage of the boy's boastful attempt at a truly horrific adult confession.) The poem has markers throughout which will be followed by historians in the future. *Letter, Part II* is superbly constructed and is a definitive statement of the deathward-tending malaise of a civilization. *Letter, Part IV* is a sustained incantation—a summoning of spiritual energies—which concludes with a lyric of the chastest beauty. And in the unfolding of *Letter,* the only poem I know of which is built to the size of our times, the miracle of the resurrection of the past actually begins to take place:

It is *not* daybreak
Provokes cockcrow but cockcrow drags forth the reluctant sun   not
Resurrection that allows us to rise and walk but the rising
Of the rebel dead founds resurrection and overthrows hell.
(*Letter I & II*, 210)

In this resurrection an alternative present begins to appear; if we cannot see an alternative future through the blue kachina haze, we can see the elements from which that alternative might be made. In despite of the "man-chilling dark," Thomas McGrath has fashioned an alternative self-image for America. He has deployed his poem as "a consciousness-expanding device":

The most terrible thing is the degree to which we carry around a false consciousness, and I think of poetry as being primarily an apparatus, a machine, a plant, a flower, for the creation of real consciousness . . .[55]

54. But please note the poet's comment, when I first published this criticism in *The Heavy Dancers* (London, 1985): "You are hopeful where I always felt the Revolution had to be firmly grounded in despair (however hopeful) and in the end I expect more of humankind than you do. In a few words: you are a protestant revolutionary and I'm a catholic-revisionist-buddhist one": McGrath to author, 13 March 1985. (He also remains Irish!)
55. *Voyages,* p. 48.

In a letter to us of 1949, when he first reached the West Coast, McGrath describes sharing a house and garden in Los Angeles with friends; since they had no access to an automobile, "we are pretty well cut off from everyone, and it is a little bit like being all alone on an island, although we are only about five miles from Hollywood." And I have thought of the extraordinary juxtaposition at that time, and through the ensuing "Great Fear" in Hollywood, with Ronald Reagan and Thomas McGrath almost as neighbors and as visitants within the same hysteric culture; and of the genesis of opposed self-images of America.[56]

The future President was at that time steadily working his way up the "levels" of Los Angeles:

                                                                    . . . at the ten
Thousand a year line (though still in the smog's sweet stench)
The Johnny Come Earlies of the middling class:
                                                           morality
                                                                 fink-size
Automatic rosaries with live Christs on them and cross-shaped purloined
Two-car swimming pools full of holy water . . .
                                              From here God goes
Uphill.
          Level to level.
                          Instant escalation of money—up!
To Cadillac country.

              Here, in the hush of the long green,
The leather priests of the hieratic dollar enclave to bless
The lush-working washing machines of the Protestant Ethic ecumenical
Laundries: to steam the blood from the bills—O see O see how
Labor His Sublime Negation streams in the firmament!
                                                        (*Letter I & II*, 113)

Here was manufactured the approved self-image of America, as television opened its "poisoned eyes" within the heads of millions, carrying that poison image from Hollywood to far Dakota:

                     The houses blacked out as if for war, lit only
With random magnesium flashes like exploding bombs (TV
Courtesy REA)
              Cold hellfire
                       screams
Tormented, demented, load the air with anguish
                                                   invisible
Over the sealed houses, dark, a troop of phantoms,
Demonic, rides: the great Indians come in the night like

56. This should have been clear from the title of his remarkable collection, *Figures from a Double World* which, as he explains in a note prefaced to *Movie,* was a publisher's error for his chosen title, *Figures of the Double World,* "the emphasis on the dialectic, on process, on states of the world rather than states of mind."

Santa Claus
>   down the electronic chimneys whooping and dead . . .
>   (*Letter I & II*, 192)

And so those lush-working washing machines laundered the "American dream" and washed the blood out of the American past. It was McGrath's neighbor who won, and who, in his triumph, threatens the whole world. At the lowest level, the poet sat by the beach and waited for the hunters. But, with the help of the "Marsh Street Irregulars" and the network of little resistance magazines, McGrath commenced his long labors of fashioning an alternative moment of contradiction, of confronting images. "Everyone everywhere in the States" (McGrath wrote in 1972) "senses that the whole system is finished, though it may endure for a time. Meanwhile there is this great emptiness that can never be paved . . ."57

If this moment should come, then it will be in such material as *Letter* that an alternative America will discover her features. It is still possible that a miracle will take place, and that the hunted poet will triumph over the powerful impostor—as Blake wrote, when discussing miracles, did not Paine "overthrow all the armies of Europe with a small pamphlet?"

The world may now be too old and lost for such miracles. But, confronted with McGrath's lifetime of loyalty to his Muse, "the grand old bitch," I can only celebrate his stamina. His loyalty has been not only to his own talent, at a time when in the scanty *samizdat* of hunted outlaws, poetry itself seemed to be an obsolescent trade. It has been also a loyalty to a notion of poetry as still, despite every evidence of defeat, a major art, a major vector of consciousness, and a major guarantor of an unextinguished human potential:

>   [. . .] all time is redeemed by the single man—
> Who remembers and resurrects.
>   And I remember.
>   I keep
> The winter count.
>   (*Letter I & II*, 119)

He has kept the count well. Homage to Thomas McGrath.

---

57. *Measure* 2 (note 39 above). Among those who read early drafts of this essay I benefited especially from the comments of my friend, the late Warren Susman. He suggested that, while McGrath's poetry is unique, I have overstated the uniqueness of his experience. Between the twin poles of the "academy" ("The 1940s and 1950s saw the triumph of the New Criticism and its favorite poets on virtually every American campus") and its "official" opposition, McGrath was not exceptional in being ignored and isolated. The forest of little journals in most parts of the States—in many of which McGrath found refuge and hospitality for his own poems—is witness to a different story, and (Susman suggests) "For the cultural historian his *typicality* as well as his uniqueness are important cultural facts."

13   An Interview with Thomas McGrath

THIS INTERVIEW WAS conducted on 19 January 1978. McGrath had given a reading of his poetry at the University of Illinois at Chicago. After the reading, in the early afternoon, he came to my office, where we talked for more than two hours, with a cassette tape recorder running. My office has a lovely view east to Lake Michigan and the Chicago skyline, and McGrath watched the sun sink lower over the lake, feeling the pressure of time because he had an engagement for dinner at the home of a friend. Thus, some topics were not explored as fully as I would have liked, so that we could get McGrath to his appointment in time. McGrath and I had met in person only once before, at a conference of the Western Literature Association, which is mentioned in several of the essays in this book, most notably by Frederick Manfred. We had been in correspondence, however, both before and after that meeting. At the time this interview was conducted, very little of Parts III and IV of Letter to an Imaginary Friend *had yet been published, though I had seen a substantial portion of Part III in typescript. In time, the interview was transcribed, as best as possible given some technical problems, to typescript. I then edited the typescript, making no substantive changes of which I am aware, and never adding to McGrath's language, but removing some of the inevitable verbal ticks, hemmings and hawings, false starts, and other dross in the language of both parties to the interview. The edited manuscript was then sent to McGrath to check the accuracy of names and other details, to correct any gross inaccuracies in fact, and to correct any impressions left that McGrath would not want. Thus, this interview is by no means an effort to catch the subject off guard, but rather a considered product with which both McGrath and I are reasonably content.*

I have used the abbreviation TM *to indicate that McGrath is speaking and the abbreviation* FS *to indicate that I am speaking. I have placed in square brackets explanatory matter added to the interview in the editing process. Unexplained references are either to material I consider too familiar to require explanation or to names and incidents (for example, "the grandfather in the buffalo coat") from* Letter to an Imaginary Friend *or other McGrath poetry, as the context indicates.*

*   *   *

FS: Tom, tell me how you relate to the Western experience, which is so much a part of your poetry and your political radicalism.

TM: That's very hard. The first thing is simply this. I grew up out there and my first experience with radicalism was there. I think also there's

150

something that has to do with the fact that, where I grew up, the frontier wasn't very far away and that the Wobblies really began in the Western Federation of Miners. Some of them weren't very far from the bad men of the West, the good bad men of the West. This may be away from your question, but there's some relationship, I think, between the violence of the frontier and the violence that existed, either in practice or in theory, among the Wobblies.

FS: You talk in your poetry, especially in *Letter to An Imaginary Friend,* about the connectedness between land and work on the land, a sense of a different America than the urban one in which most of your readers live. Can you comment?

TM: Except in the way I've talked about it in the poem, I guess I haven't thought about it. Land for a lot of the people where I grew up was a brand new thing. It was a brand new thing for the Irish peasants who were immigrants, my immediate forebears.

FS: That's the grandfather who had the buffalo coat?

TM: Yeah, both grandfathers, both of them were homesteaders out there. My father, when he was a little boy, lived at Fort Ransom. Along with the other settlers, he ran for the fort. At the time my father told me this, I didn't even know what would have been going on, but it turns out it was Wounded Knee and the Ghost Dancing. This is away from the land part, and yet, it isn't either. On the one hand, the settlers had stolen the land almost overnight, as it were, from the Indians. And my father was a very good friend of some of them. He had a good friend who was a little Indian boy. They [Indians] used to move across my grandfather's land every spring and fall and they would camp on the land where there was a place they had always camped before. So my father's sense of the Indians was quite different from that of many others. My grandfather was frightened of them, my mother's father. He was terrified of them. Of course, I suppose my father's father, whom I never knew, was frightened too, otherwise they wouldn't have taken off for Fort Ransom. My father had a different feeling about them. Here's the thing. The land had been taken away from the Indians really in my father's lifetime. Also in his lifetime, the banks were taking the land away from them [the farmers]. There was this very strange kind of thing that I know he was well aware of and that some of the older people that I knew had a sense of also, of how fast this had happened, a sense of bewilderment. On the one hand, here the Indians had lost the land in their own lifetime, and now the settlers are suddenly being pushed off the land themselves. I don't know how to relate that together except that it happened, it was that way.

FS: In *Letter to An Imaginary Friend,* you quote your father. You write of the sign your father carried saying that labor in white skin can never be free while black labor isn't free. Was your father a political radical in that sense? Is that biographical?

TM: In a certain sense he was political, and in another sense he was not. He had worked as a lumberjack and so he had contact with the Wobblies as a worker. He had also worked a little bit on the railroad at a time when the railroad unions were much more radical than they have been since, and when there were also Wobblies working on the railroad and in the harvest fields. My dad was, in a sense, what the Wobblies called "the home guard." He had settled down. He had no theory at all, but he had very strong instincts and years later he wouldn't vote. He didn't think there was much point to it. Sometimes my mother would talk him into voting. In 1940 he voted Communist, I remember. So in that sense he was political. Almost all that he had gotten he had gotten from the Wobblies, but as I say, it wasn't any kind of theory at all.

FS: How did you get from your really quite agrarian and midwestern background to modern poetry?

TM: I got to poetry, again, by way of my father, who was known far and wide, in a small circle naturally, as a wonderful storyteller who had memorized the whole *McGuffey's Readers*. He hadn't gone to more than the fourth or fifth grade, though he was probably older than people would be in those grades now. I remember many Saturday nights, when all he would do is sing, or tell stories or recite poems. I remember this particularly, at some times in the thirties. As all the farmers did then, we had a battery-operated radio. There was no electricity on the land yet out there; it didn't come until after the second World War. And the batteries would go dead and there wouldn't be money to change them, or, in the winter, if you had the money, you couldn't get to town. So, many nights, especially in the winters when there was more time, he would send us all off to sleep one by one telling us stories, singing and reciting poems, so I guess I sort of grew up with a sense of that this was just the way things were. Now I look back on it, I know damn well they weren't, that it was exceptional, though there were a lot of people who did have stories and did have songs and even bits of poems. As a result of this, I guess I was very early interested in all kinds of writing. Before I could read, I forced my mother to read to me whenever she had free time. When I learned to read, I read everything in sight, which was a very strange conglomeration of stuff. The little country school I went to had a bookcase about the size of your steel [filing] cabinets there, but it had many things in it that surprise me now. For instance, I read the *Iliad* and the *Odyssey* when I was in grade school. I read probably most of the *Edda*. Oh, hell, and of course I read junk all the time, all the bunkhouse materials that I could get my hands on after the end of the depression. The idea of reading and the idea of writing, I didn't feel that it was foreign to me at all. In grade school I recall the first time I wrote anything. I was asked by my teacher to write some little story of some sort. It was the first time I had ever written and I was very excited about that, I recall. In high school, I was interested in poetry. I wasn't reading modern poetry—all I had come across was traditional poetry of one sort or the other.

FS: Let me stop you. What were you reading? Longfellow? Emerson? American Poetry? British?

TM: Every bloody thing. I'll give you an example. I read all of Thomas Moore, can you imagine that? And all of Scott—that's another example that pops into my head.

FS: Not only the novels but the border ballads and the other poetry?

TM: Oh, the poetry, primarily the poetry. I read the novels as well, but I was more interested in reading poetry and plays than in novels. Oh, hell, it was a ragbag thing. I was reading the old *Scribner's* magazine. I was reading *Tender is the Night* and some Faulkner and Hemingway. Knowing Hemingway told you shoot to the neck and so on. But I didn't encounter modern poetry until I was about a sophomore in high school. I had a teacher, an excellent one, who gave me my first anthology of modern poetry, and then I began to pick up on other anthologies. It was very difficult to get hold of books. I remember when I bought Joyce's *Ulysses,* it cost me about three or four days of labor. Three bucks and a half I suppose at the time—a dollar a day. I wanted to read Proust. I had heard something about him and I got hold of *Swann's Way.* I remember reading it during a dust storm. It was hot as a pistol lying on the floor of a bunkhouse. I got hold of, I remember, Conrad Aiken, and—remember there was a Library?

FS: Modern Library?

TM: Yeah, it was a Modern Library, this anthology of modern poetry, and there I first ran across a whole lot of people I had never seen before. I had read the first anthology I had got, which had people like Sandburg and Frost and so on. I hadn't encountered, oh, Eliot, or Pound. I don't think that book included Hart Crane. I'm pretty sure it didn't. That would be very odd, but I remember I didn't read Crane until I was in college. He knocked me absolutely flat on my ass. I'm talking about when I first began to read contemporary poetry—no: *modern,* not contemporary, about 1932 and then in college from about '32 onward. There I could get hold of books and I read.

FS: Were you impressed particularly by Frost, or Sandburg, or any of these figures?

TM: I was struck by Sandburg. I didn't like him very much, but I was struck by the fact that he was bringing in all kinds of things that I hadn't seen in poetry—more than anybody else among the people I was reading at that time—all the folk say and so on, and the kind of openness of the work. I hadn't experienced much open-form poetry.

FS: Were you writing anything of your own then?

TM: I was. I had begun to write but it was just awful junk—terrible, terrible! Luckily none of it survived. The first poem that I wrote was probably in the summer of 1938. I remember well that I got a couple of rhymes, and it scared me because I could feel that I was getting on to something really for the first time, and that's the first time that I had a true sense that I was really into something.

FS: After high school in Sheldon, you went on to college?

TM: Yes, to North Dakota at Grand Forks.

FS: How did the family feel about that? I mean were they ready to send you?

TM: Yes. They wanted me to go to college. I had a year when I couldn't. I didn't have the money to go, but I made a start. I had a scholarship of some sort to what is now North Dakota State University, but I would have had to stay in a dormitory then, and I couldn't afford it and didn't want to. I went across the river to the place I'm teaching now, Moorhead State, and I managed to do one term there. I was staying with relatives who became ill, so I couldn't stay there anymore. I had no money to manage it; so I was out for a year. I might well have joined the Navy at that time—I considered doing it. There were no jobs, nothing, and a friend of mine went into the Navy, and I came very close to going, but my mother was very upset at that idea, and my father finally talked me out of it. Now, I'm very glad he did. Then, I don't know, I worked and I put together a little money and I got a job and a little scholarship and a little bit of this and that, a couple of jobs at UND, and then I was back in college.

FS: Where were your brothers and sisters then?

TM: They were in grade or high school. Because of the war or one thing or the other, they never got into college at all. One of my brothers did—he did a couple of years at UND after the war—but the others, the war came along and they were in the army and my brother Jim was killed during that time. My brother Joe was in the service and my sister was a Navy nurse. My youngest brothers were at home on the farm. They were too young for the war.

FS: How did they feel about having this poet brother?

TM: I think they felt quite good about it. I know they thought I was special. They didn't think I was especially loco, because they had grown up with me. They were proud of me.

FS: Are you still in touch with much of your family?

TM: Oh, sure. Not as much as I'd like to be, but, yes, the ones that remain I see. I have a brother in Minneapolis. Usually I see him fairly frequently. I have another brother in North Dakota. I see him seldom for no very good reason. We talk on the phone, he says he'll come down or I'll come down or whatever, but we don't, but we're still close.

FS: Have they read your poetry?

TM: Yeah. They've read. The brother in Minneapolis might have been a writer himself, if things had been slightly different. He has a gift and he might well have been. He's read all of it. I suppose they all have read all of it. I don't even know that that's the case, but I think so.

FS: Let me get some of the history straight. You went to North Dakota about when?

TM: I graduated from there in 1939. I graduated from high school in '34 and was out of school a year, started in the fall of '35 at UND.

FS: Did you go back to your dad's farm to work in the summers?

TM: No, usually not, because there was enough help on the farm. Beginning in high school, I worked out, worked on farms around. Then again I'd get a little construction work. It was a sort of discount construction work. It was boondoggling kind of work, you know. The county was going to do this, that, they're building a bridge or doing something or other, and people in the neighborhood, some of them, would get hired from time to time. Mostly it was working on farms.

FS: Let me take you back a minute because everybody loves that Cal story in *Letter to an Imaginary Friend*. At the reading today that was one of the things asked for, and I think for younger people it's so impressive because they really don't know anything about labor struggles, especially about agrarian labor struggles. What's the reality behind that? Is it pretty much as you describe it?

TM: Yeah, it is.

FS: So we have some right to say that the voice in *Letter* is not just an imaginary voice; it's a real Tom McGrath speaking.

TM: That story is quite close to the thing. The fighting is all there and the guy is there and so on. I can't think of anything really that I added in there. I suppose I added some of the imagery. There's a kind of list of trees and so on. Oh, they all grow there. The going to the river, that's there, and my father in the barn. On the ramp under the lantern, all of that really happened. I remember organizing a strike myself once upon a time. Towards end of the run, we were working at a place where the food was awful, and so was everything else. We went on strike, and since it was the end of the run and there were no migrants in the county, we had the guy right by the balls. That was the only strike I ever remember winning in my life. There were about five or six of us on this little toy rig and the guys we were striking against were brothers, the richos in the neighborhood. They had a business on the side. They ran an open-air dance hall and they sold a lot of bootleg booze. But these other strikes, there was a scattering of them. Every year there would be a few in those days, and sometimes they would be effective, we'd get some kind of a pay raise, sometimes not. A run would last a month or six weeks. There'd be a mass of migrant workers in the countryside, then they'd head on, go on north in a hurry, and so part of it was dependent upon the number of men around. Some of it was dependent upon whether there were any liveos among them.

FS: That's one of your words isn't it, liveos?

TM: Yeah, liveos, yeah. Actually, that's a seaman's term, you know. In the bars on 9th or 10th Avenue—"here comes the liveos," somebody's got money in his pocket. I decided that the whole world is divided into what I call liveos and mechanicals, people who just trudge along like robots in life, and others who are a little bit more awake.

FS: Let me take you back to North Dakota now, to the university. You began to read a fair amount of modern poetry. Can you say that some poets were more influential than others, that there was a particular thrust that shaped you? You've already mentioned Hart Crane in that regard.

TM: Crane was really the biggest power in me, and yet I don't see that in my work very much. Here's a poet that I was very taken with long ago: Conrad Aiken. Eliot, of course; I don't suppose anyone could have read him in those days without getting the feeling of the power and the thought and the attitudes. As much as I might have opposed the attitudes, there was no way that the poetry couldn't move me, and of course excite me too because of the way in which he worked.

FS: How about people like William Carlos Williams?

TM: I never felt close to William Carlos Williams. I still don't. There's something there I don't warm up to. Stevens, yes, the early poems, I love them. The poems in *Harmonium,* I really love those and many of the other poems too. William Carlos Williams...in a lot of the poems I felt too much of a prosiness. Not so much in the other poems. There's a poem about crossing a bridge [in *The Desert Music*]. I don't remember what it says, but I remember I hated every attitude in it, and yet that's the first time I heard a music in William Carlos Williams. A number of poems out of his old age, I think, are quite beautiful. I never liked the wheel-barrow poem. It just struck me as a piece of commodity fetishism. I've been very indignant about this, about how important objects are to some of his poems, and I don't want to go into that. I once wrote something about it. But in any case I never felt close to his work, and yet I can't understand why, because there are many things that would suggest that I should be.

FS: Let me ask you about an off-the-wall poet. How about Robinson Jeffers?

TM: Oh, yeah, I like Jeffers very, very much. That is off the wall because you're about the only person that I've spoken to who says any more than, "Oh, yeah, Robinson Jeffers." Everybody says the guy is there and all that, but that's all. I feel attracted to nature things, and here again is somebody whose attitudes are far from mine, and yet there are many things that I love about him. It has a lot to do with the sound in Jeffers. He's got long lines and...

FS: Which, of course, you write as well.

TM: Yeah, that's one of the things, and I think that oftentimes it's true that I've been attracted to poets, the work of someone or other, as much in terms of the rhythms in the work as by anything else.

FS: Did you read these guys at North Dakota? When you were at school?

TM: Yeah. You mean did I read them in class?

FS: No, not necessarily. On your own? In some way.

TM: Yeah. I read a lot of Jeffers. I blundered across Jeffers. He wasn't turning up in the anthologies yet. But I blundered across him, then I read and read him.

FS: So you graduated from North Dakota in '39, did you say?

TM: Yeah.

FS: And then what?

TM: I went from there to LSU.

FS: Did you already have the Rhodes Scholarship?

TM: Yes, I was supposed to have gone over in the fall of '39, but I couldn't and so it was postponed then. The Rhodes people just said OK. When all this [World War II] is over. So I was offered a lot of fellowships and scholarships. All of us, all the Rhodes Scholars got offers from all over hell's half acre. I had an offer from Harvard. I would have taken that, I guess, but it was too little, I couldn't have lived on it. I had a good offer from the University of Minnesota. I didn't want that because it was too close to home. Turned out I had a good offer from the University of Iowa, which I might have taken because there's a writer's school there.

FS: Was Paul Engle there by that time?

TM: Yeah, he was there. The school was just starting. There was already some reputation, but I didn't learn about that until later. So I took the one to LSU.

FS: That must have been exciting.

TM: It was. It was exciting. I went there and they said, Well, OK, you got to take this, that, and the other thing. I wound up with a bunch of junk. I was going to be taking bibliography, and God knows what all else. About the second day—I got there late, school had been going on for about a month—I was there and Brooks called me in. He had learned that I was there, that I was a Rhodes Scholar. He was a Rhodes Scholar. So he called me in and said, "What are you taking." So I showed him. He said, "Oh my God." He wouldn't have said that: he's a very gentle and very quiet man, but he did like this...[gesture of dismay] he said I think you'd better take my class in this and my class in that and the result was that I had wonderfully interesting things. One of the most interesting courses I've ever had was a history of criticism. I've forgotten who all was in it. [Alan] Swallow was in that class, probably [John Edward] Hardy, I'm not sure. Anyway, the result was that I did a very unusual kind of thing as a graduate student. I didn't have a lot of the classes I would normally have had to take, and I spent a lot of time with Brooks, a lot of time. A number of us had a lot of time with him outside of class, and at the Roosevelt Tavern where a sort of conversation had been going on when I first went there. It was still going on when I left. It was just one of these endless things. Everything was coming into it; so many things there were totally new to me. The new criticism had just been sprung upon an unsuspecting world. I remember reading Brooks's *Modern Poetry and the Tradition* which had just come out, and things of this sort. The *Southern Review* was a very exciting magazine at that time, for what it was doing. Yes, it was an exciting time.

FS: Did you clash with Brooks on political issues?

TM: Yes, that's right. We did, but it was OK. I really loved Brooks. He was a gentle type, very sweet. I don't know if he truly was that, but he certainly appeared to have all of those qualities, though we were at opposite ends on things. Brooks was an agrarian more or less, and I didn't think much of agrarianism. I remember reading *We Take Our Stand*. But I think now that I might have gotten a great deal more from Brooks if I hadn't been as politically oriented as I was, or if I had been politically more mature. If I wouldn't have felt as strong a need to assert or maintain my position, my attitude, I could have, I probably would have, gotten more from Brooks. I'm sure I would have.

FS: Tell me about [Alan] Swallow.

TM: Well, Swallow, I first met him this way: Some people were putting together a little book that they called, finally, *Signets,* a book that two people were editing. They were gathering work from among the people interested in writing at LSU, undergraduates and graduate students and so on, but not faculty I think. Anyway they were doing this one-shot thing and Swallow had got himself a little handpress and he was printing this, and somebody asked me would I give him some poems to look at for this little book. So I did. A guy named Frederick Brantley took the poems, I believe, and showed them to Swallow. I guess Brantley wasn't sure whether Swallow wanted them or not. Swallow liked them very much and told Brantley, "Send that guy around to see me." It turned out I had been walking past his place—he lived partways between downtown where I lived and the college—and so on my way walking home, I stopped in and I walked through the driveway. At the end of it, in the garage—and it was hot—there's this madman setting type, so I went in and introduced myself and he sat down, took the poems and started talking to me about the poems, saying "I don't like this line, this is good, that's bad..." Anyway, we instantly started talking as if we had known each other for a long time. It turned out we had a good deal in common in a lot of ways and so I wound up throwing back type on some days. The first day, he said, "Do you have any more of these poems?" I said, "Yeah, I got a fair number." "Good," he said, "I'm going to start a press and I want to publish your book, your first book," and as soon as he finished setting *Signets,* he set my first little book.

FS: That was before *Three Poets*?

TM: Yeah, a little pamphlet called *First Manifesto,* full of terrible poems, but in any case that was that and we were friends and continued from that time on. He was very busy, setting type, working on a thesis, but we saw each other.

FS: There's a section of *Letter* in which you talk about the LSU experience, and I have a sense in reading it—I'm really asking you to verify whether this sense I have is valid or not—a terrible sense of your alienation and separation from the rest of that world. Is that accurate?

TM: Yeah. I had a sense of separation from it. Indeed I did.

FS: What was the basis for that, do you think?…Class? Background?

TM: I think that partly it was class, partly it was acculturation maybe. It was that that scene was so different from the one I came out of, not just the one I came out of at home on the farm but also greatly different from UND. Greatly different from that. It was the whole business of the South itself which I had wanted to come to. It was a strange place and I was doing political work. I used to distribute leaflets out in the black barrios there and it was a very weird sort of experience because here I am going to LSU, and the people I know there, if they had seen me out in the barrios, they would have said who the hell is that madman?

FS: What were your political involvements?

TM: I was a member of the CP [Communist Party]. At that time we were a small, growing organization there, with people on the campus and workers and a little bit of everything. We were growing quite rapidly. Had been since 1940.

FS: Do you think there's an influence on your writing from the experience with Brooks and from that whole LSU experience?

TM: Oh, I think so.

FS: Can you describe it a little? I know that's hard.

TM: I think that, let me see how I can put this. It's not easy for me to say this, but I did get a lot from them, some sense of the poem. I got a certain idea of functionalism from them. I got something of the idea of paradox, the idea of some poems, at least, being a network of related symbols, a family. Another thing, now that I think about it, that I got from them perhaps more than any place else was the sense that wit was a useful part of poetry. I remember having mixed feelings about it. For them, irony was all important, and I remember sometimes thinking and saying that in some of the poetry they admired the irony was kind of a cop-out, that it was a way of discounting everything so that the poet has, in effect, covered all his bets, he never puts his neck out. I remember saying it to someone in this way. In retrospect, obviously, irony is something that exists in my poetry to a very considerable degree.

FS: As a matter of fact, I think one thing which the reading [that day] did for me is to emphasize how funny some of your poetry is.

TM: Yeah; that I didn't get from them because their viewpoint was more prayerful than mine was, or, to put it another way, maybe they had more high seriousness, but I always had liked jokes in poems, in some poems anyway. In some poems they don't belong and I love the idea that poetry should have a wide range. It isn't that I have a problem doing it, but it's that I don't refuse a poem if it's at the far end of my spectrum. I'd like to be able to extend that as far as possible. I'd like to be able to make poems out of everything that comes to me. I think that in some ways I would be more successful if somewhere along the line I had said, "Here is my range, here is the kind of thing I'm going to do and if a poem comes along somewhere out of this range I just reject it." I've never wanted to do that. I've always felt that I had to fish around to find a way in which the poem wanted to be said. I think it would be great to have the kind of thing that poets were told in the 1590s. "You're going to write something. Very good, here's the sonnet." And you just automatically use that form. Some poets have developed a certain kind of poem which they do, and every poem is recognizably that. I don't mean that it's repeated—every poem repeats things over and over—but I have always had a strong sense that I have to fish around for the way that the poem wants to be said. Of course, sometimes you catch the fish and sometimes you don't. As a result, one way or the other, for good or evil, I've written poems that have a very wide range of experience and that have a very wide range of tone. They run all the way from jokes, some of them in terrible taste, I suppose, to that, quote, "high seriousness."

FS: Because I'm finding that as you talk about your history you're also talking about your poetry—which is really what I'm after—let me take you on. Time: LSU 1939–1940, then where?

TM: Maine. 1940–1941.

FS: Tell us about that.

TM: Well that was a strange place. I was very young, younger than some of the students that I had. The students [at Colby College] were very strange ones too. On the other hand there was a bunch of them who came from New York City. The typical one of this sort was like this: upper-middle class, Jewish, bright, but for some reason unable to get into the Ivy Leagues, either because of the quota or because some way or other he was getting in front of himself all the time. A lot of these were like friends that I used to see in New York years later. Then there were the Mainies, kids out of the bushes in Maine; some of whom had gone to schools as bad as the one I had gone to. A very, very wide range of types. As I say, I was very young; I didn't like teaching at all, or didn't think I did, though it turns out that some of it I did like. But I didn't think I was going to stay at it. I gave up the job after a year. I didn't know what to make of my colleagues and I don't think they knew what to make of me either. I was close to one or two people, but if there was any sort of social life among the faculty of the college, I wasn't any part of it or a very small part of it. I was close to quite a few students, and the place where we lived the students were always drifting in and out.

FS: Who is the "we"?

TM: I was married to a girl named Marian who turns up in the poem. We were there for a year. I went to New York then and I worked at various odds and ends, some of them odd. For a stretch, I did legal research. Does the name Carol King mean anything to you?

FS: Of course...radical lawyer, in the thirties and forties.

TM: Yeah. She was with her brother-in-law, I think it was, a solid bourgeois lawyer type, liberal, and so on—anyway, I was working on this case of the Immigration against some CP guy from Philadelphia. It might have been Sam Darcy. There was a deportation proceeding so this lawyer wanted me to dig up as much stuff as I could lay my hands on from our radical forefathers, so that's what I did. I worked on that for some time and then, I don't know, I worked at, I've forgotten what else. Nothing very much.

FS: Let me stop you a minute, Tom, and take you back to the Maine experience because the river and the *loup garrou* [French Canadian were-wolf-like folk creature] and such things come into play in the poetry, especially in *Letter*. Did you find the landscape, setting, people, attractive in some way?

TM: Oh, yes, I did. Yes, I still think of the Kennebec as one of the tremendous rivers of the world and the Maine woods—Oh, Jesus, fabulous. I loved Maine.

FS: That echoes in some way the North Dakota experience.

TM: Yeah, in some way, in some odd way, in spite of all the differences. Before Marian came along I lived in an area that was surrounded by Syrians. I use to hear them singing on Saturday night. They had a pipe going, a drum roll, bam, bam, bam, the pipe going way up and they're singing like maniacs, just wonderful. Then the Canucks [Canadians] they were known as, they too. The whole was again quite a new experience, beautiful, I thought. In many ways, though, as I say, I wasn't mad about the teaching.

FS: Did you feel more at home with the Syrians and the Canucks as an Irish kid from North Dakota than you did with the faculty?

TM: Yes, I did. The faculty were more Eastern. I think I felt more distant from them than I did from the southerners.

FS: So now you're in New York, 1941...

TM: The war started in winter. In spring I went back to North Dakota to see my folks and say so long. I was going to go into the army. I got back to New York and I was told by the CP, "No, you ain't going to. Go over and work in that shipyard over there." That's when I went to work for Kearney Ship. It was a huge place, growing like mad and full of Christian Front guys—you remember that—a very weak union, so a number of seamen and others were told to go over, do something about that union because the place was full of saboteurs. A number of us went in there and worked the union. I became a welder of a sort. God help the ships that I helped put together.

FS: Were you writing all this time?

TM: Yes, I was writing. I wrote in Maine, some poems. In New York, I had a pretty good year. I remember I wrote a long poem there, a longish poem, I wrote a number of poems. Remember the "Third Millennium"? That has a bunch of Maine stuff in it.

FS: Yes that's the poem dedicated to Mike Gold?

TM: Yes, Mike Gold. I dedicated it to Mike Gold in spite of the fact that I had all kinds of opposition from him. I didn't know him at the time. Later I knew him on the West Coast and I loved him, but in terms of attitude and so on we were far apart, especially in those early days. I also wrote a poem called "Death Between Two Rivers," which was at that point the longest poem I'd written. I think I felt something in that poem, some sound that was important to me, one of the most important things I had felt up to that time.

FS: Is that connected in part with the longer line?

TM: Yes, though I don't know that it really shows up as the longer line, but in terms of cadence, surely it is related to it. In Maine I had written some very political poems with long lines too. I don't know whatever happened to them. They were published in various little magazines. I don't remember them as being very good.

FS: If you think of influence here, is there a Sandburg, is there a Jeffers influence in terms of the long line and the use of it?

TM: I really don't know. I suppose Jeffers, yes, probably. I can't put my finger on any particular thing, and yet, Jeffers's long line is bigger, longer than mine and it's quite different, and yet, I felt close to that. It seems to me that I ought to be able to say where in hell's name I got it, there must be some place that I can go to, but I don't know.

FS: Well, Sandburg's line is much prosier than yours.

TM: Yeah. Right.

FS: What about Whitman?

TM: For a long time I didn't like Whitman. I had a strong, strong feeling in the forties in New York. We just used to talk about Whitman. I always put Whitman down. My argument went something like this: Whitman, stay as far away from him as possible, because if you get anywhere close to him he'll clutch you to his bosom and you're finished. You know, I used to tell people, he's the greatest wrecker of poets there ever was, especially of left-wing poetry. You look at it, it seems so goddamn easy, all straight and open and all the rest of it, and the next thing you know your writing is total garbage. It's because you can't do what Whitman does in his poetry. He makes it seem easy and it isn't. That was my sense of it. Among the poems that I most loved is "Passage to India" and, of course, "When Lilacs Last in the Dooryard Bloom'd." I don't question that I did get something from Whitman. I haven't read the poem for a long time, but I know I'd like to go back and look at "Passage to India" because there I may have heard what I was listening for. There is no doubt that I must have got something from Whitman, but, as I say, I always tended to fight shy of him because of this terrific force of gravity that's involved.

FS: Alright, you were working in the shipyard, kind of organizing, I gather, doing union stuff?

TM: Yeah.

FS: And then when did the service get you?

TM: I was about to be frozen into the job and I didn't want to be, so I went over and said, "Now look, I've done my time here and the union is in good shape, so it's my doing, I've got a right to go into the army." So they said OK, and I went into the army. I thought I was going to go into an air crew. Never such a thing, no dice, color-blind. Went to the Navy; they had more men than they had ships anyway at that point . . .

FS: You really are color-blind?

TM: Partly.

FS: Red/green?

TM: Yeah. Partly red/green. Anyway, to make a long story short, I wound up in the goddamn army. They threw me into the air force. Well, it turned out they did. I was in Camp Upton and was up on shipment about ten or twenty times. Finally, one day I got on to a train and I wound up in Miami Beach.

FS: Were you being hassled, as some other radicals in the service were at that time?

TM: At that point, I don't know, I think it was just luck. Later on, probably so. You know, hard to tell, because some people, some of us, wound up there in the Aleutians and some people got out. [John] Gates, for instance, wound up there and didn't stay very long. He was shipped out and actually got into an outfit, an active outfit in Europe. Other guys wound up carrying sides of beef. I don't think there was any consistency involved, so I don't have any idea whether this was it or not. I was supposed to go to armed forces OCS, but I started to be moved, and the papers never caught up to me, so I'm overseas. We were all frozen, they said, on the [Aleutian] Islands and, finally, when it was possible after the war was over to move, armed forces OCS was out so I never got there. I kept dreaming I was going to drive around in a tank and not have to walk. My brother, Joe, said, "You're goddamn lucky."

FS: Some of the poetry that relates to the Aleutian stay is very powerful. You begin to introduce characters like Peets here. I'm essentially talking about *Letter* now. What's the connection? How do the characters like Peets begin to show up in the Aleutian material, sort of interweave with it?

TM: I don't know. I really don't, because Peets is the landlord that I had down in Louisiana, and he first appears in that section down there where it deals with an ice storm. He's just one of those voices that I keep hearing, a kind of a cynical and reactionary voice, I guess, in some ways a counter voice to some of the radical voices in the poetry.

FS: Yet you love the guy, don't you?

TM: There's something colorful about him. Yeah. Yeah. As a character he's interesting. As a man he wouldn't have been very pleasant.

FS: Was the stay in the Aleutians very difficult? Was that a tough time for you, a bad time in your life?

TM: Yes and no. We were more likely to be killed by boredom than anything else. Physically there was a lot of difficulty at times because it was, you know, it was cold and rainy and miserably wet, awful. It was bad, and one of the things that raised hell with a lot of the people there was the sense that we were going to be there forever. One guy in the last outfit that I was in had been up there four and something years. He'd been in the National Guard outfit that shipped to Alaska.

FS: How long were you up there?

TM: I was only there for two years, but it was long enough.

FS: You never got home during that time?

TM: No. There was this deadening kind of sameness to the place.

FS: Where you able to write?

TM: Yeah, I did a fair amount of writing. I didn't have a sense of any pressure in terms of time then. No, but I guess I did, I don't know how much, but I did some poems anyway in those two years. It wasn't probably as much as I have done at other times. I wound up the last part of the time up there in charge of orientation for my squadron. I didn't want the job because it only involved one hour a week of work. You had to keep busy or else; it was difficult, but I was told I was damn well gonna have that job, so I said, Then I deserve to have some stripes. I'd left a job where a week after I would have been a sergeant anyway. I was just being cantankerous. I didn't give a damn. So, anyway, I started getting stripes; then I demanded an assistant and so I got him, an assistant. I had to go over and pick up a training film every week and I got somebody to drive the jeep. Then I became a sergeant and he became a corporal, and he began to bitch and we got a third man. By that time I did nothing. I never went anywhere near the films. My corporal took care of it. His PFC went and got the film, then he put it on the machine and ran it. It got so I slept sixteen hours a day.

FS: Was your marriage still holding together while you were up there?

TM: Yes, as far as I was concerned, yes, it was. I was very much in love with Marian and I wrote a couple of poems for her while I was there. One of them was called "Celebration for June 24th." That was the date we were married down in Missouri in 1940. I don't know though, something had happened. Maybe it was just the two years or three or however much that I was away most of the time, because we didn't go back together the way we had been. We stayed together, of course, for three years or more, whatever it was, after I came out of the army, and we still loved each other, but—I don't know—something had happened, and so that was that.

FS: When you came back from the Aleutians you were mustered out in New York?

TM: In New York.

FS: And then what?

TM: I got out about November, I guess, probably the thirteenth—everything happened on the thirteenth—I came out and we stayed in North Dakota for a substantial part of the winter.

FS: Was your dad still farming then?

TM: Yeah. The whole family was at home. It was a wonderful winter. At night we would drive horses, because the country roads were jammed with snow. We would drive to one of the neighbors and play poker a good deal that winter.

FS: There's some mention of all the family being together in *Letter,* isn't there?

TM: Yeah, everyone was there—except for Jim [his brother Jim, killed during the war, for whom "Blues for Jimmy" and other poems were written]—that winter for the last time.

FS: You want to talk about Jim, or is that too painful?

TM: It is painful still, yeah. He was my little brother, which meant that I was very protective of him, but he was also the second brother, which meant that we fought like blazes, so it was both of these things. As we got older, I was in college, he was in high school; I was in the army, he was on the west coast in the army. We got closer together. One of the things that both of us most looked forward to was being together again after the war was over. We were very close as children and then I was in college and he was at home or in high school and there was some distance between us, partly age, partly physical separation, and so on. In the letters that we wrote during the war, that was the thing that we had arrived at simultaneously, that we really loved each other, and we wanted to get back together for a while after the war to renew acquaintance because we had been separated for some length of time. Then it didn't happen. I was back in the States at Wright Field. I had just come back from overseas and he was just on his way over and was killed in a crack-up and that was that.

FS: When I asked you to read "Blues for Jimmy" during your reading today, you thought that poem was too hard for you to read.

TM: Yeah, I cracked up once reading that poem. It's painful to me. I like the poem, I'm very happy I've written that poem. It's one of three poems that are about Jimmy, but it's difficult.

FS: So you got out of the service and you were there back in North Dakota. Then what?

TM: Then to New York.

FS: You hadn't done any screenwriting yet, at that time?

TM: No, I went back to New York in the spring of '47 or maybe late winter of '46. I was going to live on the 52–20 club [a federal program for veterans of World War II, who received twenty dollars per week for fifty-two weeks in order to give them time to find work or start back to school]. The only trouble was that I no sooner started than they found me a job through the State Unemployment Service. I had a job where I did nothing except tell people, Here, take this and go there. I got that in about the middle of April and on May Day I walked out to join the parade and I never came back. I didn't know what I was going to do, so I talked to my friend Mac, who had TB at that time and was housebound. We lived near him on 17th Street near 8th Avenue. I used to go over and see him almost every day. A lot of people used to drop in on him to cheer him up, a lot of the NMU [National Maritime Union] people, almost continually passing through there and my place too. Anyway, he said, "Well, goddamn it, you say you're a writer, you write poems, why don't you write a story and sell a story," and I said, "Christ, I don't know anything about writing commercial fiction. I write poems." "If you're a writer, you can write," he said, "there is a newsstand right down the stairs where you catch the subway. Go out and buy yourself some copies of pulp magazines and go home and write a pulp story." I did exactly that, and I sold it and I said, My God, this is like a license to steal, because it was so easy. Once I had got started, it was just sort of fun, so I did that for some length of time.

FS: What kind of pulps?

TM: Murders, adventures, westerns. The real old pulps with that marvelous pulp smell. Yeah, that was toward the tail end of the pulps. They disappeared shortly after. Anyway, I did that successfully for some time, then one day I thought, Jesus, I wonder. I hadn't needed to write a poem for about three months and so I thought, I wonder if I *can* write a poem. Maybe I'm finished writing poetry. It didn't worry me. If I were finished, then that was that. I had a very relaxed feeling about it. Then when I did write, I wrote in a compulsive way. I wrote because I *had* to write. I had a sense that I might stop writing anytime, do something else, you know. So I thought, I wonder if I can still write a poem? I sat down and sat and sat and something came along and I wrote a poem called "In Praise of a Dead Body." So I began writing more poetry. Then I heard from Oxford [University]. Either you come over this fall [to claim the Rhodes Fellowship] or that's the end of it. I could have gone over a year earlier, but there was no way, there was no housing, so, in the fall of '47, I went to Oxford. I was there a year. I was at New College. I lived in New College for the first term, by myself, then I found a little apartment. Marian was staying with a friend about twenty miles out and she moved in then. We lived out of college. I did a lot of writing then, especially in the first term. They hadn't gotten me an advisor. It was like being lost in the army. So all I did was get up, eat some breakfast, spend the morning going to bookstores. I bought lots of books which the government was paying for on the GI Bill [of Rights]. I had lunch at the college or else I got on my bike and I rode out along one of the rivers and went to an outlying pub and had lunch there and sat. I did a lot of writing in those little pubs. I remember one pub in particular I used to go to often. They had wonderful cheese sandwiches. There was very little food to eat. There was a pond, a huge pond, and you could sit out there, along some stream, I don't know what it was. So I would sit there and I would work for a couple of hours or so.

FS: Was work writing?

TM: Yeah, writing. Toward the end of the afternoon, I'd come back. I shared a sitting room with a guy and so maybe four o'clock, 3:30 or 4:00, until dinner at seven I would sit in front of the gas log when it was cold. I remember, I wrote most of *Long Shot O'Leary* [*'s Garland of Practical Poesie*] there, some of it up at Scotland during the winter Christmas vacation. I did a lot of reading and a lot of writing. Then I discovered that I was going to have to do some exams and I had better start going to some lectures, so I went to some odd and interesting things. I got to study the various handwritings of the fifteenth, sixteenth, and seventeenth centuries. At one time I could recognize all of them. Strange things. And then in the spring, I did all the exams, about three or four days of writing like a lunatic, from morning to night, and then I had an oral thing.

FS: Was there anyone particularly memorable there on the faculty that you worked with or liked?

TM: Well, there were, there were some people. The guy who wrote *Primitive Songs* was there, at the college next door to mine—I can't think of his name—who got the chair of poetry later, but he wasn't lecturing. Lord David Cecil was there. He was lecturing to a massive group. He was terrible. There was a guy named Wilson who lectured on some of the most out of the way stuff of the Shakespearean and seventeenth century. I can't think of which Wilson it is, it's not Norbert. Christopher Hill was there, and there were a number of other people. Among the students at the time was Ken Tynan, who was well known. He was the butterfly of the time. I don't know of anybody else at that time who was a writer who was there. I knew some English writers who were writing poetry, but I never heard anything more of them. William Jay Smith was there, I knew him. I met Roy Fuller, just sort of in passing, that's about it. I didn't know any of the English writers except Jack Beeching. I guess I wasn't in London very much.

FS: Did you find it a useful year? Was it a good year?

TM: It was a good year for me. I did quite a lot of writing. It was a wonderful year, but at the end of it I resigned the scholarship. I thought I needed to write a novel and I did write a novel. I've still got it.

FS: It's not been published?

TM: No, it was too experimental or whatever for the left and too radical for the middle. I suppose it might be publishable now. I'd like sometime to get to it and see what it looks like. [McGrath has done so, recently.]

FS: And now, you probably would want to do a lot of work on it.

TM: No—not much. I'm sure my sense of style may have changed quite a bit. I have looked at it from time to time and I'm not unhappy with it.

FS: Were there any political involvements while you were at Oxford?

TM: I was spy for the Haganah. [Israeli (at that time Palestinian) armed forces, before the State of Israel was founded.] I was in Paris at a time when the Haganah was getting powerful, and ten different varieties of left Palestinians and Arabs used to sort of follow each other around. It was a little parade, weird. At one point somebody asked me if I would chair a meeting between some Israelis and some Palestinian left groups. That didn't work out very well. That was in Paris. I came back to Oxford and I got a letter from a friend, an American who was in Paris. It was very cryptic, but it asked me, in effect, Would I go down to London and would I meet somebody, and so I said, Yes, I would. I went down there and I went to that place, went into this apartment, perfectly empty except for a guy I was supposed to meet, I've forgotten what his name was now. So this guy lets me in and we talk. Strangest sort of thing, because he's trying to find out if I'm who I'm supposed to be and I'm trying to find out if he's who he's supposed to be. Finally that gets through. Well, all he wants me to do is arrange to have a ship blown up which is in one of the ports in England and which is carrying arms to the Arabs. I'm supposed to arrange to have the ship blown up. And I knew the guy; he was an excellent sculptor and he was head of the Haganah group in Paris. Well I thought, God, this must be the two most unlikely agents that have ever met. So I said, Well, I'll see what I can do. So I call the friend. I tell him I met the guy and I'm sure he is who he says he is and this is what he wants. The guy says I think we better find out if he is who he says he is. So he had some friends who got in touch with the French CP. The French CP sent back an answer—he's a good man but he's a total nut. So then they said, "Oh what is it that he wants?" Well he would like to arrange that either this ship be blown up or that it just never gets to where it's going. "Oh, well, I suppose you'll be going back to Oxford tonight?" I said, Yeah, I suppose I will, goodbye. Sometime, probably in that week, I read that there was a strike called, I've forgotten what port, and the ship that was struck was the ship that the munitions were on. The English longshoremen were screaming that they weren't going to do anything about this goddamn ship, didn't want to send it on its way, so it was hung up there for some length of time. The strike was a wildcat and eventually the strike was busted, or anyway the ship got out and moved. It went to Italy and in Italy burned. So it never did arrive. But that was the high point of my espionage activities, if it was espionage. I don't know. I've always wanted to talk about all this. You read a spy novel and everything goes clickety-clickety-click, or you read about various enterprises that have been carried out and I wonder if half of it was as goofy as that particular thing. Did that guy have anything to do with it? Maybe it was just because the sentiments were for not sending arms, and the Italians were, you know, they were a little more militant than their English cousins. Hard to say.

FS: We're beginning to run short on time. Let's talk a little about the books. When did *Three Poets* [one of Alan Swallow's first published books, containing poems by McGrath and two other then unknown poets] come out?

TM: Came out while I was in the army. While I was in Oxford in '48 the book *To Walk a Crooked Mile* [Swallow] came out. Yes, and then in 1950, '50 or '51, *Long Shot O'Leary* [International Publishers]. Then in '55, I think it was, *Figures of the Double World.*

FS: Now, when you came back from Oxford, you went to Los Angeles? And you went to work for Los Angeles State?

TM: Yes, that's essentially what happened. I didn't go to work there immediately. There were other odds and ends. I was out there, Marian and I split up, I went to New York briefly, was back and tried to find jobs, but couldn't find anything, blundered into the one at LA State [teaching writing], worked there three and a half years. I started at midterm, after Christmas. Taught half a year, then taught three full years, and then was hauled up before the House Un-American Activities Committee [HUAC] and got deep sixed.

FS: That's when you declared yourself "a member of the unaffiliated far left?" Were you politically involved all this time?

TM: I've always had differences at different times with the leadership, but I remained in the [Communist] Party and involved. I wasn't in the Party at the time I was in front of HUAC. Put in limbo, lost in transit because I was on the outs, split over some questions with one of the panjandrums and the idea was, I guess, simply to push me away and forget about it because it was better than having a stink about it. It can happen. It did happen to a number of people. After I lost the job [at Los Angeles State] I worked at various odds and ends.

FS: You describe that in *Letter,* the carpentry type of job?

TM: Yeah, the wooden animal factory, yeah. Wonderful job, but didn't pay anything.

FS: Were you writing for film?

TM: I began to do a little work. I wrote the narration for a little animated film, and I began to have little bits and pieces of work.

FS: How did that work out? This is after all the time when people like the Hollywood Ten [ten Hollywood screenwriters blacklisted after defying HUAC] were in a deep freeze.

TM: There were certain areas in filmmaking out there in which people who were on the left or had been left were involved in little, small, very tiny enterprises, so there were jobs, not many but occasional jobs. Once in a while something would turn up where they'd think they needed a poet, and some of those jobs I got. Then I went to New York one summer on a visit and Leo Hurwitz heard that I was there. Leo, I don't know if you know him, he made *Native Land,* which you probably remember, and he worked with Pere Lorenz and others on *The River* and *The Plow That Broke the Plains.*

He had a film which he'd already cut called "Museum and the Fury." I think it was a very good film. He wanted a poet and I was in New York and out of work. I'd never met him, but he got in touch with me through Charlie Humboldt [editor of *New Masses* and, at the time McGrath is talking about, *Masses and Mainstream,* a short-lived, left-wing arts journal]. I worked on that for about a month, I guess. The film was already cut. I had to just run it, and run it, but I like that film very much, and when I was done Leo said, You ought to go over and talk with so and so at another place, and so I did. I didn't get any work there at the time, but I did later when I went back to New York, in '57, or whatever it was, and I picked up other work on the west coast in Los Angeles.

FS: Were you living essentially by yourself all this time?

TM: For the last part I was. I was living with Alice from about '51. We were together for about five or six years.

FS: Let me ask you briefly, Tom, about the group of what I think of as Walter Lowenfels' radical poets. I'm talking about people like Replansky and Mel Weisburd and some of the others. Were these ongoing kinds of contacts? I mean, was there a community of younger radical poets?

TM: These people had no connections with Walter.

FS: No, not personally, but I think of them as his because he's the one that anthologized them [in *Poets of Today: A New American Anthology* (New York: International, 1964)].

TM: Oh yeah, right. Naomi was somebody who was my age. I had read her poetry when she published in *The Worker* under a different name, and I got to know her after the war, particularly when she lived in Los Angeles for a while. Mel was one of my students [at Los Angeles State]. After I was fired, there were various people who used to turn up at a kind of informal workshop. People brought work to me. Bert Meyers, for example. I don't know if that name rings a bell, but he brought work to me. Sometimes it was a regular workshop with half a dozen people in it; sometimes it was just people who periodically brought work to me. That went on for some years after I left Los Angeles State.

FS: This was mostly California based, then?

TM: Yeah.

FS: So one really can't make a connection between Humboldt and that group of people in New York and the Los Angeles Group?

TM: No, I'm the link.

FS: You're the link. That's interesting. Why did you leave Los Angeles eventually? Why'd you go back to New York?

TM: Well, I ran out of jobs out there, that was one thing. Alice and I had been split up for some time. I don't know especially why I went East. I went first to San Francisco, but I didn't intend to live there. I went to New York partly because there were jobs. It was a much better place for this kind of work than Los Angeles was. So I went then and I did get a job.

FS: You were doing a lot of documentary film and that kind of thing?

TM: Yeah, documentary, educational, industrial.

FS: Let me just ask you about the San Francisco business. Did you have contact—this would be about the right time—with Ginsberg and Ferlinghetti and that group?

TM: No, I didn't. I knew Larry, a guy from Chicago—I can't think of his name—he wrote *The Holy Barbarians* [Lawrence Lipton]. He had brought some poems to me when I was working on the *California Quarterly*. He hadn't written poetry or anything for a long time, had been in publicity, but I took the poems in and recommended some, and people on the Board published far more than I thought they should. I didn't like them that much. I was for publishing them, but I didn't think that much of the work. Anyway, he became a kind of guru to a group of people out in Venice, which he called Venice West. They weren't capable, they weren't very good writers, but they had links with the San Francisco people. I remember in about '55 when Ginsberg and Corso came down. They were on their way to Mexico and they called me up and spent an evening talking, sort of. I think Rexroth may have given them the steer. Ginsberg washed his socks and complained that he was lonely. Corso said that when he stopped being beautiful he was going to commit suicide, and various things of this sort. We didn't go very far in any direction. I kind of liked them both. Ginsberg I had in many ways a good feeling about. Corso, I couldn't be sure. He was so madly in love with himself that it was kind of nice. You know, you sort of bask in that wonderful warmth that he's feeding into himself. Anyway. They needed money. They were going to Mexico. I called up some of the people who had been students of mine who were running a magazine called *Coastline* and said these guys are in town. This was before "Howl" had come out, or it had just come out. I said, These guys need a reading. People used to organize them periodically. So they put together a reading very rapidly and called up everybody in the world, in their world, very small, but they had a reading with maybe about fifty people there and that was the first reading where Ginsberg took his clothes off, and that became a standard thing after that. The reading had reverberations. Ginsberg had read in San Francisco and that was a big thing—began the San Francisco Renaissance I guess—but this reading in some ways had other, bigger sorts of effects, partly because of the undressing. Then they went to Mexico. I'd see Ginsberg occasionally or Corso in New York later. I never really knew them, I wasn't part of the movement.

FS: What were you working on at this time, in terms of the poetry?

TM: I finished *Letter, Part I*.

FS: It wasn't out yet, though. It hadn't been published?

TM: No, it hadn't been published. It was finished in '54 or '55 but wasn't published for years. I don't know what I was working on then. It wasn't till maybe a year or so, maybe two years after I finished *Letter,* that I realized there was more. I thought I was done, I heaved a great sigh of relief, I'm all done with that monster, and then I began to think, God Almighty, there is another section, maybe two sections. I began to get a glimpse of things in other ways. It wasn't that there wasn't more material, of course there was, but how to use it, and how to find a form for it, that's what I couldn't figure out. Then I began to get some notions for it and then I got into it. I did write some things along the way that I didn't know at the time were a part of *Letter I,* but they were. I really started to work on it in '60, I don't know precisely when. Some things I did that winter we were out on the farm. There are passages that deal with that winter, and some of the stuff was written then, but not in the form that it's now in.

FS: I guess this is as good a time as any to ask you about the line, really the format of *Letter,* which is somewhat different than other work you've done. It has a longer line, a longer stanza, the breaking of the line into two parts, frequently, and that increases as you go from *Part I* to *Part II.* Can you comment on that?

TM: When I started the poem I had no sense of form. All I wanted to do was to get the thing down. I didn't know how long it was going to be and I just leaped, started. I think anyone can see that I wasn't sure what the hell I wanted to do in the beginning. I was writing the line, simply a kind of a rhetorical phrase, what J. V. Cunningham calls "the parsing meter." Anyway, after a while I began to feel cadence more, and bit by bit I began to feel the line. Now that I think about it, it seems strange because I look back at other work and I see how often I've used the six beat line in poems way earlier, but somewhere along the way that line began to be the prime, the dominant one, and it still is. It's true that I break the line sometimes, but I've broken it very frequently only in a kind of punctuating way. In a reading, or reading it aloud off the page, I see it primarily as an aid to punctuation.

FS: Did you have a scheme in mind for the book by then?

TM: In *Part I* there's no scheme. I was just moving along with no special sense of doing anything except that I wanted to deal with certain things that had turned up in my life. That was the way it began. Then certain things began to fall into it, oh, the signs of the zodiac, and I began to see that the central imagery is fire and water in *Part I.* I guess I began to see that. I really didn't begin to see that until I was into *Part II,* and when I began to see it, I wrote this letter to Alan [Swallow]. Alan, I said, you see this poem is organized just the way they said. It's got the four elements in it. I'd give all this kind of bullshit. And yet it's not all bullshit, either, because the first book is really fire and water imagery and the next is earth and air, the rock and the wind which become earth symbols. When I think of fire, water, earth, and the air, I think in terms of medieval notions, but, of course, that's immaterial. That little poem, the short poem "The World in a Perfect Tear," has the four elements of imagery. Anyway, the line developed sort of by itself and

I'm surprised it didn't come earlier, because that kind of line turns up quite frequently in poems from way back.

FS: When you recognized the fire and water imagery in the first book, did you then consciously work with the rock and wind imagery in the second book?

TM: No, but somewhere early along in the second book, I became aware that I was using the four elements thing and the rock and the wind became symbols that I wanted to use, but I suppose it's a kind of serendipity as much as anything. The fire and water, I was aware I was using them, but at that point I wasn't thinking in terms of the four elements, and the four elements don't mean damn all to me, except once you begin to see you are doing this, this symmetry appeals to you. It does appeal to me. So those families of images run all the way through it.

FS: Tom, let me ask you about your own direction as a poet. You've been around for a long time. You've published a remarkable amount of work. Where do you think you are going to go? I know you've said that you were working on *Part III* of *Letter.*

TM: Yeah, I am. The main thing I see is to finish *Letter.* That I very strongly desire and I have a hope of doing that.

FS: Do you think *Part III* will finish it?

TM: No, I think there's a *Part IV,* but I think it's shorter. I think of it as being one section, I don't know what the hell is in it. Maybe for partly symmetry's sake, but in any case, I think there is a *Part IV* and that will be perhaps just a sort of tying up of things. After that, there are some things that are in my head. One, I keep thinking that I'm going to write some poems, I don't know what they are about, that would in some ways be a return to a tighter form, but bringing back the long line also. I sometimes think I can hear this. I can hear the sounds of this without knowing what the hell is in it.

FS: You said something in an interview about when you're very old you're going to write fixed poems, I remember that.

TM: I don't think they will be that fixed, but I think that they would be—probably—this sounds crazy, to think that one can see these things, but I sometimes have a glimpse of something, a longish poem, couple or three pages, stanzas are big and the lines are long and there's rhyme, maybe not all terminal rhyme. I sometimes think I hear something that sounds like this— as I say, I don't know what's in these poems. I also think that I may write a poem, quite loose, sort of a winter poem for Tomasito [McGrath's son]. It starts the year I was born and has as many passages as I am old by the time I finish it. All I'm trying to do in it is tell him some of the things that happened in these years. It would be a little like *Letter,* but it would be much more historical. That's the word for it. Those are things I think I see. I will always write a lot of little poems.

FS: You do an awful lot of that. Somebody's got to put all that stuff together. It's a monumental job, I think.

TM: Yeah, I think in *Open Songs* there's a blank page. They didn't print one of the poems. I've been giving away copies and I told someone jokingly, "I'll write you a poem to go on that page," and I did so. I'll always write little poems, I suppose, because when I'm busy, little poems may float in that I can do. It isn't like something where I've got to stop and have hours to work.

FS: Tell me a little bit about your work habits.

TM: Well, when I have time, when I'm free, I generally get up fairly early and waste three hours or four hours. I manage to get started about mid-morning and work until 2:00 or 3:00, four or five hours, and that's it. When I'm not free, when I'm teaching, I oftentimes try to set myself a time to work. I don't have much success with that. I can sit down, but I can't always work. I can't get to it. I need more time to work into it, I guess. The last year I've been trying to get up at five and do some work, but now mornings I have energy, but I've got this business of taking time to get into the poem, so it's hard. When I have a poem going on, I can oftentimes get to it and get some words down.

FS: Do you listen to music or anything like that in connection with it?

TM: When I'm working, no. I sometimes do, but not these mornings. I don't do anything except drink too much coffee and smoke too many cigarettes. That's what I do. Otherwise, I listen to music sometimes, but that's not a primary thing with me. When I was in Paris in '47–48, I did a lot of writing in a cafe in Paris, in a black-market cafe, because there was heat. It was very cold. The French are good about this. They'd had people writing in cafes for a long time and it's perfectly OK. You can't do that as well in America. I used to sit in bars sometimes and work. Oftentimes I feel that I can work pretty well if I have things going on around me that I have no commitment to at all. I've oftentimes worked in the library, just sat down—there's a lot of coming and going. The only problem, I can't smoke. If I could, it would be the place to work. There's something about a little bit of background noise that's useful to me.

FS: Has your work life changed any since Tomasito's birth, since what I gather in the poetry is really one of the happiest moments in your life? Is that family situation in some ways a source for your poems?

TM: Oh, yeah, sure it is. Yes, there are a lot of poems that came as a result of that. He's important to me, and all the women have been very important to me, in terms of writing. They've all been muse, you know, and I felt and still feel a very, very, strong sense of love for Marian, and Alice, too, but that's a different thing, she's a different sort of person. It's very hard for me to unlove anybody. Tomasito means a great deal, a great deal. There are many things that I didn't expect to feel. With Alice, she had a couple of children, one of them a little boy, eighteen months old. I thought that I had

had the experience of being a father. I certainly felt close to that child as a father and he to me as a son. He's living out near me now in North Dakota. But I was surprised that I could feel these things all over again and in a sense feel them more deeply. It's not just Tomasito is my child; I don't think that is it at all. But I was there when Tomasito was born and I saw him coming into the world. That was a tremendous thing for me. I held him before Genia did. He scared the shit out of me for six weeks, I guess. I'd just look at him—My God, what, where? Then, as he began to develop, he just took me in.

FS: It's just lovely to see the two of you together as I did in Sioux Falls [at a meeting of the Western Literature Association].

TM: He's beautiful. All children are beautiful, of course, and especially to their parents, but, yeah, he's a little beauty. I wish I could have more children. I wish that I might have had another child for Tomasito, for him to be with. I feel strongly, as I think of him, that he's got no family shield in the way that I had a whole family of brothers and sisters, whole flocks of cousins around. But because Tomasito came along so late, he's got no children in the family. My brother's kids, my sister's kids, are all too much older, so he hasn't got that kind of family thing, and I'm sorry about that. I wish he did have.

FS: Let me ask you about your relationship with [Robert] Bly, and other contemporary poets. What brings it to mind is seeing Bly with his son and you with your son at the same meeting, which was really quite a remarkable experience. How about you and Bly and the rest of contemporary poetry?

TM: Well, I don't know many poets very well. Of the people of my own generation, if there are any left, I guess I could say that I never really knew any. If I belonged to a generation, I never knew anybody from it. I'm a little bit younger than a certain generation, not in terms of age, but in terms of publication. In some way, I am of the time of Roethke, and Caroline Kizer is still alive, and there are one or two others, but not very many of my age. Bly is ten years younger. Yeah, and Jim Wright, who is another poet I like very much as a person and whose work I like, but I've never known many of these people. Bob [Bly] I met in New York in the 1950s or in '60, just before we came out here. I can't recall just exactly how, but, in any case, I have seen him off and on. On the way out, we stopped and stayed over with them a day or so and so on, and he came up and stayed over with me a day or so the first year I was at Fargo [at North Dakota State]. We saw each other more frequently than we do now. I used to pass back and forth to Minneapolis, or going east in the summers and coming back in the fall, and we'd always see each other. He's always read up there once a year at one of the colleges. As time has gone on, we see each other less. We're both busier, I guess. We're still, as far as I know, good friends, and I like his work a good deal, at least up until recently. I don't know exactly how I feel about the more recent poems. I haven't seen the last book.

FS: I was going to ask you about that, about the *Point Reyes Poems,* which some say mark a new departure away from the social concerns of *Light Around the Body.*

TM: Yeah, I know that, and I don't know quite what to make of it. I haven't really had a chance to talk with Bob about it. The last book that we really talked about was *Sleepers Awake.* He showed me one of the versions of that particular poem and we talked about it. He gave me a copy of the book and wrote a little thing about how I helped him with a poem, which I don't believe I did. But I felt close to that book of poems, and to *Light Around the Body.* I reviewed the first book when it first came out, *The Silence in the Summer Fields.* I had read Bly's *Poems for the Ascent of J. P. Morgan* someplace or other before I knew anything about Bly at all, and I thought, Jesus Christ, now here's somebody.

FS: Did you know he was from Minnesota?

TM: No; didn't know anything about him.

FS: There's that remarkable similarity between the two of you, just in the geography.

TM: I didn't know anything about him at all. I just saw these poems and thought, Christ, here's somebody who can write political poems. I don't know. Bob has certain interests that are quite distant from my own. I'd love to see him more and I think he'd like to see more of me, but it's probably unlikely. He's got a busy life. He goes out to read a good deal and it takes up a lot of time.

FS: Who else in contemporary poetry do you read with interest and look to with excitement? Or which journals do you read a lot?

TM: I read in a haphazard way. In a certain sense, I'm not as interested in the poetry that's being written now. Not that I put it down or anything, it's just that in a certain way I don't need to read my contemporaries in the way that I once did. Once upon a time I absolutely had to know what these people were doing, to know what they were writing. I just had to know it because the language is yours. You're in the same soup and you have to know who the hell else is around. I don't have that feeling anymore. For what reason I don't know. I guess I have the feeling that I'm living more on my own fat. I don't know what the reason is, but I don't feel the need for reading others so much.

FS: Let me suggest one reason and see how you respond. Maybe you have some certainty about your own direction and your own abilities, and your limitations?

TM: Yeah, I think that's true. I am quite sure it's true. I read. I read a fair amount of stuff in translation. I go back and reread certain people. One of the people I very much love and read—oh, strange poets sometimes, Mac-Diarmid, for example. I do read a fair amount of new work by young people, some of it sent to me, some of it I just pick up by chance and read. I look at a lot of magazines, but I don't read them cover to cover the way I once did.

FS: Are there any magazines you find particularly interesting?

TM: I suppose the magazine that I most enjoy reading and I read fairly often is *Kayak*. Beyond that, I don't know. I read *American Poetry Review*. It's sent to me, so I read it, and I read the *Dakota Territory* because it's there and some of the other magazines from around, *Moons and Liontails,* which is published in Minneapolis. I don't have a sense of there being a magazine that I need in the way that once I needed to read *Poetry*. Once upon a time that was the prime magazine, and a few other magazines that I needed to read. I don't have that sense.

FS: How about critical stuff? I mean, do you read the *New York Review* [*of Books*]?

TM: Yeah, I used to read that until the last six months or so, but I used to read it pretty regularly, with mixed feelings. I don't read the literary quarterlies as much as I did. I don't read criticism as much as I did. There are still times when I'll get interested, you know, in some particular thing that comes along. I had some interest in structuralism and read about it. It didn't turn me on. I read some of [Harold] Bloom, for instance. I once taught criticism and, of course, then I read a lot as a trade kind of thing. I don't any longer.

FS: You mostly just teach writing?

TM: I teach that, and I teach freshman English and that's it.

FS: How do you see the relationship in our time, and in this culture between the poet and the political left?

TM: First of all, I believe that the poet ought to have some kind of political orientation and commitment. I do believe that. I think it's healthy for him. Secondly, I think that the relationship of the poet to the political party is always going to be uneasy, and probably should be, and that the poet, among other things, has got the job of blowing up and blasting a lot of things that the politicals want and accept. The poet himself may agree in some ways, but it's important that he not let these things become sacerdotal, and that he not allow attitudes to become sanctified. I think that's important for the poet. So I assume it's always going to be an uneasy relationship. I think the poet ought to recognize that. The poet, standing for all artists, and the politicals need to recognize that there's going to be an uneasy relationship between the artist and the political and to accept that. Then they would get along and work together a hell of a lot better, I think. I think that the poet oftentimes tends to be overly romantic about the political side of things. On the other hand, once the artist has accepted the revolutionary, political point of view, he ought to put the shoulder to the wheel and do things in a way that is totally in aid of whatever the given line is, with a difference. I don't think a poet or the artist can commit all of his work in that kind of way. He can paint a poster for May Day, I think that's fine, but I think it's a mistake to believe that's all that the artist ought to do. He's giving up too much. If he's any good at all, he must be discovering in his own life and in his own *political* life those things that must be valuable to the Movement, and in his own political life those things may be out of popularity from time to time. I think it very important that he manifest them.

FS: Do you see a place for yourself on the contemporary American left anywhere.

TM: Oh, I think I've got one. I wouldn't know how to define it.

FS: That's what I'm asking. Obviously you're a part of that left, but I mean, do you have a commitment to a particular grouping or faction or anything of that sort?

TM: Yeah, yes and no. It's hard to say. I certainly have commitments to particular things that are going on, particular efforts to do this, that, and the other, and in that I feel I'm willing to work with just about anybody going, that's the first thing. As to whether there is a particular group that I feel close to—is that what you mean?

FS: Yes, that, or a journal, or that kind of thing.

TM: I feel closer now to the CP than I have in a long time, and that may be because other things have left the scene. Also it's because I think the CP attitude is different from what it was in the past, when I was on the outs with it. I assume that I will always be, from time to time, on the outs with any political organization, because I can commit myself to any particular action for a period of time, but I can't commit myself indefinitely. I know myself enough to know that, right or wrong, I have a maverick approach to things, and I assume I'm going to go on having that maverick approach.

FS: Do you see some younger poets on the radical left coming to the fore who will, as it were, follow the path you have followed?

TM: I don't see anybody quite like me. I see some people who are on the left and were doing some work in a magazine like *West End,* for example. I think of a writer like Margaret Randall. Our system, our ways of working are quite different, but I think of the two of us going certainly in the same direction. As to other poets, there are a few younger ones that I know who seem to me to be going in the direction that I am going in and have gone.

FS: But no voice you see as yet to which you react the way you described your first contact with Bly's work?

TM: No, I haven't seen that for a while. No, I haven't. There are poets that I think of very highly. Don Gordon—there's an example, but he's a little older than I am. He's been around for a long time. Naomi Replansky. There are such people, but of the young I don't see many; I see the people who are writing for a magazine like *West End* and I see other political poems here and there, but I don't see anything quite like the thing I'd like to see. Except for Dale Jacobson, Bob Edwards, and a few other young ones.

FS: Do you see a shift away in the last three or four years from political poetry? There was a spate of that in the late 60s, early 70s.

TM: There's less of it now, yeah. There is a shift away, at least numerically, but I don't know exactly what that means, because during the time of the Vietnamese War, you know, everybody was writing anti-Vietnam war poems, but it was plain to me that when that war was over that was going to disappear, that it was a momentary commitment to a thing and it really wasn't political.

FS: Is that how you think of a guy like Galway Kinnell, or a poet like Bly himself?

TM: No, Galway is a very powerful poet. I don't know where he's going, but at least he's been going for some time, and he's always had some kind of social commitments, strong ones. He was involved in the, you know, Southern civil rights movement. I don't think that he's ever been very deeply political. It's a particular thing like the civil rights movement or something like it, that he's got to latch on to. In slack times he's not likely to feel much politically. I think maybe the same thing is true of Bob, but I don't think that is the case, because you see he was political in a sense before the Vietnamese War. I have a feeling that what's happening now is an interim for him. I think that he'll come back to political, social commitments or what have you.

FS: Is it fair to say, if I were to compare you and the people we've just been talking about, that we can think of you as a poet who has a real theory about society? You can overcome the slack moments because you have a more long-range view of social change?

TM: That may be true. I hope it's true. I think that I do have that and I think I can do that.

14   A Biographical Sketch of Thomas McGrath

THOMAS MCGRATH WAS born in 1916, the oldest son of James and Catherine (Shea) McGrath. There were four younger brothers, Jim (killed in World War II), Joe, Martin, and the youngest, Jack. His sister Kathleen was born between Joe and Martin. His parents were farmers, the second generation of them, working the land in Ransom County, North Dakota, near the town of Sheldon, about forty miles west of the Minnesota border, between the Maple and Sheyenne Rivers.

McGrath went to grade and high school in Sheldon, and then started somewhat delayed and intermittent University studies at Moorhead State University. Eventually, he attended the University of North Dakota at Grand Forks, where he earned a B.A. in 1939. Awarded a Rhodes Scholarship, he found that he could not use it immediately, because of the outbreak of World War II. He had received offers from a number of universities to begin work on an advanced degree—as had the other Rhodes Scholars that year—and accepted an offer from Louisiana State University at Baton Rouge. There he studied, most intensely with Cleanth Brooks, was involved in radical political activity, wrote, and met Alan Swallow, who published McGrath's first book of poems as part of the development of The Swallow Press.

In the 1940–1941 academic year McGrath taught at Colby College in Maine, but he did not find teaching there entirely satisfactory and thus left at the end of the academic year to go to New York City. There he wrote, organized, did legal research for attorneys engaged in "political" cases, and worked at the Kearney Shipyards, until he entered the armed forces in 1942. Most of his time in the service was spent on Amchitka Island. He was discharged with the rank of sergeant in 1945. After a period of adjustment he was finally able to undertake the year of study provided by the Rhodes Scholarship and spent 1947–1948 at New College, Oxford, England.

Returning to the United States after some travel, McGrath engaged in various occupations and eventually found a faculty position at Los Angeles State University, where he taught from 1951 to 1954. His dismissal from this institution was directly connected with his appearance as an unfriendly witness before the House Committee on Un-American Activities, when that infamous body brought its hearings to Los Angeles in 1953.

From 1954 to 1960 McGrath worked variously as a secondary school teacher at a private institution, for a company that manufactured carved wooden animals, and at other jobs that might earn him his keep. He wrote film and television scripts from time to time, several of the former for director Mike Cimino. In 1960 he resumed his academic career, teaching at C. W.

Post College (now part of Long Island University) in New York. At about this time he founded, with his wife Genia, the journal *Crazy Horse*.

In 1962 he returned to North Dakota, where he taught for five years at North Dakota State University at Fargo. In 1969 McGrath accepted a faculty position at Moorhead State University in Minnesota, where he had first begun his studies as an undergraduate. At the end of the 1982–1983 academic year, he retired from Moorhead State and moved to Minneapolis, where he now lives.

McGrath has held a variety of significant editorial positions and has been awarded a variety of distinguished prizes and fellowships for his work as a poet. Among the former, in addition to his founding editorship of *Crazy Horse,* he has been a contributing editor of *Mainstream* (later *Masses and Mainstream*) and has served on the editorial board of the *California Quarterly*. He has held an Amy Lowell Traveling Fellowship in Poetry (1965), has twice been awarded National Endowment for the Arts Fellowships (1974, 1982), was a Guggenheim Fellow in 1967, and was twice a Bush Fellow (1976, 1981). In May 1981 the University of North Dakota awarded him a Doctorate of Letters. In 1977 he received the Distinguished Achievement Award from the Society for Western Literature. In 1986, The Associated Writing Programs presented McGrath an award at a dinner in Chicago, at which tributes to him were presented by author "Studs" Terkel and poets Philip Levine and Michael Anania. In the same year, a "Ceili" was held by Minneapolis's "the Loft," at which many distinguished poets and writers celebrated McGrath's seventieth birthday.

McGrath has been married three times, to Marion, Alice, and Eugenia (Genia), all of whom appear in his poetry. He is the father of a son, Tomasito, to whom much poetry from McGrath's later work is addressed and dedicated.

15 A Bibliography of Works by and about Thomas McGrath

THIS BIBLIOGRAPHY DOES not include periodical publications of individual poems, editorial work by McGrath (such as with *Crazy Horse, California Quarterly,* and *Mainstream* magazine), translations, appearances in anthologies, or reviews by McGrath. Additionally, some secondary sources and reviews published in un-indexed or less well-known journals may be missing, although an attempt at a complete listing of these has been made here. Entries marked with an asterisk indicate those which this bibliographer was unable to locate and, thus, for which some information may be lacking. Material published from 1987 onward is not as completely provided here as earlier work.

BOOKS BY THOMAS MCGRATH

A Sound of One Hand. St. Peter: Minnesota Writer's Publishing House, 1975.

About Clouds. Illustrated by Chris Jenkyns. Los Angeles: Melmont Publishers, 1959.

The Beautiful Things. Illustrated by Chris Jenkyns. Los Angeles: Melmont Publishers, 1959.

This Coffin Has No Handles (novel). *North Dakota Quarterly* 52, 4, (1986). Rpt. New York: Thunder's Mouth Press, 1988.

Echoes Inside the Labyrinth. New York: Thunder's Mouth Press, 1983.

Figures from a Double World. Denver: Alan Swallow, 1955.

First Manifesto. Baton Rouge: Alan Swallow, 1940.

The Gates of Ivory, the Gates of Horn (novel). New York: Mainstream Publishers, 1957. Rpt. Chicago: Another Chicago Press, 1987.

Letter to An Imaginary Friend. Denver: Alan Swallow, 1962.

Letter to An Imaginary Friend, Parts I & II. Chicago: Swallow Press, 1970.

Letter to An Imaginary Friend, Part III: The Christmas Section. American Poetry Review 3, 1 (1974).

Letter to An Imaginary Friend, Part III, The Christmas Section II. Poetry Now 2 (Fall 1975): n.p.

Letter to An Imaginary Friend Parts Three & Four. Port Townsend, Wash.: Copper Canyon Press, 1985.

Letter to Tomasito. Minneapolis: Holy Cow! Press, 1977.

Longshot O'Leary Counsels Direct Action. Minneapolis: West End Press, 1983.

Longshot O'Leary's Garland of Practical Poesie. New York: International
    Publishers, 1949.
The Movie at the End of the World: Collected Poems. Chicago: Swallow
    Press, 1973.
New and Selected Poems. Denver: Alan Swallow, 1964.
9 Poems. New York: Mandrill Press, n.d.
Open Songs: Sixty Short Poems. Mount Carroll, Ill.: Uzzano Press, 1977.
Passages Toward the Dark. Port Townsend, Wash.: Copper Canyon Press,
    1982.
*Three Young Poets: Thomas McGrath, William Peterson, James Franklin
    Lewis.* Selected by Alan Swallow. Prairie City, Ill.: The Press of J. A.
    Decker, 1942.
Trinc: Praises II. Port Townsend: Copper Canyon Press, 1979.
*Voices from Beyond the Wall: A Sampler of Poems from Movie at the End of
    the World.* Moorhead, Minnesota: The Territorial Press, 1974.
*Voyages to the Inland Sea, Essays and Poems by R. E. Sebenthall, Thomas
    McGrath, and Robert Dane.* Ed. John Judson, Center for Contemporary
    Poetry. LaCrosse: University of Wisconsin, 1973.
To Walk a Crooked Mile: Poems. New York: Swallow Press, 1947.
Waiting for the Angel. Menomonie, Wis.: Uzzano (#14), 1979.
Witness to the Times! Poems. Los Angeles: Students of Thomas McGrath,
    1953.

INTERVIEWS AND OTHER PROSE

Statement. U.S. Congress. Hearings before the Committee on Un-American
    Activities, House of Representatives, 83d Congress, First Session. Investi-
    gation of Communist Activities in the Los Angeles Area—Part 5. Wash-
    ington: United States Government Printing Office, 1953, pp. 862–63.
    Reprinted in *Dream Champ—A Festschrift for Thomas McGrath*, ed.
    Fred Whitehead.
"Manifesto: No More Cattlemen or Sheepmen—We Want Outlaws!!"
    Crazy Horse 2 (1962?). Reprinted in *Dream Champ—A Festschrift for
    Thomas McGrath*, ed. Fred Whitehead.
Interview by Richard Lyons. *Dacotah Territory* 1 (1971): 8–17; 2 (1972):
    8–17.
"The Outrider." Editorial. *Dacotah Territory* 3 (Summer 1972): 45. Guest-
    edited by McGrath.
"Poetry and Place." Interview with Mark Vinz. *Voyage to the Inland Sea* 3
    (1973): 33–48.
"McGrath on McGrath." Edited by James Bertolino. *Epoch* 22 (1973): 207–
    19. Reprinted in *Dream Champ—A Festschrift for Thomas McGrath*, ed.
    Fred Whitehead.

"On My Work." *American Poetry Review* 3, 1 (1974): 26.

"A Conversation on Literature and Place." With John Milton and Frederick Manfred. *Dacotah Territory* 8 and 9 (1974–1975): 19–26.

Interview by William Childress. *Poetry Now* 2, 4 (1975): cover, 1, 38.

*"Problems of the Revolutionary Poet in Contemporary Times." Mimeographed paper for a forum of the Midwest Modern Language Association Convention, November 1976.

"Some Notes on Walter Lowenfels." *Praxis* 4 (1978): 87–91.

"Edward Dahlberg: A Memorial." With Meridel LeSueur, Jack Conroy, David Cumberland, and Fred Whitehead. *Quindaro* 3 (1979): 29–37.

Interview with Paul Buhle. *Cultural Correspondence* 9 (1979): 42–3.

Interview. *Another Chicago Magazine* 5 (1980): 72–78.

"Language, Power, and Dream." In *Claims for Poetry*. Ed. Donald Hall. Ann Arbor: University of Michigan Press, 1982, pp. 286–95.

"Surviving as a Writer: The Politics of Poetry / The Poetry of Politics." Interview with Jim Dochniak. *Sez* 2 and 3 (1981): special section.

"Panel on the Frontiers of Language." With Jack Conroy, Meridel LeSueur, Truman Nelson, and Fred Whitehead. *Quindaro* 8–9 (1981): 27–34. Partially reprinted in *Dream Champ—A Festschrift for Thomas McGrath,* ed. Fred Whitehead.

"North Dakota is Everywhere." *North Dakota Quarterly* 50, 3 (Summer 1982): 6–7.

Gibbons, Reginald and Terrence Des Pres. "An Interview with Thomas McGrath, January 30–February 1, 1987." *TriQuarterly* 70 (Fall 1987): 38–102.

Weiner, Joshua. "More Questions: An Interview with Thomas McGrath, June 4, 1987." *TriQuarterly* 70 (Fall 1987): 193–210.

FILMSCRIPT TITLES

"Limit High" (or "A Building is Many Buildings"). Graphic Films, L.A. (documentary).

"The Museum and the Fury." Leo Hurwitz and Frontier Films, NYC (documentary).

"The Little Boat" (from the short story by Malcolm Lowry). Sextant, NYC.

"Conquering Horse" (from the Frederick Manfred novel). Mike Cimino and Universal Films, L.A.

"The Supply Manager's Dilemma" (animated film on inventory systems). Graphic Films, L.A.

"The Ages of Time." NY (documentary).

"Everlasting Morning" (documentary).

"Choruses for the City" (documentary).

"Home Again." Mike Greshoff, L.A.

"Kef." Mike Cimino, L.A.

"Paradise." Mike Cimino, L.A.
"Genesis." Francis Thompson, Inc., NYC.
"American Moments." Collaboration for Francis Thompson (documentary).
Revision of script for "Stakeout on Dope Street." L.A. "The Naked Hunt."

ARTICLES ABOUT MCGRATH

Butwin, Joseph. "'The Winter Count': Politics in the Poetry of Thomas McGrath." McGrath Festschrift in *North Dakota Quarterly* 50, 4 (Fall 1982): 59. A comprehensive discussion of McGrath's poetry as an enterprise deliberately courting contradictions. Focuses on how various worlds (political/poetic, West/East, personal/public, present/past, community/isolation) are negotiated and provides biographical and historical material as context.

Cardona-Hine, Alvarado. "Knowing McGrath A Little." McGrath Festschrift in *North Dakota Quarterly* 50, 4 (Fall 1982): 52. A personal reminiscence of McGrath in 1957, discussing his work in general and relating a few telling anecdotes.

Des Pres, Terrence. "Thomas McGrath." *TriQuarterly* 70 (Fall 1987): 158–92. A discussion of McGrath's poetry in terms of Marxist history and in light of such figures as Bakhtin, Caudwell, and others.

Doyle, Joe. "Longshot O'Leary: Tom McGrath's Years on the Waterfront." McGrath Festschrift in *North Dakota Quarterly* 50, 4 (Fall 1982): 32. Discusses *Longshot O'Leary's Garland of Practical Poesie* in the context of McGrath's experiences on the Chelsea waterfront in 1941. Focuses on the Irish American Chelsea neighborhood radicals the poem is dedicated to and provides a history of the local politics McGrath was involved in and influenced by.

Engel, Bernard F. "From Here We Speak." *The Old Northwest* 2, 1 (March 1976): 37–44. Questions various assumptions about a particularly Midwestern "flavor" or influence and discusses the use of regional material by William Stafford, James Wright, and Thomas McGrath.

———. "Thomas McGrath's Dakota." *Midwestern Miscellany. Society for the Study of Midwestern Literature Newsletter* 4, n.d. A discussion of *Letter to an Imaginary Friend* emphasizing its assured and optimistic qualities, and focusing on its treatment of personal experience, labor, North Dakota, and McGrath's idea of a "revolution of pure potential."

———. "The Utopian Dakota of Thomas McGrath." *Late Harvest Bookmark* (1977). Discusses McGrath's use of his native place.

Frumkin, Gene. "A Note on Tom McGrath: The Early 50's." McGrath Festschrift in *North Dakota Quarterly* 50, 4 (Fall, 1982): 46. A reminiscence of McGrath's teaching activities in the fifties, providing history of his experiences during McCarthyism and of the foundation of the Sequoia school, the Marsh St. irregulars, and the magazine *Coastlines*.

Gibbons, Reginald and Terrence Des Pres, eds. *Thomas McGrath: Life and the Poem. TriQuarterly* 70 (Fall 1987). A special McGrath issue of the journal.

Gibbons, Reginald. "A Personal Introduction." *TriQuarterly* 70 (Fall 1987): 7-15. Explains motives for the special issue of the journal Gibbons edits and discusses both McGrath's work and the work of some of the contributors to the special issue.

Gurian, Jay. "The Possibility of a Western Poetics." *Colorado Quarterly* 15 (Summer 1966): 69-85. Argues the need for a thoughtful, analytical western poetics and cites McGrath's "The Buffalo Coat" as exemplifying the potential for a poetry that fuses Western and literary traditions.

Hall, Donald. "McGrath's Invective." In *Goatfoot, Milktongue, Twinbird.* Ann Arbor: University of Michigan Press, 1978. Reprinted in *Dream Champ—A Festschrift for Thomas McGrath,* ed. Fred Whitehead. Discusses the lack of curse and invective in American poetry and presents McGrath as our best example of its use.

Hamill, Sam. "The Problem of Thomas McGrath." McGrath Festschrift in *North Dakota Quarterly* 50, 4 (Fall 1982): 92. Discusses McGrath's use of multiple (and supposedly contradictory) traditions and argues that attempts to label his poetry fail to understand its strengths.

Hazard, Mike. "Movie Moonlighting, or the Other Career of Tom McGrath." McGrath Festschrift in *North Dakota Quarterly* 50, 4 (Fall 1982): 101. Discusses making the film, "The Movie at the End of the World," McGrath's writing for the movies, and links between his cinematic and poetic work.

Holscher, Rory. "Receiving Thomas McGrath's *Letter.*" *Moons and Lion Tails, A Midwestern Journal of Poetry and Comment* 4 (January 1976): 29-48. Reprinted in *Dream Champ— A Festschrift for Thomas McGrath,* ed. Fred Whitehead. A comprehensive review essay of *Letter to an Imaginary Friend* focusing on qualities of language and vision and linking these to qualities of historical events and experiences.

Jacobson, Dale. "The Mythical Element in *Letter to an Imaginary Friend.*" McGrath Festschrift in *North Dakota Quarterly* 50, 4 (Fall 1982): 71. A complex discussion of the book as "an attempt to resurrect the power of myth" by exposing false myths and creating a new one with community, not the individual, as the hero. Argues that McGrath's poem does for our understanding of society what traditional myth did for an earlier people's understanding of nature.

Levine, Philip. "Small Tribute to Tom McGrath." *TriQuarterly* 70 (Fall 1987): 103-5. This is the tribute Levine delivered at the "Tribute to Thomas McGrath," a dinner of the Associated Writing Programs Annual Meeting in Chicago, 12 April 1986.

Matchie, Thomas. "The Function of the Hopi Kachina in Tom McGrath's *Letter to an Imaginary Friend.*" *South Dakota Review,* 22, 3 (1984): 7-21.

Merer, Harry. "Alaska." McGrath Festschrift in *North Dakota Quarterly* 50, 4 (Fall 1982): 41. A personal memoir of time spent in the Air Corps with McGrath and Charley Wallant in Amchitka, Alaska, 1943–1944.

Moore, James. "The Strength of Wounds." Review Essay. *Dacotah Territory* 14 (Spring-Summer 1977): 79–90. Discusses *Letter to an Imaginary Friend* in terms of McGrath's idea of "harvest from a massacre," focusing on movements from confusion to chaos as rites of passage into mystery and personal power.

Shpak, Valery. "A Soviet View." McGrath Festschrift in *North Dakota Quarterly* 50, 4 (Fall 1982): 86. Considers McGrath's work in terms of democratic/socialist and surrealist/realist tendencies.

Smeall, Joseph F. S. "Thomas McGrath: A Review Essay." *North Dakota Quarterly* 40, 1 (1972): 29–38. A discussion of McGrath's use of the familiar (or "near"), his "returns inward" to North Dakota, and his publication experiences and expectations.

Stern, Frederick C. "'The Delegate for Poetry': McGrath as communist Poet." In *Where the West Begins: Essays on Middle Border and Siouxland Writing in Honor of Herbert Krause*, eds. Arthur R. Huseboe and William Geyer. Sioux Falls, South Dakota: Center for Western Studies Press, 1978. Reprinted in *Dream Champ—A Festschrift for Thomas McGrath*, ed. Fred Whitehead. Discusses how McGrath's politics provide "a framework of conviction and thought and imagery" for his poetry. Explains references, historical events, and uses of language important to an understanding of the poetry.

———. "Thomas McGrath." In *Literary History of the American West*, ed. Thomas J. Lyons. Fort Worth, Tex.: Texas Christian University Press, 1986.

Vinz, Mark. "Thomas McGrath: Words for a Vanished Age: A Memoir." *Great River Review* 4, 2 (1983). Reprinted in *Dream Champ—A Festschrift for Thomas McGrath*, ed. Fred Whitehead. A discussion of McGrath's poetry (by the former editor of *Dacotah Territory*) praising its celebratory, revolutionary, and "marvelous" qualities and emphasizing the complexity of McGrath's politics and sense of place.

Whitehead, Fred, ed. *Dream Champ—A Festschrift for Thomas McGrath*. *North Dakota Quarterly* 50, 4 (Fall 1982). Contains essays by McGrath, essays and poetry about McGrath, memoirs, reviews, bibliography, chronology, and photos. With an introduction by Fred Whitehead.

Wilson, Mark. "American Surrealism 1971?" *New: American and Canadian Poetry*. New York: Crossing Press, No. 15 (April-May 1971): 4–8, 97–100. An anti-surrealist polemic that mentions McGrath's *Crazy Horse Manifesto* as pointing toward imaginative poetics.

REVIEWS OF MCGRATH'S BOOKS

of *First Manifesto* (1940):

Howells, Thomas. *Poetry* 56, 6 (September 1940): 340.

of *To Walk a Crooked Mile* (1947):

Blau, Milton. *Masses and Mainstream* 1, 1 (March 1948): 77–80.
Elton, William. *Partisan Review* 15 (1948): 598.
Fibb, Hugh. *New York Times Book Review,* 7 March 1948, 4.
Maurer, Deane. *New Mexico Quarterly* 18 (1948): 253.
Meyer, Gerard Previn. *Saturday Review* 31, 16 (17 April 1948): 51.
Morgan, Frederick. *Hudson Review* 1 (1948): 258.
Theobald, John. *Poetry* 74, 1 (April 1949): 50.

of *Figures From a Double World* (1955):

Meredith, William. *New York Times Book Review,* 18 December 1955, 4.
Viertel, Tom and Mel Weisburd. *Coastlines* 1 (Summer 1955): 39–43.
Van Duyn, Mona. *Poetry* 88, 5 (August 1956): 329.
Wells, Christopher. *Mainstream* 10, 1 (January 1957): 63–64.

of *The Beautiful Things* (1960):

Low, Alice. *New York Times Book Review,* 26 February 1961, 44.

of *Letter to an Imaginary Friend* (1962):

Simpson, Louis. *Hudson Review* 16, 1 (Spring 1963): 131.
Creeley, Robert. *Poetry* 102, 1 (April 1963): 42.
Pendleton, Conrad. *Voices* (January-April 1963): 56.
Rosenthal, M. L. *New York Times Book Review,* 21 April 1963, 38.
Rubinstein, Annette T. *Mainstream* (March 1963): 55.
*Scherill, James. *San Francisco Chronicle "This World" Magazine,* (19 May
     1963?): 28.

of *Letter to an Imaginary Friend* (1970):

Anonymous. *Antioch Review* 30, 3 and 4 (Fall 1970): 465.
Bernardin, J. *Poetry Review* (Autumn 1970): 254.
Anonymous. *Times Literary Supplement,* 11 December 1970, 1436.
Fuson, Ben. *Library Journal* 95, 14 (August 1970): 2689.
National Observer 9 (30 November 1970): 24.
Anonymous. *Publisher's Weekly* 197 (2 March 1970): 79.
Atlas, James. *Poetry* 119, 1 (October 1971): 45.
Dicky, R. P. *Western American Literature* 6, 1 (Spring 1971): 65.
Anonymous. *Choice* 18 (June 1971): 552.

of *New and Selected Poems* (1964):

Rexroth, Kenneth. *New York Times Book Review,* 21 February 1965, 4.
Carruth, Hayden. *Hudson Review* 18 (1965): 133.
Howard, Richard. *Poetry* 106, 4 (July 1965): 296.

of *Movie at the End of the World* (1973):

Anonymous. *New Republic* 168 (21 April 1973): 27.
Anonymous. *Choice* 10 (September 1973): 980.
Anonymous. *Virginia Quarterly Review* 56, 4 (Autumn 1980): 144.
Anonymous. *New York Times Book Review,* 13 April 1980, 43.

of *Open Songs* (1977):

Anonymous. *Booklist* 74 (15 April 1978): 1319.
American Book Review 2 (June 1980): 2.
Anonymous. *Booklist* 76 (15 March 1980): 1033.

of *Waiting for the Angel* (1979):

Stern, Frederick C. *Southwest Review* 65, 1 (Winter 1980): 108.

of *Passages Toward the Dark* (1982):

Smeall, Joseph F. S. McGrath Festschrift in *North Dakota Quarterly* 50, 4
    (Fall 1982): 139–141.
San Francisco *Review of Books* 7 (November 1982): 29.
Stern, Frederick C. *Western American Literature* 19 (Spring 1984): 50.
Wakoski, Diane. *American Book Review* 5 (May 1983): 18.

of *Echoes Inside the Labyrinth* (1983):

Anonymous. *Publisher's Weekly* 224, 18, (28 October 1983): 64.
Anonymous. *Choice* 21 (February 1984): 822.
Kliatt Paperback Book Guide 18 (Spring 1984): 28.
Los Angeles Times Book Review 13 (1983): 9.
Stern, Frederick C. *Chicago* (April 1984): 135–36.

FILMS

*"The Movie at the End of the World." Produced by Mike Hazard, 1981(?).
    Documentary about McGrath and his work. Available from CIE, Box
    3343, St. Paul, Minnesota, 55165.

Works Cited

de Man, Paul. "Shelley Disfigured." *Deconstruction and Criticism*. Harold Bloom, Paul de Man, Jacques Derrida, et al. New York: Continuum, 1979.

Eliot, T. S. *The Complete Poems and Plays 1900–1950*. New York: Harcourt, Brace & Co., 1952.

Matthiessen, F. O. *American Renaissance Art and Expression in the Age of Emerson and Whitman*. New York: Oxford University Press, 1941.

Miller, J. Hillis. "Steven's Rock and Criticism as Cure." *Georgia Review* 30 (1976): 5–31.

———. "Steven's Rock and Criticism as Cure II." *Georgia Review* 30 (1976): 330–48.

Mills, Ralph J., Jr. "On Creation's Very Self: On the Personal Element in Recent American Poetry." *The Cry of the Human: Essays on Contemporary American Poetry*. Urbana, Ill.: University of Illinois Press, 1975.

Nelson, Cary. *Our Last First Poets Vision and History in Contemporary American Poetry*. Urbana, Ill.: University of Illinois Press, 1981.

Neruda, Pablo. "Winter Encounter III," from *Stones of Chile*. Trans. Ben Belitt. In *Pablo Neruda: A New Decade (Poems 1958–1967)*. Trans. Ben Belitt and Alastair Reid. New York: Grove Press, 1969.

Pound, Ezra. *The Cantos of Ezra Pound*. New York: New Directions, 1970.

Quasimodo, Salvatore. *The Selected Writings of Salvatore Quasimodo*. Trans. Allen Mandelbaum. New York: Farrar, Strauss & Cudahy, 1960.

Rosenthal, M. L. *The Modern Poets: A Critical Introduction*. New York: Oxford University Press, 1963.

Shapiro, Karl Jay. *Collected Poems 1940–1978*. New York: Random House, 1978.

Stern, Frederick C. *F. O. Matthiessen: Christian Socialist as Critic*. Chapel Hill: University of North Carolina Press, 1981.

———. "Interview with Thomas McGrath." In this volume.

Stevens, Wallace. *The Collected Poems*. New York: Alfred A. Knopf, 1974.

Williams, William Carlos. *Paterson*. Harmondsworth: Penguin, 1983 (1963).

Wordsworth, William. "Preface to the Second Edition of *Lyrical Ballads*," in *Anthology of Romanticism,* 3d ed. Ed. Ernest Bernbaum. New York: Ronald Press, 1948.

Yeats, William Butler. *The Collected Poems of William Butler Yeats*. New York: The Macmillan Co., 1956, 1962.

Contributors

James Bertolino is a well-known poet and poetry editor, who now teaches at Skagit Valley Community College in the State of Washington. He taught for many years at the University of Cincinnati.

Joseph Butwin teaches English at the University of Washington.

Hayden Carruth, one of the nation's most distinguished poets and anthologists, has been publishing books of poetry since 1950. His anthology of American poetry, *The Voice That Is Great Within Us* has been in print continuously since 1970. His *Selected Poetry* appeared in 1985. Earlier volumes of verse included *Snow and Rock, From Chaos, The Bloomingdale Papers,* and *Nothing for Tigers.*

Bernard F. Engel is Professor of American Thought and Language at Michigan State University. He has written books about Marian Moore, Richard Eberhart and "H.D."

Gene Frumkin is the author of many volumes of poetry. Among them are *The Rainbow-Walker, Dostoevsky and Other Nature Poems,* and *Locust Cry: Poems 1958–65.* He is the co-editor of *The Indian Rio Grande: Recent Poems from Three Cultures.* He teaches at the University of New Mexico at Albuquerque.

Carla Kaplan is a poet and editor. She holds an MA in Creative Writing from the University of Illinois at Chicago and is now a doctoral candidate in English at Northwestern University. She has accepted a faculty appointment at Yale for the fall of 1988.

Frederick Manfred is a widely known and admired novelist whose subject is most often the land of the South Dakota-Iowa border he has called "Siouxland." Early novels were published under the name "Feike Feikema." His novels include *Conquering Horse, Morning Red,* and *Wanderlust,* the last of these a combination of several of the Feikema novels.

Joel Oppenheimer is a prize-winning poet and teacher of poetry who has published many books of verse. Among them are *In Time: Poems 1962–82* and *The Woman Poems.*

Robert Schuler is a widely known poet and editor who for some years published the journal *Uzzano.* He teaches at the University of Wisconsin-Stout.

Frederick C. Stern teaches English at the University of Illinois at Chicago. He is the author of *F. O. Matthiessen: Christian Socialist as Critic.*

"Studs" (Louis) Terkel is the distinguished Pulitzer Prize-winning writer, as well as an actor and radio and TV personality. His on-going radio program on Station WFMT (Chicago) is a continuation of his many-years-long pioneering work in radio and television. Among his books are *Working, Division Street: America,* and *Giants of Jazz.*

E. P. Thompson is one of Britain's outstanding historians, and a major and leading figure in the peace and disarmament movement of Europe. His best-known book is *The Making of the English Working Class*. Among other works he has edited the volume *Star Wars* and written *The Poverty of Theory and other Essays*.

Diane Wakoski is a widely known and admired poet. She has published a remarkably large number of books of verse, most recently *The Rings of Saturn* and *The Collected Greed*. Among her earlier volumes, *Pachelbel's Canon* indicates her deep involvment with music. She has also published *Toward a New Poetry*. She teaches at Michigan State University.

Index

(The titles of McGrath's books of verse have not been indexed here, because they appear throughout the work. Footnotes have been indexed only when it seems useful.)